Book of data

Editor
R. D. Harrison

Nuffield Advanced Science
Published for the Nuffield Foundation by Penguin Books

Penguin Books Ltd, Harmondsworth, Middlesex, England
Penguin Books Inc., 7110 Ambassador Road, Baltimore, Md 21207, U.S.A.
Penguin Books Ltd, Ringwood, Victoria, Australia

Filmset in 'Monophoto' Times New Roman
and made and printed in Great Britain
Reprinted 1974
by Tinling (1973) Ltd, Prescot, Lancs,
(a member of the Oxley Printing Group Ltd.)

Design and art direction by Ivan and Robin Dodd
Illustrations designed and produced by Penguin Education

Foreword

It is almost a decade since the Trustees of the Nuffield Foundation decided to sponsor curriculum development programmes in science. Over the past few years a succession of materials and aids appropriate to teaching and learning over a wide variety of age and ability ranges has been published. We hope that they may have made a small contribution to the renewal of the science curriculum which is currently so evident in the schools.

The strength of the development has unquestionably lain in the most valued part that has been played in the work by practising teachers and the guidance and help that has been received from the consultative committees to each Project.

Advanced courses are at once both a difficult and an interesting venture. They have been designed to be of value to teacher and student, be they in sixth forms or other forms of education in a similar age range. Furthermore, it is expected that teachers in universities, polytechnics, and colleges of education may find some of the ideas of value in their own work.

In the preparation of published materials suitable for Advanced courses in the sciences, it was clear that it would be convenient to the schools to have available a single *Book of data* appropriate for sixth form students taking Chemistry, Physical Science, or Physics. The Foundation secured the services of Roger Harrison, then senior lecturer at Newcastle-upon-Tyne Polytechnic and now of the Open University, to edit this book. We are particularly grateful to him for the manner in which he has fulfilled this onerous task.

K. W. Keohane
Co-ordinator of the Nuffield Foundation Science Teaching Project

Contents

Code

Code

Introduction

I have long felt a need for an up-to-date compilation of basic physical data in SI units for use by my students, and had already begun to consider producing one when it was decided that there should be a book of data for the Nuffield Advanced courses in Physics, Physical Science, and Chemistry. I was therefore delighted when I was asked to undertake the task of compiling and editing this work: it has been a labour of love.

The selection of data posed a number of problems. Obviously all items required specifically for the Nuffield programmes must be included, but I felt it would be missing an opportunity if the data were to be tied too closely to the requirements of these particular courses. Students following other courses also have need of data and it is to be expected that the Nuffield courses themselves will be modified as time goes on. I therefore decided to include as much data as possible in the hope that this will provide flexibility for future developments and save others from the not inconsiderable labour of producing a similar work. I have also included a small amount of material which is probably more appropriate to first year degree work, in the hope that the book will also prove valuable in higher education. By constant reference to numerical data, students may learn to be more critical of both theory and experiment. By learning to work with tabulated data rather than committing facts to memory, they stand more chance of coping with the rising tide of information. I hope this book will encourage these developments, and in particular, I hope that students may be allowed to use it in examinations.

At the same time, I have tried to avoid including so much material that students may be confused or find it difficult to locate what they want. Early on, a few trial sheets were tested on a number of sixth forms to determine the maximum number of rows and columns that could safely be included on a page; thereafter each page has been designed in the light of this information and a number of interesting items were omitted because there just was not room to include them.

I have tried to include data for all common properties of a relatively few representative materials and these have been grouped by material rather than by property to give an overall picture of the various types of material of importance in the modern world.

Most of the data and the mathematical tables have been rounded to three figure accuracy, since this is enough for slide rule calculations and it is mostly a waste of time to attempt to compute with greater precision: additional significant figures are often doubtful. Even to this degree of accuracy, however, it often proved remarkably difficult to obtain reliable data. No attempt was made to go to original sources, which would have involved far too much time and effort. Instead, the information was abstracted from existing tables and handbooks and converted to SI units. Wherever possible, two such sources were consulted. This revealed a surprisingly large number of more than trivial discrepancies. A list of sources is given at the back of the book.

Explanation has been cut to the minimum. The notation used follows very recent international recommendations and should prove clear and easy to use.

I am grateful to the Newcastle-upon-Tyne Polytechnic for permitting me to undertake this work partly during working hours and to use the Polytechnic computer and other facilities.

It is a pleasure to acknowledge the help received in preparing possible tables from various outside consultants, friends, colleagues, students, technicians, and the Nuffield headquarters teams, among them B. Britton, T. Burns, R. Day, A. E. Dodd (of the British Ceramic Research Association), P. J. Doyle (of the British Glass Industry Research Association), Sister D. Furtado, R. F. Hearman (of the Forest Products Research Laboratory), E. Henshall, R. Hodgson, D. J. Hucknall, J. A. Hunter, L. V. Kite, T. R. Manley, G. G. Matthews, T. Priest (of Exeter University), P. Pullar-Strecker (of C.I.R.I.A.), P. Roe, I. S. Simpson, J. Thompson, B. Tunnard, R. W. Tyler, and Miss C. A. Wigglesworth. My special thanks are due to Professor M. L. McGlashan, who went to enormous trouble to advise on the correct use of the new conventions. The remaining faults are due to me alone. Mrs E. Hadwin typed most of the script and Miss M. Nicholson punched the computer cards.

Despite the care taken to eliminate errors, it is inevitable that there will be a number of copying and other mistakes in a work of this nature. I shall be grateful to readers who will point these out, or who wish to make suggestions for the improvement of future editions: these should be addressed to the Nuffield Foundation Science Teaching Project. We shall be only too happy to make use of measurements carried out in schools to fill in some of the numerous gaps in the tables, provided that their reliability can be demonstrated. Attempting to fill these gaps could be the starting point for any number of 'projects'.

R. D. Harrison
The Open University
1971

How to use this book

All the table headings are given in the Contents list, and there is also an index at the end of the book. Each table (or set of related tables) has been given a three letter code, which is printed on the top righthand corner of each page of the table, e.g. **PTO** for the table of '**P**hysical, **T**hermochemical and other properties of **O**rganic compounds'. A few tables had to be inserted wherever there was space and are therefore not in any obvious grouping.

Most of the tables are arranged to cover groups of similar or related substances, rather than by property. For example, to find the density of cadmium oxide, turn to the table of 'Physical, thermochemical and other properties of inorganic compounds' **PTI**.

The *symbols* defining the quantities recorded are given at the head of the first page of the table, or in the introduction to the table. The *units* are given at the head of each column.

Entries which do not relate directly to the definition at the head of the column are generally printed in bold with the appropriate qualification as a superscript. Entries where no appropriate data could be found are left blank, and entries for which there is no appropriate data (e.g. half-life of a stable nuclide) are given a dash. Entries marked * relate to values which vary between specimens. Entries marked † show disagreement between the sources consulted, and entries marked ‡ were stated in the sources to be uncertain. The sources used are listed under code letters R1, R2, etc. as footnotes to each table, and full details are given in the References at the end of the book.

SI units

The International System of Units, which is abbreviated SI (Système International d'Unités), forms a coherent system of units based on the seven basic and two subsidiary (the radian and steradian) units listed on the next page. It should be used for measurements in all branches of science, technology, industry, and commerce as well as in everyday life, and is recognized throughout the world. The great advantages of the SI over earlier systems of measurement, such as the British (foot, pound, second) system and the earlier metric (centimetre, gramme, second) system, are that it is completely decimal and completely coherent, which greatly simplifies calculations based on measurement. By coherent, we mean that all the derived units are formed by simple multiplication or division of the basic units, without the introduction of any numerical factor, even a power of ten. In consequence, when measurements expressed in basic units of the SI are substituted in an equation, the result will automatically be in the appropriate basic unit of the SI.

Unit names and symbols

Names like 'metre' or 'coulomb' are the names of the standard quantities and are used in sentences like ordinary nouns. We write 'twenty coulombs' or '20 coulombs', 'one tenth of a coulomb' or '0.1 coulomb'. Even the units named after scientists are spelt with a small letter. A hyphen is used between a number and a unit name to form an adjective, thus, a 'five-litre flask'.

Symbols like m or C denote one metre length or one coulomb charge respectively. They may be multiplied by numbers, so that 5 m means five times one metre, and 0.1 C means one tenth times one coulomb. They may also be multiplied or divided by other symbols, for example, m^2, N m (or N × m), $\mathrm{m\ s^{-1}}$ (or m/s), $\mathrm{W\ m^{-2}\ K^{-4}}$ (or $\mathrm{W/(m^2\ K^4)}$) but *not* $\mathrm{W/m^2/K^4}$. Can you see why not?)

Unit symbols are used algebraically and follow all the usual rules of algebra. In particular, they do not need a full stop (to denote an abbreviation) nor an s (to denote the plural), because in spite of appearances they are *not* abbreviations. Symbols for units named after men or women start with a capital letter.

Prefixes (see following page) may be used to indicate sub-units or multiples of units. The prefix and the unit symbol together form a single algebraic symbol. Thus km means 1000 m and $\mathrm{km^{-2}}$ means $(1000\ \mathrm{m})^{-2}$, or $10^{-6}\ \mathrm{m^{-2}}$. mN means a thousandth of a newton. We must be careful to distinguish this from m N which would mean metre multiplied by newton – it is safer to write N m or N × m. Not more than one prefix should be attached to any one unit symbol – more would be clumsy. It is usually most convenient to choose the prefix so that the number multiplying the unit will lie in the range 0.1 to 999.9.

Do not forget to write out the multiplier as a power of 10 before substituting a value into an equation. This is a frequent source of error. If you often make this mistake, avoid using prefixes at all.

Non-dimensional numbers may be formed by dividing a quantity symbol by an appropriate unit symbol. Thus instead of writing $l = 5$ m, where l denotes a length, we may write $l/\mathrm{m} = 5$, so that the righthand side does not contain a unit. This trick is useful for heading columns of figures in tables (see almost any page of this book), for labelling the axes of graphs, and for writing empirical equations (see page 35, **NUC**).

It is sometimes convenient to include a power of ten, or some other number, in the divisor to leave the numbers with manageable values. Thus the axis of a graph might be labelled $l/(10^4\ \mathrm{m})$ to give values in the range 1 to 10.

Gravitational units of force are not SI but are occasionally useful. They are written kgf, tonf, etc.

Temperature. The SI unit is the kelvin, symbol K (not °K), but the Celsius scale is generally used for practical measurement. 273 K is approximately 0 °C (note the space between the zero and the degree sign). The name centigrade should be avoided as this word stands for a unit of angle.

Metre The unit of length is equal to 1 650 763.73 wavelengths in vacuum of the radiation corresponding to the transition $2p_{10}$–$5d_5$[C] of the krypton-86 atom. *Unit symbol:* m

Kilogramme The unit of mass is equal to the mass of the *International Prototype* kilogramme (a platinum-iridium cylinder) kept at the Bureau International des Poids et Mesures (BIPM), Sèvres, Paris. *Unit symbol:* kg

Second The unit of time is the duration of exactly 9 192 631 770 periods of the radiation corresponding to the transition between the two hyperfine levels of the ground state of the caesium-133 atom. *Unit symbol:* s

Ampere The unit of electric current is that constant current which, if maintained in two parallel rectilinear conductors, of infinite length and negligible circular cross section, placed 1 metre apart in a vacuum, would produce a force between these conductors equal to 2×10^{-7} newton per metre of length. *Unit symbol:* A

Kelvin The unit of thermodynamic temperature is the fraction 1/273.16 (exactly) of the thermodynamic temperature at the triple point of water. *Unit symbol:* K

Mole The unit of amount of substance is the amount of substance which contains as many elementary units as there are atoms in 12 grammes[D] (exactly) of pure carbon-12. The elementary unit must be specified and may be an atom, a molecule, an ion, a radical, an electron, a photon, etc. or a group of such entities. *Unit symbol:* mol

Candela The unit of luminous intensity is the luminous intensity, in the perpendicular direction, of a surface of 1/60 square centimetre of a black body at the freezing temperature of platinum under a pressure of 101 325 pascal (1 atm). *Unit symbol:* cd

Radian The unit of angle is the angle subtended at the centre of a circle by an arc of the circumference equal in length to the radius of the circle. *Unit symbol:* rad

Steradian The unit of solid angle is the solid angle subtended at the centre of a sphere of radius r by a portion of the surface of the sphere having an area r^2. *Unit symbol:* sr

Multiplying prefixes may be used with any unit symbols to indicate decimal multiples or fractions.

10^{12}	tera	T	10^2	hecto[A]	h	10^{-3}	milli	m	10^{-15}	femto	f
10^9	giga	G	10	deka[A]	da	10^{-6}	micro	µ	10^{-18}	atto	a
10^6	mega	M	10^{-1}	deci[A]	d	10^{-9}	nano	n			
10^3	kilo	k	10^{-2}	centi[A]	c	10^{-12}	pico	p			

Units with special SI names

Frequency	hertz[B]	$Hz = s^{-1}$	Electric charge	coulomb	$C = A\,s$
Force	newton	$N = kg\,m\,s^{-2}$	e.m.f.; p.d.	volt	$V = kg\,m^2\,s^{-3}\,A^{-1}$
Energy	joule	$J = kg\,m^2\,s^{-2}$	Resistance	ohm	$\Omega = kg\,m^2\,s^{-3}\,A^{-2}$
Power	watt	$W = kg\,m^2\,s^{-3}$	Capacitance	farad	$F = A^2\,s^4\,kg^{-1}\,m^{-2}$
Luminous flux	lumen	$lm = cd\,sr$	Magnetic flux	weber	$Wb = kg\,m^2\,s^{-2}\,A^{-1}$
Illumination	lux	$lx = cd\,sr\,m^{-2}$	Flux density	tesla	$T = kg\,s^{-2}\,A^{-1}$
Pressure	pascal	$Pa = kg\,m^{-1}\,s^{-2}$	Inductance	henry	$H = kg\,m^2\,s^{-2}\,A^{-2}$
			Conductance	siemens	$S = \Omega^{-1} = kg^{-1}\,m^{-2}\,s^3\,A^2$

Notes

[A] It is suggested that these prefixes should be used in scientific work only where they are already well established, e.g. cm, dm^3, etc. mm is preferable to cm for measurements of laboratory equipment, etc.

[B] Some authors consider that Hz should be used only when referring to periodic phenomena and not, for instance, for radioactive count rates.

[C] This is the spectroscopists' notation to show which spectral line is used.

[D] Note that the mole is based on the gramme, not the kilogramme.

References: R15, R60.

Physical quantities, recommended symbols, and SI units

A physical quantity may be represented by a single letter algebraic symbol, such as l to denote a length, or I to denote a current. As far as possible, we should always use the internationally recommended symbols listed below for each physical quantity, so that formulae, etc, may be more readily recognized. The table also gives the appropriate basic SI unit (unit without prefix) for the quantity. If you have any difficulty in interpreting or using quantity symbols, the following notes may be useful.

Typeface

Quantity symbols are generally *printed* in italic (sloping) script to help distinguish them from mathematical constants, unit symbols, and symbols for chemical elements, all of which are printed in roman (upright) type. Vector quantities are printed in bold (Clarendon) type.

Definitions

A quantity symbol should always be defined precisely the first time it is used because its meaning cannot necessarily be guessed by the reader, and each letter of the alphabet is used for several different quantities in different contexts. There are a number of ways of getting over difficulties caused by running out of letters of the Greek and Latin alphabets. Sometimes there are alternative recommended letters. Sometimes we may use a small letter instead of the corresponding capital, or vice versa. Generally, however, it is necessary to attach distinguishing marks to the letters.

Distinguishing marks

i Numerical subscripts: V_1, V_2, and V_3 for the e.m.f.s of three cells.
ii Alphabetic subscripts: ρ_m for mass density and ρ_e for charge density; $C_{V,\mathrm{m}}$ for molar heat capacity at constant volume.
iii Parentheses: ρ (air) and ρ (water) for densities of air and water.
iv Standard superscripts:

G L S X aq	gaseous, liquid, solid, or crystalline state, or aqueous solution
$\ominus$	standard state, which must be defined (very often this denotes 298 K and 101 kPa (1 atm) pressure)
$\cdot$	pure substance
+ −	positive or negative ion, or electrode

v Standard subscripts:

∞	limiting value at infinite dilution
c	critical state or critical value
f fus e s tr d	formation, fusion, evaporation, sublimation, transition, or dilution
m b	are used in this book to denote normal melting and boiling. This avoids the ambiguity of $_\mathrm{f}$ for fusion and $_\mathrm{f}$ for formation. There is no generally accepted symbol for boiling at 101 kPa (1 atm) pressure.

Particular values

A symbol such as ρ is used to refer to density in general. If we wish to refer to the density of air at a particular temperature and pressure we may indicate this in parentheses after the symbol, for example, ρ (air, 273 K, 1 atm). This is a bit bulky to write down repeatedly in equations and it may be simpler to abbreviate it to $\rho_\mathrm{a}^\ominus$ and *state in a separate sentence* that $\rho_\mathrm{a}^\ominus$ denotes the density of air at a temperature of 273 K and a pressure of 1 atmosphere.

Thermodynamic quantities

There is a special convention to help decide whether what is being referred to is a total quantity for the system, a molar quantity, or a specific* quantity. 'Molar' means 'divided by amount of substance' and 'specific' means 'divided by mass'. That is, the units are ... per mole or ... per kilogramme respectively.

Upper case (capital) letters relate to total quantities: for example, H for total enthalpy, C for total heat capacity.

Upper case letters with subscript $_{\mathrm{m}}$ relate to the molar quantities: for example, H_{m} for molar enthalpy, C_{m} for molar heat capacity. (But in many cases the subscript $_{\mathrm{m}}$ is omitted where it has already been stated that molar quantities are intended.)

Upper case letters with subscript $_{\mathrm{B}}$ (where $_{\mathrm{B}}$ denotes a chemical species) denote the partial molar quantity: for example, H_{Al} for the partial molar enthalpy of aluminium.

The corresponding lower case (small) letters denote specific quantities: for example, h for specific enthalpy, c for specific heat capacity (N.B. not specific heat). Note also that c_p stands for specific heat capacity at constant pressure; and c_V for specific heat capacity at constant volume.

Units and physical quantities

A quantity symbol such as l means a length (of, say, a rod) irrespective of the units the length is measured in. Thus we may write $l = 1$ inch $= 2.54$ cm $= 0.0254$ m, that is, l is a number multiplied by a unit, not just the number. It is therefore algebraically incorrect to write l cm (which would in fact represent an area, namely a length l multiplied by a length 1 cm). If you wish to remind yourself of the appropriate (SI) units for a particular quantity, say so separately. For example, 'The self inductance of the coil is L (L will be measured in henries.)'.

Similarly, avoid writing equations containing numbers which depend on units. It is far better to say '$p = k\,h$, where p denotes pressure, h denotes height of water, and $k = 1.33 \times 10^5$ N m^{-3}' than 'Pressure $= 1.33 \times 10^5\,h$ Pa' which does not tell us what to do if we want to measure h in inches. Alternatively, write '$p = 1.33 \times 10^5(h/\mathrm{m})$Pa', where h/m is now a non-dimensional quantity. This is a very convenient way of writing empirical equations (see page 4).

A general point

It is clumsy to perform algebraic operations on words or abbreviations. It is better to say:
'$p = \rho g h$, where p denotes pressure,...' *rather than* 'pressure $= \rho g h$'.
'$V^{3/2}$, where V denotes potential difference' *rather than* '(p.d.)$^{3/2}$'.
'Square metre' *rather than* 'metre^2'.

* Note that specific should not be used in any other sense. Specific gravity and specific resistance are obsolete – use relative density and resistivity instead.
References: R15, R60.

Physical quantities, recommended symbols and SI units

	Quantity	Symbol	SI unit
1	absorption coefficient (acoustic)	α_a	—
2	absorption factor (radiation)	α	—
3	acceleration	a	m s^{-2}
4	acceleration of free fall	g	m s^{-2}
5	acceleration, angular	α	rad s^{-2}
6	activation energy	$E, E^{\ddagger}$	J mol^{-1}
7	activity (radioactive)	A	s^{-1}
8	activity coefficient of substance B	F_B, γ_B, y_B	—
9	amount of substance	n	mol
10	amplitude	a or x_0 etc	as appropriate
11	angle	$\alpha, \beta, \gamma, \theta, \phi$ etc	rad▲
12	angle of contact	θ	rad▲
13	angle of deviation	D	rad▲
14	angle of prism	A	rad▲
15	angle of optical rotation	α	rad▲
16	angular acceleration	α	rad s^{-2}
17	angular momentum	b, p_θ, L	J s
18	angular velocity	ω	rad s^{-1}
19	area	A, S	m^2
20	average speed	$\bar{c}, \bar{u}$	m s^{-1}
21	atomic number	Z	—
22	attenuation coefficient (particles)	μ	m^{-1}
23	Avogadro constant	L, N_A	mol^{-1}
24	Boltzmann constant	k	J K^{-1}
25	Bragg angle	θ	rad▲
26	breadth	b	m
27	bulk modulus	K	N m^{-2}
28	capacitance	C	F

	Quantity	Symbol	SI unit
29	charge density (surface)	σ	C m^{-2}
30	charge density (volume)	ρ	C m^{-3}
31	charge number of ion	z	—
32	coefficient of friction	μ	—
33	compressibility	κ	m^2 N^{-1}
34	conductance	G	S = Ω^{-1}
35	conductivity, electrical	σ, γ	S m^{-1}
36	conductivity, thermal	λ, k	W m^{-1} K^{-1}
37	coordinate (Cartesian)	x, y, z	m
38	cubic expansivity	γ, α	K^{-1}
39	decay constant, radioactive	λ	s^{-1}
40	degree of dissociation	α	—
41	density	ρ	kg m^{-3}
42	diameter	d	m
43	dispersive power	ω	—
44	distance along path	s, L	m
45	electric charge	Q	C
46	electric current	I	A
47	electric current density	J	A m^{-2}
48	electric dipole moment	p, μ	C m
49	electric displacement	D	C m^{-2}
50	electric field strength	E	V m^{-1}
51	electric flux	Ψ	C
52	electric flux density	D	C m^{-2}
53	electric polarization	P	C m^{-2}
54	electric potential	V, ϕ	V
55	electric potential difference	V, U	V
56	electric susceptibility	χ_e	—

▲ In practice, these will generally be measured in degrees (°).

	Quantity	Symbol	SI unit
57	electrolytic conductivity	κ	$S\,m^{-1}$
58	electromagnetic moment	m	$A\,m^2$
59	electromotive force	E	V
60	electron mass	m_e	kg
61	elementary (electron) charge	e	C
62	emissivity	ε	—
63	energy	E, W	J
64	energy, internal (of gas)	U, E	J
65	energy, kinetic	E_k, T, K	J
66	energy, potential	E_p, V, Φ	J
67	energy, radiant	Q, Q_e	J
68	enthalpy	H	J
69	entropy	S	$J\,K^{-1}$
70	equilibrium constant	K	as appropriate
71	expansivity, cubic	γ, α	K^{-1}
72	expansivity, linear	α, λ	K^{-1}
73	Faraday constant	F	$C\,mol^{-1}$
74	field strength, electric	E	$V\,m^{-1}$
75	field strength, magnetic	H	$A\,m^{-1}$
76	focal length	f	m
77	force	F	N
78	frequency	ν, f	Hz, s^{-1}
79	frequency, angular (pulsatance)	ω	rad s^{-1}
80	frequency, rotational	n	s^{-1}
81	Gibbs free energy function	G	J
82	gravitational constant	G	$N\,m^2\,kg^{-2}$
83	grating spacing or slit separation	d	m
84	half-life (radioactive)	$T_{\frac{1}{2}}, t_{\frac{1}{2}}$	s

	Quantity	Symbol	SI unit
85	Hall coefficient	R_H	$m^3\,C^{-1}$
86	heat capacity	C	$J\,K^{-1}$
87	heat flow rate	Φ	W
88	heat, quantity of	Q	J
89	height	h	m
90	Helmholtz free energy function	A, F	J
91	image distance	v	m
92	impedance	Z	Ω
93	impulse	p	N s
94	intensity of gravitational field	g	$N\,kg^{-1} = m\,s^{-2}$
95	internal energy (of gas)	U, E	J
96	ionic strength	I	$mol\,kg^{-1}$
97	kinetic energy	E_k, T, K	J
98	latent heat	$L, \Delta H$	J
99	length	l	m
100	light, quantity of	Q, Q_v	J or lm s
101	linear expansivity	α, λ	K^{-1}
102	luminance	L, L_v	$cd\,m^{-2}$
103	luminous flux	Φ, Φ_v	lm
104	luminous intensity	I, I_v	cd
105	magnetic field strength	H	$A\,m^{-1}$
106	magnetic flux	Φ	Wb
107	magnetic flux density	B	T
108	magnetic moment	m	$A\,m^2$
109	magnetic polarization	J	T
110	magnetic susceptibility	χ_m	—
111	magnetization	M	$A\,m^{-1}$
112	magnetomotive force	F_m	A

Physical quantities, recommended symbols and SI units – *(continued)*

	Quantity	Symbol	SI unit
113	magnification, linear	m	—
114	magnifying power	M	—
115	mass	m	kg
116	mass excess	Δ	kg
117	mass number	A	—
118	mass of electron	m_e	kg
119	mass of neutron	m_n	kg
120	mass of proton	m_p	kg
121	mean free path	l, λ	m
122	mean life (radioactive)	τ	s
123	molality	m_B	$mol\ kg^{-1}$
124	molar conductivity (conductance)	Λ	$S\ m^2\ mol^{-1}$
125	molar volume	V_m	$m^3\ mol^{-1}$
126	molar mass of a compound B	M_B	$kg\ mol^{-1}$
127	molar mass of an element	A	$kg\ mol^{-1}$
128	molecular mass	m	kg
129	molecular velocity	c, u	$m\ s^{-1}$
130	mole fraction of substance B	x_B, y_B	—
131	moment of couple	T	N m
132	moment of force	M	N m
133	moment of inertia	I, J	$kg\ m^2$
134	momentum	p	N s
135	mutual inductance	M, L_{12}	H
136	neutron number	N	—
137	nucleon number	A	—
138	number density of molecules	n	m^{-3}
139	number of molecules	N	—
140	number of turns on coil	N	—
141	number of turns per unit length of coil	n	m^{-1}
142	object distance	u	m
143	order of reflection or interference	n	—
144	osmotic pressure	Π	Pa
145	packing fraction	f	—
146	Peltier coefficient	Π	V
147	period	T	s
148	permeability (magnetic)	μ	$H\ m^{-1}$
149	permeability of vacuum	μ_0	$H\ m^{-1}$
150	permeability, relative	μ_r	—
151	permittivity	ε	$F\ m^{-1}$
152	permittivity of vacuum	ε_0	$F\ m^{-1}$
153	permittivity, relative	ε_r	—
154	phase angle	ϕ	rad (or °)
155	Planck constant	h	J s
156	Planck constant divided by 2π	$\hbar$	J s
157	Poisson ratio	μ, ν	—
158	potential energy	E_p, V, Φ	J
159	power	P	W
160	power factor	$\cos \phi$	—
161	power of lens	F	$rad\ m^{-1}$
162	pressure	p, P	Pa ($= N\ m^{-2}$)
163	pulsatance (angular frequency)	ω	$rad\ s^{-1}$
164	quantum number (principal)	n	—
165	radius	r	m
166	radius of gyration	k	m
167	rate constant of $(n+1)^{th}$ order reaction	k, k_r	$m^{3n}\ mol^{-3n}\ s^{-1}$
168	ratio $C_p/C_V = c_p/c_V$	γ	—

	Quantity	Symbol	SI unit
169	reactance	X	Ω
170	reflection coefficient (factor)	ρ	—
171	refractive index	n	—
172	relative atomic mass of an element (atomic weight)	A_r	—
173	resistance	R	Ω
174	resistivity	ρ	Ω m
175	self inductance	L	H
176	shear modulus	G	Pa (= N m^{-2})
177	slit separation or grating spacing	d	m
178	solid angle	Ω, ω	sr
179	sound intensity	I, J	W m^{-2}
180	specific charge (electron)	e/m_e	C kg^{-1}
181	specific heat capacity	c	J kg^{-1} K^{-1}
182	specific heat capacity at constant pressure	c_p	J kg^{-1} K^{-1}
183	specific heat capacity at constant volume	c_V	J kg^{-1} K^{-1}
184	speed	u, v, w	m s^{-1}
185	speed of electromagnetic waves (light) in vacuum	c	m s^{-1}
186	speed of sound	c	m s^{-1}
187	Stefan–Boltzmann constant	σ	W m^{-2} K^{-4}
188	strain, linear	ε, e	—
189	strain, shear	γ	—
190	strain, volume	θ	—
191	stress, normal	σ	Pa (= N m^{-2})
192	stress, shear	τ	Pa (= N m^{-2})
193	stress, volume	p	Pa (= N m^{-2})
194	surface tension	γ, σ	N m^{-1}
195	temperature, common (Celsius)[A]	θ, t	°C
196	temperature, thermodynamic (absolute)	T	K
197	temperature difference	θ	K
198	thermal capacity	C	J K^{-1}
199	thermal conductivity	λ, k	W m^{-1} K^{-1}
200	thermoelectric power (differential)	S	V K^{-1}
201	thickness	d, δ	m
202	Thomson coefficient	μ	V K^{-1}
203	time	t	s
204	time constant	τ	s
205	torque	T	N m
206	transmission coefficient (transmittance)	τ	—
207	transport number	t	—
208	van der Waals coefficients	a and b	N m^4 mol^{-2}, m^3 mol^{-1}
209	velocity	u, v, w	m s^{-1}
210	viscosity (dynamic)	η, μ	N s m^{-2}
211	viscosity (kinematic)	ν	m^2 s^{-1}
212	volume	V	m^3
213	volume expansivity	γ, α	K^{-1}
214	wavelength	λ	m
215	wave number	$\sigma, \tilde{\nu}$	m^{-1}
216	weight	W, G, P	N
217	work	W, A	J
218	work function	ϕ	V
219	Young modulus	E	N m^{-2}

[A] By definition, common temperature is expressed in non-SI units.

Mathematical symbols: The Greek alphabet

Symbol	Meaning
$=$	is equal to
$\neq$, $\neq$	is not equal to
$\equiv$	is identically equal to
$\hat{=}$	corresponds to (see page 14)
$\approx$	is approximately equal to
$\sim$, $\propto$	is proportional to
$\rightarrow$	tends towards, approaches
A/B, $\frac{A}{B}$, AB^{-1}	A divided by B (/ is called a solidus)
a^n	a raised to power n
$a^{\frac{1}{2}}$, $\sqrt{a}$, $\sqrt{a}$	square root of a
$a^{1/n}$, $\sqrt[n]{a}$	n^{th} root of a
$\lim_{x \to a} f(x)$	limit of $f(x)$as $x \rightarrow a$
∞	infinity
Δx	finite increment of x
δx	infinitesimal increment of x; variation of x
$\frac{df}{dx}$, df/dx, $f'(x)$	differentiation of $f(x)$ wrt[▲] x
$\frac{d^n f}{dx^n}$, $d^n f/dx^n$, $f^{(n)}(x)$	,, ,, $f(x)$ wrt x n times
$\dot{x}$	differentiation of x wrt t
$>$	is larger than
$\gg$	is much larger than
$\geqslant$, $\geqq$, $\geq$	is larger than or equal to
$<$	is less than
$\ll$	is much less than
$\leqslant$, $\leqq$, $\leq$	is less than or equal to
$\pm$	plus or minus
$\parallel$	is parallel to } mainly used in pure mathematics
$\perp$	is perpendicular to } mainly used in pure mathematics
$\angle A$, $\hat{A}$	angle A } mainly used in pure mathematics
$r!$	factorial $r = r(r-1)(r-2)\ldots \times 2 \times 1$
$\binom{n}{r}$	binomial coefficient $= \frac{n!}{r!(n-r)!}$
x_{av}, $\bar{x}$, $\langle x \rangle$	average value of x
x_m or $\hat{x}$	maximum value of x
x_{min} or $\check{x}$	minimum value of x
x_{eff} or $\tilde{x}$	root mean square (r.m.s.) value of x
$\int f(x)\,dx$	indefinite integral of f wrt x
$\int_a^b f(x)\,dx$	definite integral of f wrt x
$\oint f(x)\,dx$	integral of $f(x)$ round a closed path
$\sum x_i$ or $\sum_{i=1}^{n} x_i$	sum of members of the set $x_1, \ldots x_n$
$\prod x_i$ or $\prod_{i=1}^{n} x_i$	product of members of the set $x_1, \ldots x_n$

▲ wrt means 'with respect to'.

Symbol	Meaning
$|x|$	the modulus function or absolute value of x
$|A|$	determinant of the square set A_{ij}
e^x, exp x	exponential function of x
e	base of natural logarithms
ln x, $\log_e x$	natural logarithm of x
lg x, log x, $\log_{10} x$	logarithm to base 10 of x (common logarithm)
$\log_a x$	logarithm to base a of x
lb x, $\log_2 x$	binary logarithm of x
sin x, cos x, tan x, sec x, cosec x, cot x	trigonometric functions
arcsin x, or $\sin^{-1} x$, etc.	argument of trigonometric function

Names of modifying signs

$^-$ bar	$\cdot$ dot	$_x$ subscript
† dagger	$\hat{}$ hat	^{x} superscript
′ dash	* star (asterisk)	~ tilde
() parentheses	[] brackets	{} braces

Conventions followed in writing numbers and mathematical statements

The decimal point is indicated by a dot on the line or, in continental texts, by a comma: e.g. 123.45 or 123,45. A zero should be placed before the point in numbers less than unity: e.g. 0.123 **not** .123.

Long numbers should be written in groups of three digits, with a space between groups: e.g. 1 234.567 89. Commas should **not** be used to separate thousands (except for amounts of money) to avoid confusion with the continental decimal point.

The argument of a function should be enclosed in brackets (except for standard functions with not more than two symbols in the argument). Thus $f(x)$, $\exp\{(\tau - \tau_0)/\lambda\}$ but e^{kx}, sin wt.

The Greek Alphabet

Letter		Name	Letter		Name
A	α	Alpha	N	ν	Nu
B	β	Beta	Ξ	ξ	Xi
Γ	γ	Gamma	O	o	Omicron
Δ	δ	Delta	Π	π	Pi
E	$\varepsilon\ \epsilon$	Epsilon	P	ρ	Rho
Z	ζ	Zeta	Σ	σ	Sigma
H	η	Eta	T	τ	Tau
Θ	$\theta\ \vartheta$	Theta	Υ	υ	Upsilon
I	ι	Iota	Φ	$\phi\ \varphi$	Phi
K	κ	Kappa	X	χ	Chi
Λ	λ	Lambda	Ψ	ψ	Psi
M	μ	Mu	Ω	ω	Omega

References: R15, R60.

Miscellaneous units: names and conversion factors into SI; SI units with special names

Non-SI units are now defined in terms of SI, except those marked *. (Quantities not *definable* in terms of SI units are not considered satisfactory units.) Exact values are printed in bold type. Multiples and submultiples of some of the non-SI units may be formed, where appropriate, by prefixes as in the SI, provided that this can be done without ambiguity (*not* min for 0.001 in, etc). Names of units within the SI are underlined. (This table may also be used to find out the meaning of unfamiliar units and unit symbols.)

Students are advised to convert all non-SI units and non-basic SI units to basic SI units before carrying out calculations. Compound units not given in this list may be converted by the use of the appropriate conversion factor for each factor of the unit symbol, for example, 1 lb ft^{-3} = {0.4536 (kg lb^{-1})/(0.3048)^3 (m ft^{-1})^3} lb ft^{-3} = 16.0 kg m^{-3}.

Unit	Symbol	SI equivalent			$\log_{10}$
acre (=4840 yd^2)	acre	4.047	$\times 10^{3}$	m^2	3.6071
ångström	Å	**1.000**	$\times \mathbf{10^{-10}}$	**m**	$\overline{10}$.0000
astronomical unit (Earth–Sun)*	au	1.496	$\times 10^{11}$	m	11.1750
atmosphere (760 Torr)	atm	1.013	$\times 10^{5}$	N m^{-2}	5.0056
atomic mass unit (unified)*	u	1.660	$\times 10^{-27}$	kg	$\overline{27}$.2201
bar	bar	**1.000**	$\times \mathbf{10^{5}}$	**N m^{-2}**	5.0000
barn (unit of nuclear area)	barn	**1.000**	$\times \mathbf{10^{-28}}$	**m^2**	$\overline{28}$.0000
biot (CGS: e.m.u. current)[A]	Bi	**1.000**	$\times \mathbf{10^{-1}}$	**A**	$\overline{1}$.0000
British thermal unit	Btu	1.055	$\times 10^{3}$	J	3.0233
	Btu h^{-1}	2.931	$\times 10^{-1}$	W	$\overline{1}$.4670
bushel (UK) (=8 gal)	bushel (UK)	3.637	$\times 10^{-2}$	m^3	$\overline{2}$.5607
calorie (thermochemical)	cal (thermochem)	**4.184**		**J**	0.6216
coulomb (SI: electric charge)	C	**1.000**		**A s**	—
cubic foot	ft^3	2.832	$\times 10^{-2}$	m^3	$\overline{2}$.4521
cubic yard	yd^3	7.646	$\times 10^{-1}$	m^3	$\overline{1}$.8834
curie (radioactivity)	Ci	**3.7**	$\times \mathbf{10^{10}}$	**s^{-1}**	10.5682
day	d	**8.6400**	$\times \mathbf{10^{4}}$	**s**	4.9365
debye	D	3.336	$\times 10^{-30}$	C m	$\overline{30}$.5237
decibel[B]	dB				
degree (angular)	...°	1.745	$\times 10^{-2}$	rad	$\overline{2}$.2407
degree Celsius[C]	°C	**1.000**		**K**	—
degree Fahrenheit[C]	°F	5.556	$\times 10^{-1}$	K	$\overline{1}$.7448
dyne (CGS: force)	dyn	**1.000**	$\times \mathbf{10^{-5}}$	**N**	$\overline{5}$.0000
electronvolt*	eV	1.602	$\times 10^{-19}$	J	$\overline{19}$.2046

* Experimental, not defined.

[A] The biot or the franklin is used when a fourth fundamental electrical unit is required in CGS calculations.

[B] The decibel is used to express $10 \log_{10} P/P^{\ominus}$, where P is a power and $P^{\ominus}$ a standard power, which must be specified. In acoustics, $P^{\ominus}$ is generally 10^{-2} W. Sound intensities are generally expressed in dB, with $I^{\ominus} = 10^{-2}$ W m^{-2}. In electrical engineering, amplification ratios are expressed in dB, and e.m.f.s are given in dB as $20 \log_{10} V/V^{\ominus}$, where $V^{\ominus}$ is often 10^{-6} V. The decibel is not strictly a unit in the sense of the other units in this table. It is very useful for measurements which range over many powers of ten when expressed in basic SI units.

[C] The degrees defined above are temperature intervals. Temperatures convert according to the formulae: $t_c/°C = (5/9)\{(t_f/°F) - 32.0\} = 0.556\{(t_f/°F) - 32.0\} = T/K - 273.15$.

Note

The relationship between CGS and SI units in these tables is that of correspondence (≙) and not of equality, because SI electrical units are based on four fundamental units (m, kg, s, A) and CGS units on only three (cm, g, s). It is incorrect to write, for example, 1 abamp = 10 A because if these two units were expressed in terms of, say, (ft, lb, s, (A)), the equality would no longer hold.

Unit	Symbol	SI equivalent			$\log_{10}$
erg (CGS: energy)	erg	**1.000**	$\times \mathbf{10^{-7}}$	**J**	$\bar{7}.0000$
farad (SI: capacitance)	F	**1.000**		$\mathbf{C\,V^{-1}}$	—
foot	ft	**3.048**	$\times \mathbf{10^{-1}}$	**m**	$\bar{1}.4840$
foot pound-force	ft lbf	1.356		N m (or J)	0.1323
franklin (CGS: e.s.u. charge)[A]	Fr	3.336	$\times 10^{-10}$	C	$\overline{10}.5237$
gallon (UK)	gal (UK)	4.546	$\times 10^{-3}$	m^3	$\bar{3}.6577$
gauss (CGS: e.m.u. flux density)[F]	G	$\hat{=}$ **1.000**	$\times \mathbf{10^{-4}}$	$\mathbf{T(=Wb\,m^{-2})}$	$\bar{4}.0000$
hectare (land area)	ha	**1.000**	$\times \mathbf{10^{4}}$	$\mathbf{m^2}$	4.0000
henry (SI: inductance)	H	**1.000**		$\mathbf{J\,A^{-2}}$	—
hertz (SI: frequency)	Hz	**1.000**		$\mathbf{s^{-1}}$	—
hour	h	**3.600**	$\times \mathbf{10^{3}}$	**s**	3.5563
horsepower	hp	7.457	$\times 10^{2}$	W	2.8726
horsepower hour	hp h	2.685	$\times 10^{6}$	J	6.4289
hundredweight (long, UK)	cwt	5.080	$\times 10$	kg	1.7059
inch	in	**2.54**	$\times \mathbf{10^{-2}}$	**m**	$\bar{2}.4048$
joule (SI: energy)	J	**1.000**		**N m**	—
kilogramme-force (kilopond)	kgf (kp)	9.807		N	0.9915
kilowatt hour	kWh	**3.600**	$\times \mathbf{10^{6}}$	**J**	6.5563
knot (international)	kn	5.144	$\times 10^{-1}$	$m\,s^{-1}$	$\bar{1}.7113$
light year*	light year	9.461	$\times 10^{15}$	m	15.9759
litre[B]	l	**1.000**	$\times \mathbf{10^{-3}}$	$\mathbf{m^3}$	$\bar{3}.0000$
litre atmosphere	l atm	1.013	$\times 10^{2}$	J	2.0056
lambert	lambert	3.183	$\times 10^{4}$	$cd\,m^{-2}$	4.5029
lumen (SI: luminous flux)	lm	**1.000**		**cd sr**	—
lux (SI: illumination)	lx	**1.000**		$\mathbf{lm\,m^{-2}}$	—
maxwell (CGS: e.m.u. magnetic flux)[F]	maxwell	**1.000**	$\times \mathbf{10^{-8}}$	**Wb**	$\bar{8}.0000$
mho (reciprocal ohm)[C]	mho	**1.000**		$\mathbf{S(=\Omega^{-1})}$	—
micron (micrometre)[C]	μm (μ)	**1.000**	$\times \mathbf{10^{-6}}$	**m**	$\bar{6}.0000$
mile (nautical)	n mile	1.852	$\times 10^{3}$	m	3.2677
mile (statute)	mile	1.609	$\times 10^{3}$	m	3.2066
mile per hour	mile h^{-1}	4.704	$\times 10^{-1}$	$m\,s^{-1}$	$\bar{1}.6725$
minute (angle)	. . .	2.909	$\times 10^{-4}$	rad	$\bar{4}.4638$
minute (time)	min[E]	**6.0**	$\times$ **10**	**s**	1.7782
newton (SI: force)	N	**1.000**		$\mathbf{kg\,m\,s^{-2}}$	—
oersted (CGS: e.m.u. magnetic field)[F]	Oe	$\hat{=}$ 79.58		$A\,m^{-1}$	1.9008
		$\hat{=}$ 1.0	$\times 10^{-4}$	T (in vacuo)	$\bar{4}.0000$
ohm (SI: resistance)	Ω	**1.000**		$\mathbf{V\,A^{-1}}$	—
ounce (avoirdupois)	oz	2.835	$\times 10^{-2}$	kg	$\bar{2}.4526$

* Experimental, not defined.

[A] The biot or the franklin is used when a fourth fundamental electrical unit is required in CGS calculations.

[B] The definition of the litre as 1000.028 cm^3 was abandoned in 1964. Because of the possibility of ambiguity, the litre should not be used for high precision work: dm^3 is unambiguous.

[C] These words are not used in the Advanced Science materials, although they may be found in some books and journals.

[E] m is used in time of day, for example, 18 h 23 m.

[F] Care is needed when converting CGS magnetic quantities to SI units because rationalization introduces a factor of 4π into the conversion factor and removes it from the defining equations. A magnetic field of 1 Oe produces a magnetic flux density of 10^{-4} T in vacuum. When magnetic materials are present, it is convenient to introduce a subsidiary quantity, the magnetic field strength denoted by H, which is measured in Oe in the CGS system and in $A\,m^{-1}$ in SI units. We thus have $B = \mu_r\mu_0 H$ as the equation for the magnetic flux density, which is also known as the magnetic induction. μ_r generally depends on B in ferromagnetics. See 'Properties of magnetic materials', **SLD**.

Miscellaneous units: names and conversion factors into SI; SI units with special names – *(continued)*

Unit	Symbol	SI equivalent			$\log_{10}$
ounce (fluid UK)	fl oz (UK)	2.841	$\times 10^{-5}$	m^3	$\bar{5}.4535$
parsec*	parsec	3.084	$\times 10^{16}$	m	16.4892
pascal (SI: pressure)	Pa	**1.000**		**$N\,m^{-2}$**	—
phon (loudness level)[C]	phon				
pint (UK)	pt (UK)	5.682	$\times 10^{-4}$	m^3	$\bar{4}.7545$
poise (CGS: dynamic viscosity)	P	**1.000**	**$\times 10^{-1}$**	**$kg\,m^{-1}\,s^{-1}$**	$\bar{1}.0000$
pound	lb	4.536	$\times 10^{-1}$	kg	$\bar{1}.6567$
pound-force	lbf	4.448		N	0.6482
pound-force foot	lbf ft	1.356		N m	0.1323
pound-force per sq. inch[D]	$lbf\,in^{-2}$	6.895	$\times 10^{3}$	$N\,m^{-2}$	3.8385
pound-force per sq. foot	$lbf\,ft^{-2}$	4.788	$\times 10$	$N\,m^{-2}$	1.6801
rad or röntgen (radiation dosage)	R	1.00	$\times 10^{-2}$	$J\,kg^{-1}$	$\bar{2}.0000$
rem (radiation dosage)[B]	Rem				
second (angle)	. . .″	4.848	$\times 10^{-6}$	rad	$\bar{6}.6855$
siemens (SI: reciprocal ohm)	S	**1.000**		**Ω^{-1}** $(=A\,V^{-1})$	—
square foot	ft^2	9.290	$\times 10^{-2}$	m^2	$\bar{2}.9680$
square inch	in^2	6.452	$\times 10^{-4}$	m^2	$\bar{4}.8097$
square mile	$mile^2$	2.590	$\times 10^{6}$	m^2	6.4133
square yard	yd^2	8.361	$\times 10^{-1}$	m^2	$\bar{1}.9223$
stokes (CGS: kinematic viscosity)	St	**1.000**	**$\times 10^{-4}$**	**$m^2\,s^{-1}$**	$\bar{4}.0000$
talbot	talbot	1.000		lm s	—
tesla (SI: magnetic flux density)	T	**1.000**		**$Wb\,m^{-2}$** $(=V\,s\,m^{-2})$	—
therm (100 000 Btu)	therm	1.055	$\times 10^{8}$	J	8.0233
ton (UK long, 2240 lb)	ton	1.016	$\times 10^{3}$	kg	3.0069
ton-force	ton f	9.964	$\times 10^{3}$	N	3.9984
ton-force per square inch	$tonf\,in^{-2}$	1.544	$\times 10^{7}$	$N\,m^{-2}$	7.1886
tonne (metric ton)[A]	t	**1.000**	**$\times 10^{3}$**	**kg**	3.0000
torr (=mmHg to 1 in 10^7)	Torr	1.333	$\times 10^{2}$	$N\,m^{-2}$	2.1248
volt (SI: e.m.f. and p.d.)	V	**1.000**		**$J\,C^{-1}$**	—
watt (SI: power)	W	**1.000**		**$J\,s^{-1}$**	—
weber (SI: magnetic flux)	Wb	**1.000**		**V s** $(J\,s\,C^{-1})$	—
X unit (approx. 0.001 Å)	Xu	1.002	$\times 10^{-13}$	m	$\overline{13}.0008$
yard	yd	9.144	$\times 10^{-1}$	m	$\bar{1}.9611$
year (tropical)*	a	3.156	$\times 10^{7}$	s	7.4976

Notes
* Experimental, not defined.
[A] Tonne is used for commercial and engineering purposes but is not SI. Mg is preferable for scientific work.
[B] 1 Rem of any ionizing radiation produces the same biological effect in human beings as 1 R of X-rays.
[C] The phon is a subjective (that is, depends on the individual) unit of loudness on a decibel scale (see page 14).
[D] The abbreviation psi is often used, but is not recommended.
Reference: R2 (page F204).

Conversion table: energy units and related quantities

This table contains factors for converting energy units and quantities related to energy which are frequently used in atomic physics and chemistry.

The numbers in this table have 'units' $U L^{-1}$, where U denotes the entry at the head of the column and L that at the left of the row.

A These are defined energy units.

B These are units of energy per amount of substance which may be converted to the corresponding energy per atom or other elementary entity by dividing by the Avogadro constant, L.

C The electronvolt is widely used as a unit of energy (per atom, etc.) although it is strictly not a unit but a unit divided by a physical quantity subject to experimental error, namely J/e.

D Hz and cm^{-1} are related to energy by the Planck equation $E = (h)\nu = (hc)\tilde{\nu}$, where ν is measured in Hz and $\tilde{\nu}$ has generally been measured in cm^{-1}. The table entries are related by the quantities in parentheses.

E The kelvin is related to energy by the equation $E = (k)T$.

F The masses are related to energy by the Einstein equation $E = m(c^2)$.

D, **E**, and **F** are not energy units, but units of quantities proportional to energy.

		J	cal	l atm	$kJ\ mol^{-1}$	$kcal\ mol^{-1}$	eV	Hz	cm^{-1}	K	kg
A	J	1	2.39×10^{-1}	0.99×10^{-2}	6.02×10^{20}	1.44×10^{20}	6.24×10^{18}	1.51×10^{33}	5.04×10^{22}	7.25×10^{22}	1.11×10^{-17}
	cal	4.18	1	4.13×10^{-2}	2.52×10^{21}	6.02×10^{20}	2.61×10^{19}	6.32×10^{33}	2.11×10^{23}	3.03×10^{23}	4.65×10^{-17}
	l atm	1.01×10^{2}	24.22	1	6.10×10^{22}	1.46×10^{22}	6.33×10^{20}	1.53×10^{35}	5.10×10^{24}	7.34×10^{24}	1.13×10^{-15}
B	$kJ\ mol^{-1}$	1.66×10^{-21}	3.97×10^{-22}	1.64×10^{-23}	1	2.39×10^{-1}	1.04×10^{-2}	2.51×10^{12}	83.6	1.20×10^{2}	1.85×10^{-38}
	$kcal\ mol^{-1}$	6.95×10^{-21}	1.66×10^{-22}	6.86×10^{-23}	4.18	1	4.34×10^{-2}	1.05×10^{13}	3.5×10^{2}	5.04×10^{2}	7.73×10^{-38}
C	eV	1.60×10^{-19}	3.83×10^{-20}	1.58×10^{-21}	96.5	23.1	1	2.42×10^{14}	8.07×10^{3}	1.16×10^{4}	1.78×10^{-34}
D	Hz	6.63×10^{-34}	1.58×10^{-34}	6.54×10^{-36}	3.99×10^{-13}	9.54×10^{-14}	4.14×10^{-15}	1	3.34×10^{-11}	4.80×10^{-11}	7.37×10^{-51}
	cm^{-1}	1.99×10^{-23}	4.75×10^{-24}	1.96×10^{-25}	1.20×10^{-2}	2.86×10^{-3}	1.24×10^{-4}	3.00×10^{10}	1	1.44	2.21×10^{-40}
E	K	1.38×10^{-23}	3.30×10^{-24}	1.36×10^{-25}	8.31×10^{-3}	2.99×10^{-3}	8.61×10^{-5}	2.08×10^{10}	6.95×10^{-1}	1	1.54×10^{-40}
F	kg	8.99×10^{16}	2.15×10^{16}	8.87×10^{14}	5.41×10^{37}	1.29×10^{37}	5.61×10^{35}	1.36×10^{50}	4.53×10^{39}	6.51×10^{39}	1
	u	1.49×10^{-10}	3.57×10^{-11}	1.47×10^{-12}	8.98×10^{10}	2.15×10^{10}	9.31×10^{8}	2.25×10^{23}	7.51×10^{12}	1.08×10^{13}	1.66×10^{-27}
	m_e	8.19×10^{-14}	1.96×10^{-14}	8.08×10^{-16}	4.93×10^{7}	1.18×10^{7}	5.11×10^{5}	1.14×10^{20}	4.12×10^{9}	5.93×10^{9}	9.11×10^{-31}

For example

$1\ J = 0.99 \times 10^{-2}$ 1 atm, 1 J(per particle) $\hat{=}\ 6.02 \times 10^{20}\ kJ\ mol^{-1}$, $1\ kJ\ mol^{-1}\ \hat{=}\ 1.66 \times 10^{-21}$ J(per particle).

1 eV (per particle) $= 1.60 \times 10^{-19}$ J (per particle) $\hat{=}\ 1.58 \times 10^{-13}$ 1 atm $\hat{=}$ quantum frequency of 2.42×10^{14} Hz, etc.

Conversion table: millimetres of mercury to kilopascals

1 mmHg = (13 595.1 kg m^{-3}) × (9.806 65 N kg^{-1}) × (0.001 m) ≈ 0.1333 kPa

mmHg	0	1	2	3	4	5	6	7	8	9
100	13.33	13.47	13.60	13.73	13.87	14.00	14.13	14.27	14.40	14.53
110	14.67	14.80	14.93	15.07	15.20	15.33	15.47	15.60	15.73	15.87
120	16.00	16.13	16.27	16.40	16.53	16.67	16.80	16.93	17.07	17.20
130	17.33	17.47	17.60	17.73	17.87	18.00	18.13	18.27	18.40	18.53
140	18.67	18.80	18.93	19.07	19.20	19.33	19.47	19.60	19.73	19.87
150	20.00	20.13	20.27	20.40	20.53	20.66	20.80	20.93	21.06	21.20
160	21.33	21.46	21.60	21.73	21.86	22.00	22.13	22.26	22.40	22.53
170	22.66	22.80	22.93	23.06	23.20	23.33	23.46	23.60	23.73	23.86
180	24.00	24.13	24.26	24.40	24.53	24.66	24.80	24.93	25.06	25.20
190	25.33	25.46	25.60	25.73	25.86	26.00	26.13	26.26	26.40	26.53
200	26.66	26.80	26.93	27.06	27.20	27.33	27.46	27.60	27.73	27.86
210	28.00	28.13	28.26	28.40	28.53	28.66	28.80	28.93	29.06	29.20
220	29.33	29.46	29.60	29.73	29.86	30.00	30.13	30.26	30.40	30.53
230	30.66	30.80	30.93	31.06	31.20	31.33	31.46	31.60	31.73	31.86
240	32.00	32.13	32.26	32.40	32.53	32.66	32.80	32.93	33.06	33.20
250	33.33	33.46	33.60	33.73	33.86	34.00	34.13	34.26	34.40	34.53
260	34.66	34.80	34.93	35.06	35.20	35.33	35.46	35.60	35.73	35.86
270	36.00	36.13	36.26	36.40	36.53	36.66	36.80	36.93	37.06	37.20
280	37.33	37.46	37.60	37.73	37.86	38.00	38.13	38.26	38.40	38.53
290	38.66	38.80	38.93	39.06	39.20	39.33	39.46	39.60	39.73	39.86
300	40.00	40.13	40.26	40.40	40.53	40.66	40.80	40.93	41.06	41.20
310	41.33	41.46	41.60	41.73	41.86	42.00	42.13	42.26	42.40	42.53
320	42.66	42.80	42.93	43.06	43.20	43.33	43.46	43.60	43.73	43.86
330	44.00	44.13	44.26	44.40	44.53	44.66	44.80	44.93	45.06	45.20
340	45.33	45.46	45.60	45.73	45.86	46.00	46.13	46.26	46.40	46.53
350	46.66	46.80	46.93	47.06	47.20	47.33	47.46	47.60	47.73	47.86
360	48.00	48.13	48.26	48.40	48.53	48.66	48.80	48.93	49.06	49.20
370	49.33	49.46	49.60	49.73	49.86	50.00	50.13	50.26	50.40	50.53
380	50.66	50.80	50.93	51.06	51.20	51.33	51.46	51.60	51.73	51.86
390	52.00	52.13	52.26	52.40	52.53	52.66	52.80	52.93	53.06	53.20
400	53.33	53.46	53.60	53.73	53.86	54.00	54.13	54.26	54.40	54.53
410	54.66	54.80	54.93	55.06	55.20	55.33	55.46	55.60	55.73	55.86
420	56.00	56.13	56.26	56.40	56.53	56.66	56.80	56.93	57.06	57.20
430	57.33	57.46	57.60	57.73	57.86	58.00	58.13	58.26	58.40	58.53
440	58.66	58.80	58.93	59.06	59.20	59.33	59.46	59.60	59.73	59.86
450	60.00	60.13	60.26	60.40	60.53	60.66	60.80	60.93	61.06	61.19
460	61.33	61.46	61.59	61.73	61.86	61.99	62.13	62.26	62.39	62.53
470	62.66	62.79	62.93	63.06	63.19	63.33	63.46	63.59	63.73	63.86
480	63.99	64.13	64.26	64.39	64.53	64.66	64.79	64.93	65.06	65.19
490	65.33	65.46	65.59	65.73	65.86	65.99	66.13	66.26	66.39	66.53
500	66.66	66.79	66.93	67.06	67.19	67.33	67.46	67.59	67.73	67.86
510	67.99	68.13	68.26	68.39	68.53	68.66	68.79	68.93	69.06	69.19
520	69.33	69.46	69.59	69.73	69.86	69.99	70.13	70.26	70.39	70.53
530	70.66	70.79	70.93	71.06	71.19	71.33	71.46	71.59	71.73	71.86
540	71.99	72.13	72.26	72.39	72.53	72.66	72.79	72.93	73.06	73.19
mmHg	0	1	2	3	4	5	6	7	8	9

mmHg	0	1	2	3	4	5	6	7	8	9
550	73.33	73.46	73.59	73.73	73.86	73.99	74.13	74.26	74.39	74.53
560	74.66	74.79	74.93	75.06	75.19	75.33	75.46	75.59	75.73	75.86
570	75.99	76.13	76.26	76.39	76.53	76.66	76.79	76.93	77.06	77.19
580	77.33	77.46	77.59	77.73	77.86	77.99	78.13	78.26	78.39	78.53
590	78.66	78.79	78.93	79.06	79.19	79.33	79.46	79.59	79.73	79.86
600	79.99	80.13	80.26	80.39	80.53	80.66	80.79	80.93	81.06	81.19
610	81.33	81.46	81.59	81.73	81.86	81.99	82.13	82.26	82.39	82.53
620	82.66	82.79	82.93	83.06	83.19	83.33	83.46	83.59	83.73	83.86
630	83.99	84.13	84.26	84.39	84.53	84.66	84.79	84.93	85.06	85.19
640	85.33	85.46	85.59	85.73	85.86	85.99	86.13	86.26	86.39	86.53
650	86.66	86.79	86.93	87.06	87.19	87.33	87.46	87.59	87.73	87.86
660	87.99	88.13	88.26	88.39	88.53	88.66	88.79	88.93	89.06	89.19
670	89.33	89.46	89.59	89.73	89.86	89.99	90.13	90.26	90.39	90.53
680	90.66	90.79	90.93	91.06	91.19	91.33	91.46	91.59	91.73	91.86
690	91.99	92.13	92.26	92.39	92.53	92.66	92.79	92.93	93.06	93.19
700	93.33	93.46	93.59	93.73	93.86	93.99	94.13	94.26	94.39	94.53
710	94.66	94.79	94.93	95.06	95.19	95.33	95.46	95.59	95.73	95.86
720	95.99	96.13	96.26	96.39	96.53	96.66	96.79	96.93	97.06	97.19
730	97.33	97.46	97.59	97.73	97.86	97.99	98.13	98.26	98.39	98.53
740	98.66	98.79	98.93	99.06	99.19	99.33	99.46	99.59	99.73	99.86
750	99.99	100.1	100.3	100.4	100.5	100.7	100.8	100.9	101.1	101.2
760	101.3	101.5	101.6	101.7	101.9	102.0	102.1	102.3	102.4	102.5
770	102.7	102.8	102.9	103.1	103.2	103.3	103.5	103.6	103.7	103.9
780	104.0	104.1	104.3	104.4	104.5	104.7	104.8	104.9	105.1	105.2
790	105.3	105.5	105.6	105.7	105.9	106.0	106.1	106.3	106.4	106.5
800	106.7	106.8	106.9	107.1	107.2	107.3	107.5	107.6	107.7	107.9
810	108.0	108.1	108.3	108.4	108.5	108.7	108.8	108.9	109.1	109.2
820	109.3	109.5	109.6	109.7	109.9	110.0	110.1	110.3	110.4	110.5
830	110.7	110.8	110.9	111.1	111.2	111.3	111.5	111.6	111.7	111.9
840	112.0	112.1	112.3	112.4	112.5	112.7	112.8	112.9	113.1	113.2
850	113.3	113.5	113.6	113.7	113.9	114.0	114.1	114.3	114.4	114.5
860	114.7	114.8	114.9	115.1	115.2	115.3	115.5	115.6	115.7	115.9
870	116.0	116.1	116.3	116.4	116.5	116.7	116.8	116.9	117.1	117.2
880	117.3	117.5	117.6	117.7	117.9	118.0	118.1	118.3	118.4	118.5
890	118.7	118.8	118.9	119.1	119.2	119.3	119.5	119.6	119.7	119.9
900	120.0	120.1	120.3	120.4	120.5	120.7	120.8	120.9	121.1	121.2
910	121.3	121.5	121.6	121.7	121.9	122.0	122.1	122.3	122.4	122.5
920	122.7	122.8	122.9	123.1	123.2	123.3	123.5	123.6	123.7	123.9
930	124.0	124.1	124.3	124.4	124.5	124.7	124.8	124.9	125.1	125.2
940	125.3	125.5	125.6	125.7	125.9	126.0	126.1	126.3	126.4	126.5
950	126.7	126.8	126.9	127.1	127.2	127.3	127.5	127.6	127.7	127.9
960	128.0	128.1	128.3	128.4	128.5	128.7	128.8	128.9	129.1	129.2
970	129.3	129.5	129.6	129.7	129.9	130.0	130.1	130.3	130.4	130.5
980	130.7	130.8	130.9	131.1	131.2	131.3	131.5	131.6	131.7	131.9
990	132.0	132.1	132.3	132.4	132.5	132.7	132.8	132.9	133.1	133.2
mmHg	0	1	2	3	4	5	6	7	8	9

Conversion table: thermochemical calories to joules

1 cal (thermochem) = 4.1840 J

cal	0	1	2	3	4	5	6	7	8	9
100	418.4	422.6	426.8	431.0	435.1	439.3	443.5	447.7	451.9	456.1
110	460.2	464.4	468.6	472.8	477.0	481.2	485.3	489.5	493.7	497.9
120	502.1	506.3	510.4	514.6	518.8	523.0	527.2	531.4	535.6	539.7
130	543.9	548.1	552.3	556.5	560.7	564.8	569.0	573.2	577.4	581.6
140	585.8	589.9	594.1	598.3	602.5	606.7	610.9	615.0	619.2	623.4
150	627.6	631.8	636.0	640.2	644.3	648.5	652.7	656.9	661.1	665.3
160	669.4	673.6	677.8	682.0	686.2	690.4	694.5	698.7	702.9	707.1
170	711.3	715.5	719.6	723.8	728.0	732.2	736.4	740.6	744.8	748.9
180	753.1	757.3	761.5	765.7	769.9	774.0	778.2	782.4	786.6	790.8
190	795.0	799.1	803.3	807.5	811.7	815.9	820.1	824.2	828.4	832.6
200	836.8	841.0	845.2	849.4	853.5	857.7	861.9	866.1	870.3	874.5
210	878.6	882.8	887.0	891.2	895.4	899.6	903.7	907.9	912.1	916.3
220	920.5	924.7	928.8	933.0	937.2	941.4	945.6	949.8	954.0	958.1
230	962.3	966.5	970.7	974.9	979.1	983.2	987.4	991.6	995.8	1000
240	1004	1008	1013	1017	1021	1025	1029	1033	1038	1042
250	1046	1050	1054	1059	1063	1067	1071	1075	1079	1084
260	1088	1092	1096	1100	1105	1109	1113	1117	1121	1125
270	1130	1134	1138	1142	1146	1151	1155	1159	1163	1167
280	1172	1176	1180	1184	1188	1192	1197	1201	1205	1209
290	1213	1218	1222	1226	1230	1234	1238	1243	1247	1251
300	1255	1259	1264	1268	1272	1276	1280	1284	1289	1293
310	1297	1301	1305	1310	1314	1318	1322	1326	1331	1335
320	1339	1343	1347	1351	1356	1360	1364	1368	1372	1377
330	1381	1385	1389	1393	1397	1402	1406	1410	1414	1418
340	1423	1427	1431	1435	1439	1443	1448	1452	1456	1460
350	1464	1469	1473	1477	1481	1485	1490	1494	1498	1502
360	1506	1510	1515	1519	1523	1527	1531	1536	1540	1544
370	1548	1552	1556	1561	1565	1569	1573	1577	1582	1586
380	1590	1594	1598	1602	1607	1611	1615	1619	1623	1628
390	1632	1636	1640	1644	1648	1653	1657	1661	1665	1669
400	1674	1678	1682	1686	1690	1695	1699	1703	1707	1711
410	1715	1720	1724	1728	1732	1736	1741	1745	1749	1753
420	1757	1761	1766	1770	1774	1778	1782	1787	1791	1795
430	1799	1803	1807	1812	1816	1820	1824	1828	1833	1837
440	1841	1845	1849	1854	1858	1862	1866	1870	1874	1879
450	1883	1887	1891	1895	1900	1904	1908	1912	1916	1920
460	1925	1929	1933	1937	1941	1946	1950	1954	1958	1962
470	1966	1971	1975	1979	1983	1987	1992	1996	2000	2004
480	2008	2013	2017	2021	2025	2029	2033	2038	2042	2046
490	2050	2054	2059	2063	2067	2071	2075	2079	2084	2088
500	2092	2096	2100	2105	2109	2113	2117	2121	2125	2130
510	2134	2138	2142	2146	2151	2155	2159	2163	2167	2171
520	2176	2180	2184	2188	2192	2197	2201	2205	2209	2213
530	2218	2222	2226	2230	2234	2238	2243	2247	2251	2255
540	2259	2264	2268	2272	2276	2280	2284	2289	2293	2297
cal	0	1	2	3	4	5	6	7	8	9

cal	0	1	2	3	4	5	6	7	8	9
550	2301	2305	2310	2314	2318	2322	2326	2330	2335	2339
560	2343	2347	2351	2356	2360	2364	2368	2372	2377	2381
570	2385	2389	2393	2397	2402	2406	2410	2414	2418	2423
580	2427	2431	2435	2439	2443	2448	2452	2456	2460	2464
590	2469	2473	2477	2481	2485	2489	2494	2498	2502	2506
600	2510	2515	2519	2523	2527	2531	2536	2540	2544	2548
610	2552	2556	2561	2565	2569	2573	2577	2582	2586	2590
620	2594	2598	2602	2607	2611	2615	2619	2623	2628	2632
630	2636	2640	2644	2648	2653	2657	2661	2665	2669	2674
640	2678	2682	2686	2690	2694	2699	2703	2707	2711	2715
650	2720	2724	2728	2732	2736	2741	2745	2749	2753	2757
660	2761	2766	2770	2774	2778	2782	2787	2791	2795	2799
670	2803	2807	2812	2816	2820	2824	2828	2833	2837	2841
680	2845	2849	2853	2858	2862	2866	2870	2874	2879	2883
690	2887	2891	2895	2900	2904	2908	2912	2916	2920	2925
700	2929	2933	2937	2941	2946	2950	2954	2958	2962	2966
710	2971	2975	2979	2983	2987	2992	2996	3000	3004	3008
720	3012	3017	3021	3025	3029	3033	3038	3042	3046	3050
730	3054	3059	3063	3067	3071	3075	3079	3084	3088	3092
740	3096	3100	3105	3109	3113	3117	3121	3125	3130	3134
750	3138	3142	3146	3151	3155	3159	3163	3167	3171	3176
760	3180	3184	3188	3192	3197	3201	3205	3209	3213	3217
770	3222	3226	3230	3234	3238	3243	3247	3251	3255	3259
780	3264	3268	3272	3276	3280	3284	3289	3293	3297	3301
790	3305	3310	3314	3318	3322	3326	3330	3335	3339	3343
800	3347	3351	3356	3360	3364	3368	3372	3376	3381	3385
810	3389	3393	3397	3402	3406	3410	3414	3418	3423	3427
820	3431	3435	3439	3443	3448	3452	3456	3460	3464	3469
830	3473	3477	3481	3485	3489	3494	3498	3502	3506	3510
840	3515	3519	3523	3527	3531	3535	3540	3544	3548	3552
850	3556	3561	3565	3569	3573	3577	3582	3586	3590	3594
860	3598	3602	3607	3611	3615	3619	3623	3628	3632	3636
870	3640	3644	3648	3653	3657	3661	3665	3669	3674	3678
880	3682	3686	3690	3694	3699	3703	3707	3711	3715	3720
890	3724	3728	3732	3736	3740	3745	3749	3753	3757	3761
900	3766	3770	3774	3778	3782	3787	3791	3795	3799	3803
910	3807	3812	3816	3820	3824	3828	3833	3837	3841	3845
920	3849	3853	3858	3862	3866	3870	3874	3879	3883	3887
930	3891	3895	3899	3904	3908	3912	3916	3920	3925	3929
940	3933	3937	3941	3946	3950	3954	3958	3962	3966	3971
950	3975	3979	3983	3987	3992	3996	4000	4004	4008	4012
960	4017	4021	4025	4029	4033	4038	4042	4046	4050	4054
970	4058	4063	4067	4071	4075	4079	4084	4088	4092	4096
980	4100	4105	4109	4113	4117	4121	4125	4130	4134	4138
990	4142	4146	4151	4155	4159	4163	4167	4171	4176	4180
cal	**0**	**1**	**2**	**3**	**4**	**5**	**6**	**7**	**8**	**9**

Length, speed, time, mass: some useful values

The following provide a progression of lengths, masses, etc, which may be useful for estimations and checking calculations. Students are advised to consult this table frequently until they are familiar with the magnitudes involved.

Orders of magnitude of physical quantities such as enthalpy or tensile strength may be obtained by consulting the appropriate tables.

Length

10^{-15} m	radius of proton	0.25 m	length of standard brick
10^{-12} m	wavelength of gamma ray (0.8 MeV)	0.3 m	recommended 'module' for house building
10^{-10} m	lower limit of resolution of electron microscope	1.8 m	height of man
10^{-10} m	diameter of hydrogen atom	5.0 m	height of modern two storey house to eaves
10^{-7} m	mean free path of air molecule (S.T.P.)	20 m	length of cricket pitch
5×10^{-7} m	wavelength of visible light	294 m	length of R.M.S. *Queen Elizabeth II*
10^{-6} m	diameter of finest drawn quartz fibre	300 m	wavelength of radio waves (1 MHz)
2×10^{-6} m	diameter of staphylococcus (small bacterium)	450 m	height of Empire State Building
5×10^{-6} m	length of human chromosome	8800 m	height of Mount Everest
7.5×10^{-6} m	diameter of human blood corpuscle	10^{4} m	maximum depth of the ocean
2×10^{-5} m	diameter of finest commercial glass capillary	1.7×10^{6} m	radius of Moon
10^{-4} m	thickness of paper (this book)	6×10^{6} m	radius of Earth
2×10^{-4} m	diameter of single strand of lighting flex	4×10^{8} m	distance Earth – Moon
10^{-3} m	diameter of single stranded 5 A conductor	1.5×10^{11} m	distance Earth – Sun
1.4×10^{-3} m	thickness of new penny piece	9.5×10^{15} m	1 light year
0.02 m	width of stamp; diameter of one penny piece	4.6×10^{16} m	distance of nearest star
		10^{21} m	radius of local galaxy (Milky Way)
0.03 m	diameter of fifty penny piece	10^{22} m	average distance between galaxies
0.212 m × 0.3 m	A 4 paper[A]	3×10^{26} m	radius of observable universe

Speed

3×10^{8} m s^{-1}	light in vacuum	283 m s^{-1}	land speed record
6×10^{5} m s^{-1}	electron (1 eV)	147 m s^{-1}	water speed record
1.1×10^{4} m s^{-1}	escape velocity from earth	47 m s^{-1}	fastest bird
2×10^{3} m s^{-1}	neutron (0.025 eV)	30 m s^{-1}	speed limit on motorways (70 mile h^{-1})
500 m s^{-1}	air molecule (S.T.P.)	27 m s^{-1}	fastest land animal
330 m s^{-1}	speed of sound in air (S.T.P.)	13 m s^{-1}	fastest sprint (Man)

Note

[A] successive paper sizes in the A range halve the longest dimension. A 4 is the metric size of paper which will be increasingly used for school work. Pages of this book are A 5.

Time

3×10^{-24} s	light crossing proton
10^{-22} s	proton revolution within nucleus
3×10^{-19} s	light crossing atom
10^{-16} to 10^{-20} s	period of electron revolution around nucleus
2×10^{-15} s	period of visible light
10^{-13} s	vibration period of ion in solid
10^{-12} s	period of molecular spin (infra red)
10^{-11} s	period of millimetric wave
10^{-9} s	lower limit of direct timing
10^{-8} s	light crosses a room
10^{-7} s	dead time of scintillation counter
10^{-6} s	period of M.W. radio signal
10^{-5} s	stroboscopic light flash
2×10^{-5} s	dead time of geiger counter
10^{-4} s	period of sound (highest audible frequency)
2×10^{-2} s	period of a.c. mains oscillation
0.1 to 0.2 s	human reaction time
0.7 s	comfortable reverberation time of living room
60 s	1 minute
500 s	light from Sun to Earth
10^{5} s	1 day
3×10^{7} s	1 year
2×10^{9} s	human life span
5×10^{10} s	half life of radium
10^{14} s	antiquity of man (*Homo sapiens*)
10^{17} s	age of Earth and of oldest rocks
1.4×10^{17} s	half life of uranium
10^{18} s	expected life of Sun as a bright star

Mass

10^{-30} kg	electron
1.7×10^{-27} kg	proton
4×10^{-25} kg	uranium atom
10^{-22} kg	haemoglobin molecule
4×10^{-15} kg	staphylococcus
6×10^{-10} kg	limit of direct weighing
10^{-7} kg	grain of sand (2×10^{-4} m radius)
2.5×10^{-3} kg	smallest English mammal (pygmy shrew)
1.5×10^{-2} kg	house mouse
4 kg	standard house brick
5 kg	cat
65 kg	man
100 kg	earth satellite (Sputnik I)
650 kg	car ('Mini')
10^{3} kg	cubic metre of water
2×10^{4} kg	elephant
10^{5} kg	blue whale
3×10^{6} kg	heaviest tree
3×10^{8} kg	laden oil super-tanker
5×10^{18} kg	total mass of atmosphere
10^{21} kg	total mass of oceans
7×10^{22} kg	mass of Moon
6×10^{24} kg	mass of Earth
2×10^{30} kg	mass of Sun
10^{41} kg	mass of local galaxy (Milky Way)
10^{52} kg	total mass of observable universe

Chemical elements (alphabetical order)

Name, symbol, atomic number, molar mass, isotopic composition, radius, natural abundance, and price.

Z atomic number
A molar mass for the naturally occurring isotopic composition (≙ chemical atomic weight) to maximum precision so far attained.
r_{cov} atomic radius in covalent bonds.
$Q_{r\oplus}$ terrestrial abundance of element by mass relative to that of silicon: $Q_{r\oplus}$ (Si) = 100.
p approximate price (1971) of the element. See note **4**.

Notes

1 **Molar mass**

To convert A to the old scale based on $A(^{16}O) = 16.000\,000\,0$ g mol^{-1}, multiply by 1.000 320 3. Apart from the following exceptions, it is believed that the naturally occurring isotopic composition, and hence the value of A, is constant for each element throughout the Solar system and possibly throughout the Universe.

The following elements marked * are found to exhibit variability in A due to variation in isotopic composition.

H	B	C	O	Si	S	
±0.000 01	±0.003	±0.000 05	±0.000 1	±0.001	±0.003	g mol^{-1}

The following elements marked ‡ have rather large experimental uncertainties in A.

Ne	Cl	Cr	Fe	Cu	Br	Ag	
±0.003	±0.001	±0.001	±0.003	±0.001	±0.002	±0.003	g mol^{-1}

2 **Mass numbers**

Those in italic denote radioactive nuclides. NR denotes a naturally occurring radionuclide and AR an artificial radionuclide. The names of elements not found naturally on Earth are in italic.

3 **Abundance**

The values given relate to the whole Earth and there are very significant local variations. Some of the figures quoted may be in error by a factor of 10 or more. See also p. 63 **TCE**.

The absolute terrestrial abundance of Si is believed to be 27.72 per cent by mass.

In other parts of the Universe, the relative abundance of the less volatile elements probably approximates to that on Earth, but the relative abundance of gases and volatile elements depends very much on the size and thermal history of the body containing them. The following Solar abundances, also relative to silicon ($Q_{r\odot}$(Si) = 100), probably approximate to the values for the Universe as a whole.

Element	H	He	C	N	O	Mg	Fe
$Q_{r\odot}$	110 000	91 000	730	150	1700	68	24

4 **Price**

The price of a substance depends basically on its rarity, availability, and cost of extraction. It also depends on the purity, physical state, and amount supplied. The prices here are for small consignments (1 g to 10 kg depending on the element), of 'chemical' purity (always better than 99 %, often better than 99.9 %); and are from the 1971 catalogues of BDH Ltd and BOC Ltd. Commercial prices of some important elements are given in parentheses, and are from the FT commodity index and the *Metal Bulletin*. Prices of the cheapest isotope of radioactive materials are given in pounds sterling per millicurie, and are from the Radiochemical Centre catalogue.

References: R1, R24, R65. Prices: see note **4**.

Chemical elements (alphabetical order)

Element	Symbol	Z	A/g mol^{-1}	Stable mass numbers and percentage abundances (in brackets)	r_{cov}/nm	$Q_{r\oplus}$	p/£ kg^{-1}
Actinium	**Ac**	89	227.0000	*227* (NR), *228* (NR)	—	1.3×10^{-15}	8/mCi
Aluminium	**Al**	13	26.9185	**27**(100)	0.125	35.8	3(0.26)
Americium	**Am**	95	243.0000	*243* (AR)	—	—	0.05/mCi
Antimony	**Sb**[A]	51	121.7550	**121**(57.25), *123*(42.75)	0.141	4.4×10^{-4}	3.09(0.71†)
Argon	**Ar**[B]	18	39.9480	**36**(0.34), **38**(0.063), **40**(99.6)	—	1.8×10^{-5}	0.70
Astatine	**At**	85	210.0000	*206* (NR), *215* (NR)	—	—	—
Arsenic	**As**	33	74.9216	**75**(100)	0.121	2.2×10^{-3}	4
Barium	**Ba**	56	137.3400	**130**(0.101), **132**(0.097), **134**(2.42), **135**(6.59), **136**(7.81), **137**(11.32), **138**(71.66)	0.198	5.7×10^{-1}	42.5
Berkelium	**Bk**	97	249.0000	*249* (AR)	—	—	—
Beryllium	**Be**	4	9.0122	**9**(100)	0.089	2.6×10^{-3}	278[O]
Bismuth	**Bi**	83	208.9800	*209*(100)	0.152	8.8×10^{-5}	20
Boron	**B**	5	10.8110*	**10**(19.7*), **11**(80.3*)	0.080	1.3×10^{-3}	10.7[O]
Bromine	**Br**	35	79.9090‡	**79**(50.52), **81**(49.48)	0.114	7.1×10^{-4}	0.98
Cadmium	**Cd**	48	112.4000	**106**(1.22), **108**(0.88), **110**(12.39), **111**(12.75), **112**(24.07), **113**(12.26), **114**(28.86), **116**(7.58)	0.141	6.6×10^{-5}	12
Caesium[C]	**Cs**	55	132.9050	**133**(100)	0.235	3.1×10^{-3}	45[Cl]
Calcium	**Ca**	20	40.0800	**40**(96.97), **42**(0.64), **43**(0.15), **44**(2.06), **46**(0.003), **48**(0.19)	0.174	16.0	9.5
Californium	**Cf**	98	251.0000	*251* (AR)	—	—	—
Carbon	**C**	6	12.0111*	**12**(98.89), **13**(1.11) {limestone CO_2} : *14*(**NR)	0.077	1.4×10^{-1}	1[N]
Cerium	**Ce**	58	140.1200	*136*(0.193), **138**(0.23), **140**(88.48), *142*(11.07)	—	2.0×10^{-2}	120
Chlorine	**Cl**	17	35.4530‡	**35**(75.53), **37**(24.47)	0.099	1.4×10^{-1}	0.52
Chromium	**Cr**	24	51.9960‡	**50**(4.31), **52**(83.76), **53**(9.55), **54**(2.38)	0.117	4.4×10^{-2}	4.8
Cobalt	**Co**	27	58.9332	**59**(100)	0.116	1.0×10^{-2}	10(2)
Columbium	**Cb** now known as niobium						
Copper	**Cu**[D]	29	63.5400‡	**63**(69.1), **65**(30.9)	0.117	3.1×10^{-2}	2.(0.5†)
Curium	**Cm**	96	247.0000	*247* (AR)	—	—	0.3/mCi
Deuterium	**D** synonym for ^{2}H				—	8.5×10^{-5}	2340
Dysprosium	**Dy**	66	162.5000	*156*(0.05), *158*(0.09), **160**(2.29), **161**(18.88), **162**(25.53), **163**(24.97), **164**(28.18)	—	2.0×10^{-3}	800[O]

* Variable isotopic compositions, see p. 24. **Variable because of radioactivity. ‡ Experimental uncertainty see p. 24.
[A] stibium [B] Formerly A was used to denote Argon. [C] The spelling cesium is frequently used. [D] cuprum.
† price subject to violent fluctuations. [O] supplied as oxide. [Cl] supplied as chloride. [N] wood charcoal.

Chemical elements (alphabetical order) – *(continued)*

Element	Symbol	Z	A/g mol^{-1}	Stable mass numbers and percentage abundances (in brackets)	r_{cov}/nm	$Q_{r\oplus}$	p/£ kg^{-1}
Einsteinium	**Es**	99	254.0000	*254* (AR)	—	—	—
Emanation	**Em**	obsolete for radon					
Erbium	**Er**	68	167.2600	**162**(0.14), **164**(1.56), **166**(33.41), **167**(22.94), **168**(27.07), **170**(14.88)	—	1.1×10^{-3}	720°
Europium	**Eu**	63	151.9600	**151**(47.77), **153**(52.23)	—	4.7×10^{-4}	6360°
Fermium	**Fm**	100	253.0000	*253* (AR)	—	—	—
Fluorine	**F**	9	18.9984	**19**(100)	0.072	4.0×10^{-1}	155
Francium	**Fr**	87	223.0000	*223* (NR)	—	—	—
Gadolinium	**Gd**	64	157.2500	**152**(0.20), **154**(2.15), **155**(14.7), **156**(20.47), **157**(15.68), **158**(24.9), **160**(21.9)	—	2.1	750°
Gallium	**Ga**	31	69.7200	**69**(60.2), **71**(39.8)	0.125	6.6×10^{-3}	1900
Germanium	**Ge**	32	72.5900	**70**(20.55), **72**(27.37), **73**(7.67), **74**(36.74), *76*(7.67)	0.122	3.1×10^{-3}	1000
Gold	**Au^{D}**	79	196.9670	**197**(100)	0.134	2.2×10^{-6}	2500(536^{P})
Hafnium	**Hf**	72	178.4900	**174**(0.16), **176**(5.21), **177**(18.56), **178**(27.1), **179**(13.75), **180**(35.22)	0.144	2.0×10^{-3}	2500
Helium	**He**	2	4.0026	**3**(0.00013) {atmosphere}, **4**($\approx$ 100)	—	1.3×10^{-6}	44
Holmium	**Ho**	67	164.9300	**165**(100)	—	5.1×10^{-4}	1800
Hydrogen	**H**	1	1.0079*	**1**(99.985), **2**(0.015), *3*(**NR)	0.037	5.7×10^{-1}	4.2
Indium	**In**	49	114.8200	**113**(4.23), *115*(95.77)	0.150	4.4×10^{-5}	149
Iodine	**I**	53	126.9044	**127**(100)	0.133	1.3×10^{-4}	5
Ionium	**Io**	obsolete for ^{230}Th					
Iridium	**Ir**	77	192.2000	**191**(38.5), **193**(61.5)	0.126	4.4×10^{-7}	9500
Iron	**Fe^{E}**	26	55.8470‡	**54**(5.84), **56**(91.68), **57**(2.17), **58**(0.31)	0.116	22.0	1(0.06^{Q})
Krypton	**Kr**	36	83.8000	**78**(0.35), **80**(2.27), **82**(11.56), **83**(11.55), **84**(56.90), **86**(17.37)	—	4.3×10^{-8}	170
Lanthanum	**La**	57	138.9100	*138*(0.09), **139**(99.91)	0.169	8.1×10^{-3}	29°
Lawrencium	**Lr**	103	257.0000	*257* (AR)	—	—	—
Lead	**Pb^{F}**	82	207.1900**	*202*(0.5), **204**(1.40), **206**(25.1), **207**(21.7), **208**(52.3)	0.154	7.0×10^{-3}	0.92(0.11)
Lithium	**Li**	3	6.9390	**6**(7.42), **7**(92.58)	0.123	2.9×10^{-2}	46
Lutetium	**Lu**	71	174.9700	*175*(97.4), *176*(2.60)	—	3.3×10^{-4}	13 600°
Magnesium	**Mg**	12	24.3120	**24**(78.60), **25**(10.11), **26**(11.29)	0.136	9.2	2.6(0.36)
Manganese	**Mn**	25	54.9380	**55**(100)	0.117	4.4×10^{-1}	2.7(0.25)

* Variable isotopic composition, see p. 24. ** Variable because of radioactivity. ‡ Experimental uncertainty see p. 24.
^{D} aurum. ^{E} ferrum. ^{F} plumbum. ^{O} supplied as oxide. ^{P} price fixed by financial policy. ^{Q} mild steel bars.

Element	Symbol	Z	A/g mol^{-1}	Stable mass numbers and percentage abundances (in brackets)	r_{cov}/nm	$Q_{r\oplus}$	p/£ kg^{-1}
Mendelevium	**Md**	101	256.0000	***256*** (AR)		—	
Mercury	**Hg**[G]	80	200.5900	***196***(0.15), **198**(10.02), **199**(16.84), **200**(23.13), **201**(13.22), **202**(29.80), **204**(6.85)	0.144	2.2×10^{-4}	18(6.2)
Molybdenum	**Mo**	42	95.9400	***92***(15.86), **94**(9.12), **95**(15.70), **96**(16.50), **97**(9.45), **98**(23.75), ***100***(9.62)	0.129	6.6×10^{-3}	31
Neodymium	**Nd**	60	144.2400	**142**(27.13), **143**(12.20), ***144***(23.87), ***145***(8.29), **146**(17.18), **148**(5.72), ***150***(5.6)	—	1.1×10^{-2}	292
Neon	**Ne**	10	20.1830‡	**20**(90.92), **21**(0.26), **22**(8.82)	—	3.1×10^{-8}	194
Neptunium	**Np**	93	237.0000	***237*** (AR), ***239*** (AR)	—	—	—
Nickel	**Ni**	28	58.7100	**58**(67.76), **60**(26.16), **61**(1.25), **62**(3.66), **64**(1.16)	0.115	3.5×10^{-2}	4.3(1.24)
Niobium	**Nb**	41	92.9060	**93**(100)	0.134	1.1×10^{-2}	160
Nitrogen	**N**	7	14.0067	**14**(99.63), **15**(0.37)	0.074	9.0×10^{-2}	0.16
Nobelium	**No**	102	254.0000	***254*** (AR)	—	—	—
Osmium	**Os**	76	190.2000	**188**(13.3), **189**(16.1), **190**(26.4), ***192***(41.0)	0.126	2.2×10^{-6}	12 500
Oxygen	**O**	8	15.9940*	**16**(99.759), **17**(0.037), **18**(0.204) {air}	0.074	2.1×10^{2}	0.16
Palladium	**Pd**	46	106.4000	**102**(1.0), **104**(11.0), **105**(22.2), **106**(27.3), **108**(26.7), **110**(11.8)	0.128	4.4×10^{-6}	2500
Phosphorus	**P**	15	30.9738	**31**(100)	0.110	5.2	3.6
Platinum	**Pt**	78	195.0900	***190***(0.01), ***192***(0.78), **194**(32.9), **195**(33.8), **196**(25.2), **198**(7.2)	0.129	2.2×10^{-6}	4600(1540†)
Plutonium	**Pu**	94	242.0000	***238*** (AR), ***239*** (AR), ***242*** (AR)	—	—	15 000[R]
Polonium	**Po**	84	210.0000	***210*** (NR)	—	1.3×10^{-1}	0.5/mCi
Potassium	**K**[H]	19	39.1020	**39**(93.22), ***40***(0.12), **41**(6.77)	0.203	11.4	13.3
Praseodymium	**Pr**	59	140.9070	***141***(100)	—	2.4×10^{-3}	396
Promethium	**Pm**	61	145.0000	***145*** (AR)	—	—	0.04/mCi
Protactinium	**Pa**	91	231.0000	***231*** (NR precursor)	—	3.5×10^{-10}	2/mCi
Radium	**Ra**	88	226.0500	***226*** (NR), ***228*** (NR), ***224*** (NR), ***223*** (NR) {order of decreasing abundance}		5.7×10^{-9}	11 000[Cl]
Radon	**Rn**	86	222.0000	***222*** (NR), ***220*** (NR) {order of decreasing abundance}		—	—
Rhenium	**Re**	75	186.2000	**185**(37.07), ***187***(62.93)	0.128	4.4×10^{-8}	3000
Rhodium	**Rh**	45	102.9050	**103**(100)	0.125	4.4×10^{-7}	9500
Rubidium	**Rb**	37	85.4700	**85**(72.15), ***87***(27.85)	0.216	1.4×10^{-1}	356[Cl]
Ruthenium	**Ru**	44	101.0700	**96**(5.46), **98**(1.87), **99**(12.63), **100**(12.53), **101**(17.02), **102**(31.60), **104**(18.87)	0.124	1.8×10^{-6}	3070[O]
Samarium	**Sm**	62	150.3500	**144**(3.16), ***147***(15.07), ***148***(11.27), ***149***(13.82), **150**(7.47), **152**(26.63), **154**(22.53)	—	2.8×10^{-3}	420[O]
Scandium	**Sc**	21	44.9560	**45**(100)	0.144	2.2×10^{-3}	7300[O]

* Variable isotopic composition, see p. 24. ** Variable because of radioactivity. ‡ Experimental uncertainty see p. 24.
[G] hydrargyrum. [H] kalium. † price subject to violent fluctuations. [O] supplied as oxide. [Cl] supplied as chloride. [R] there is no free market in Pu.

Chemical elements (alphabetical order) – *(continued)*

Element	Symbol	Z	A/g mol^{-1}	Stable mass numbers and percentage abundances (in brackets)	r_{cov}/nm	$Q_{r\oplus}$	p/£ kg^{-1}
Selenium	**Se**	34	78.9600	**74**(0.89), **76**(9.02), **77**(7.58), **78**(23.52), **80**(49.82), ***82***(9.19)	0.117	4.0×10^{-5}	66
Silicon	**Si**	14	28.0860*	**28**(92.18), **29**(4.71), **30**(3.12)	0.117	1.0×10^{2}	3.3
Silver	**Ag**[J]	47	107.8700‡	**107**(51.35), **109**(48.65)	0.134	4.4×10^{-5}	104(22†)
Sodium	**Na**[K]	11	22.9898	**23**(100)	0.157	12.5	1.8
Strontium	**Sr**	38	87.6200	**84**(0.56), **86**(9.86), **87**(7.02), **88**(82.56)	0.191	1.3×10^{-1}	7.60[Cl]
Sulphur	**S**	16	32.0640*	**32**(95), **33**(0.76), **34**(4.22), **36**(0.01)	0.104	2.3×10^{-1}	0.60
Tantalum	**Ta**	73	180.9480	***180***(0.01), **181**(99.99)	0.134	9.2×10^{-4}	190
Technetium	**Tc**	43	99.0000	***99*** (AR)	—	—	4/mCi
Tellurium	**Te**	52	127.6000	**120**(0.09), **122**(2.46), **123**(0.87), **124**(4.61), **125**(6.99), **126**(18.71), **128**(31.79), ***130***(34.49)	0.137	8.8×10^{-7}	22.5
Terbium	**Tb**	65	158.9240	***159***(100)	—	4.0×10^{-4}	4100[O]
Thallium	**Tl**	81	204.3700	**203**(29.5), **205**(70.5)	0.155	1.3×10^{-3}	20
Thorium	**Th**	90	232.0380	***232*** (100 NR precursor)	—	5.1×10^{-3}	30[O]
Thoron	**(Tn)**	synonym for ^{220}Rn			—		
Thulium	**Tm**	69	168.9340	***169***(100)	—	8.8×10^{-5}	10 300[O]
Tin	**Sn**[L]	50	118.6900	**112**(0.95), **114**(0.65), **115**(0.34), **116**(14.24), **117**(7.57), **118**(24.01), **119**(8.58), **120**(32.97), **122**(4.71), **124**(5.98)	0.140	1.8×10^{-2}	5.7(1.5)
Titanium	**Ti**	22	47.9000	**46**(7.99), **47**(7.32), **48**(73.99), **49**(5.46), **50**(5.25)	0.132	1.4	13.5(1.17)
Tungsten	**W**[M]	74	183.8500	***180***(0.14), ***182***(26.4), ***183***(14.4), **184**(30.6), ***186***(28.4)	0.130	3.0×10^{-2}	10(4)
Tritium	**T**	Synonym for ^{3}H (NR and AR)			—		0.75/Ci[S]
Uranium	**U**	92	238.0300	***234***(0.0057), ***235***(0.7196), ***238***(99.276) {all NR : proportions in natural U}	—	1.8×10^{-3}	11[O]
Vanadium	**V**	23	50.9420	***50***(0.25), **51**(99.75)	0.122	6.6×10^{-2}	13
Xenon	**Xe**	54	131.3000	**124**(0.013), **126**(0.09), **128**(1.92), **129**(26.44), **130**(4.08), **131**(21.18), **132**(26.89), **134**(10.4), **136**(8.87)	—	5.3×10^{-10}	1070
Ytterbium	**Yb**	70	173.0400	**168**(0.14), **170**(3.03), **171**(14.31), **172**(21.82), **173**(16.13), **174**(31.84), **176**(12.73)	—	1.2×10^{-3}	1720[O]
Yttrium	**Y**	39	88.9050	**89**(100)	0.162	1.2×10^{-2}	380[O]
Zinc	**Zn**	30	65.3700	***64***(48.89), **66**(27.81), **67**(4.11), **68**(18.56), ***70***(0.62)	0.125	5.8×10^{-2}	0.75(0.12)
Zirconium	**Zr**	40	91.2200	**90**(51.46), **91**(11.23), **92**(17.11), **94**(17.40), ***96***(2.80)	0.145	9.7×10^{-2}	4[O]

* Variable isotopic composition, see p. 24. ** Variable because of radioactivity. ‡ Experimental uncertainty see p. 24.
[J] argentum. [K] natrium. [L] stannum. [M] wolfram. † price subject to violent fluctuations. [O] supplied as oxide.
[Cl] supplied as chloride. [S] per curie, *not* per millicurie.

Chart of the nuclides

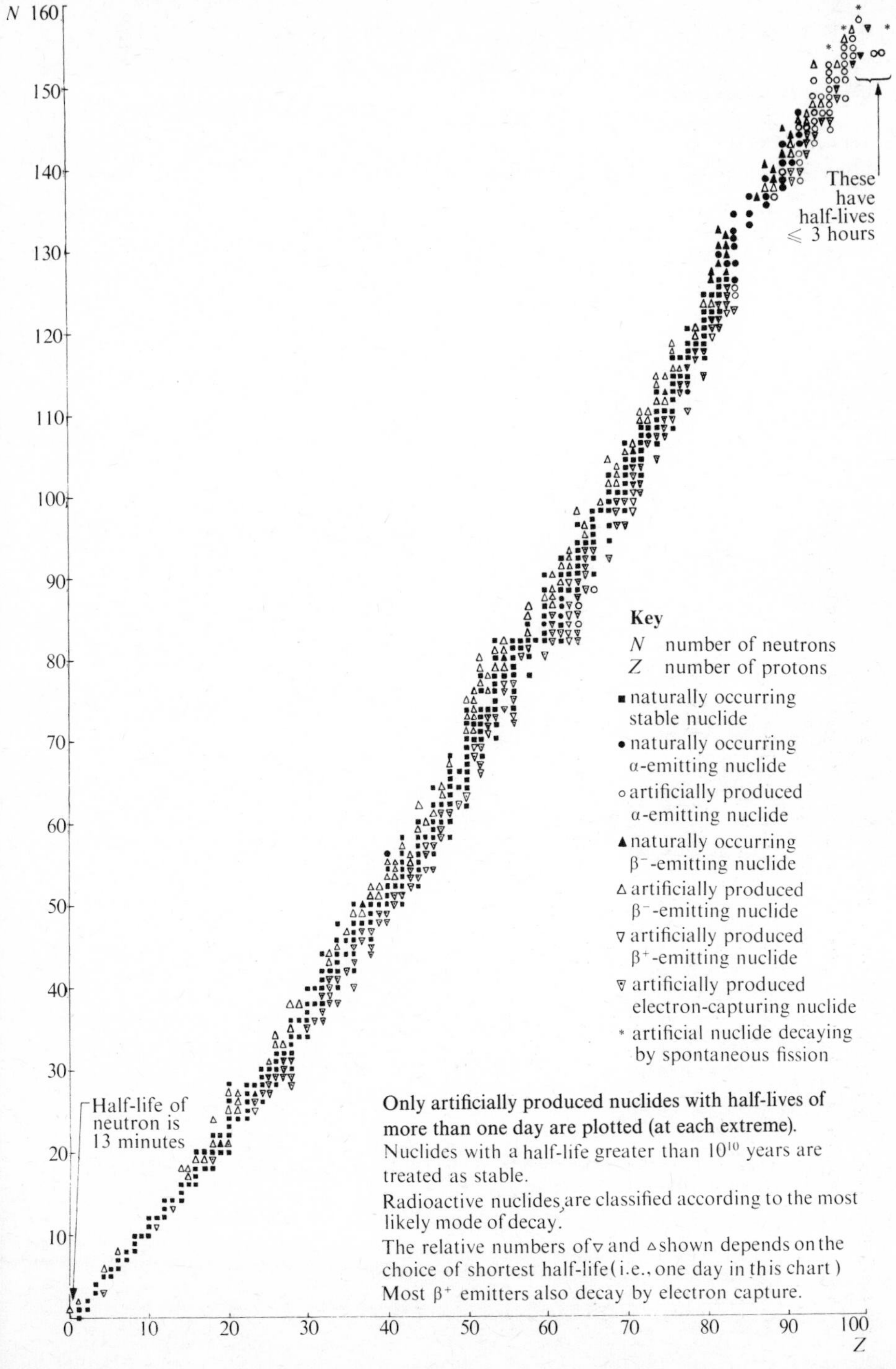

Only artificially produced nuclides with half-lives of more than one day are plotted (at each extreme).

Nuclides with a half-life greater than 10^{10} years are treated as stable.

Radioactive nuclides are classified according to the most likely mode of decay.

The relative numbers of ▽ and △ shown depends on the choice of shortest half-life (i.e., one day in this chart)

Most β^+ emitters also decay by electron capture.

Radioactive decay chains

A mass number *Z* atomic number

Branches involving less than 1 % of the atoms have been omitted. Gamma radiation is emitted after the majority of the decays.

Thorium series $A = 4n$

Symbols in brackets are the old symbols for the nuclide (no longer used).

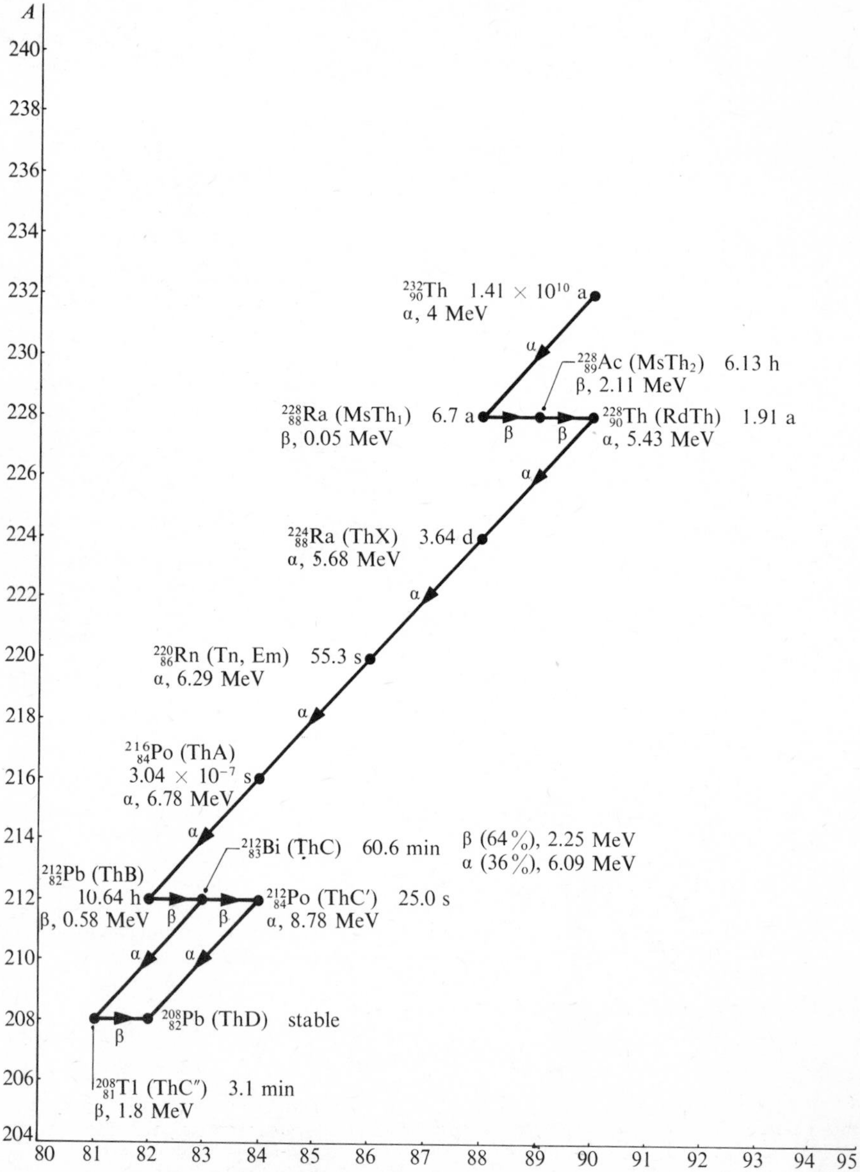

Neptunium series $A = 4n+1$

This series does not occur in nature. The precursors are formed in nuclear reactors.

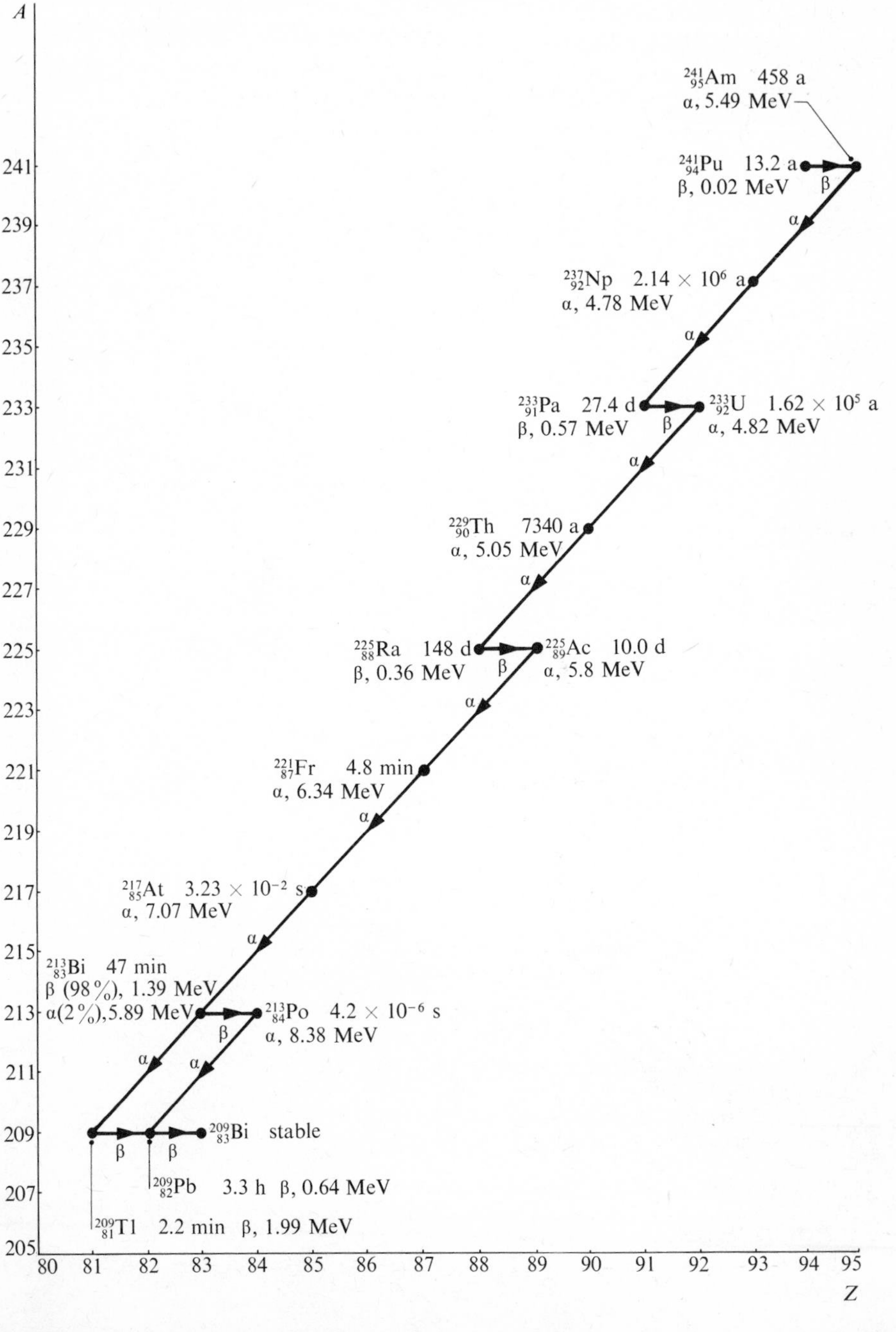

Radioactive decay chains

Uranium series $A = 4n+2$

Symbols in brackets are the old symbols for the nuclide (no longer used).

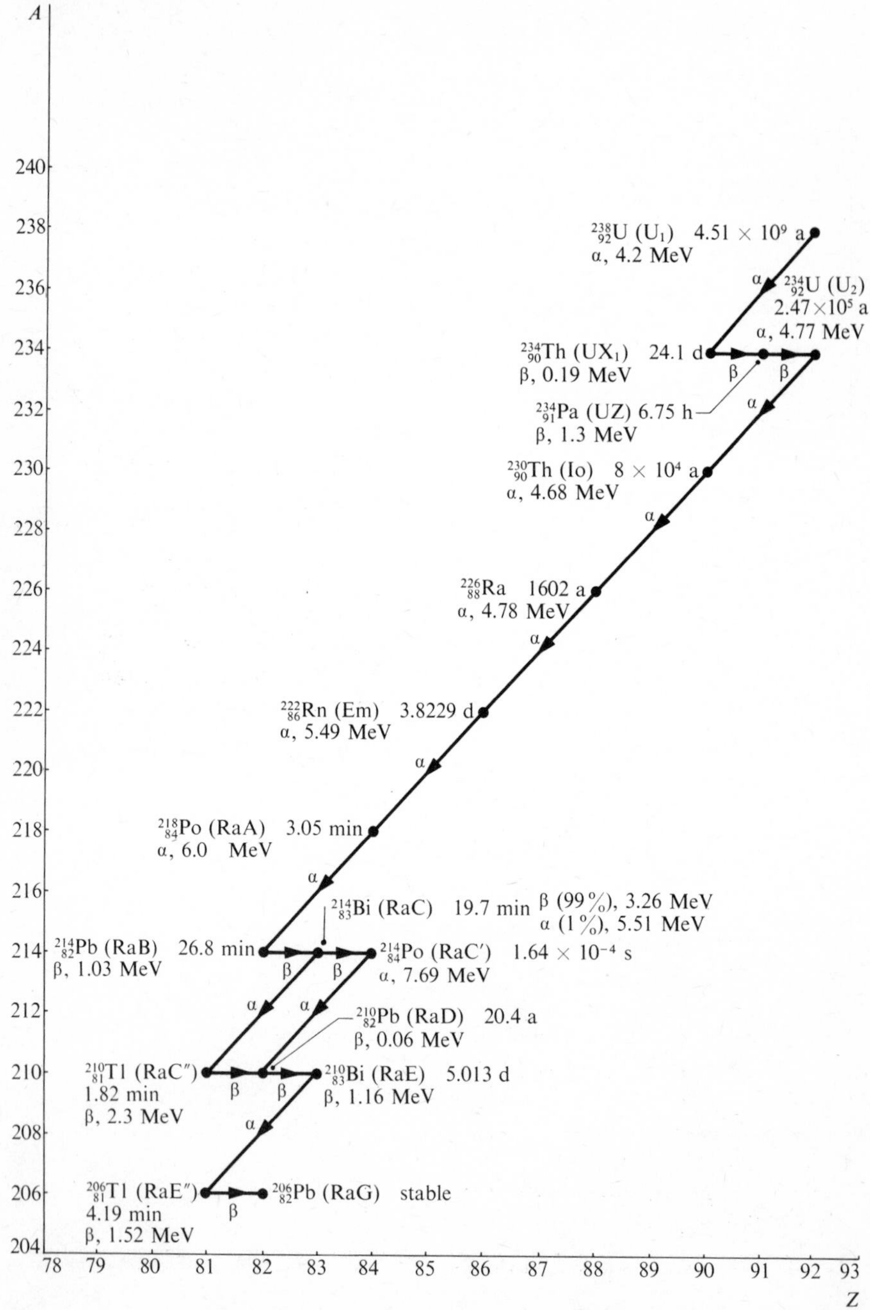

Actinium series $A = 4n+3$
Symbols in brackets are the old symbols for the nuclide (no longer used).

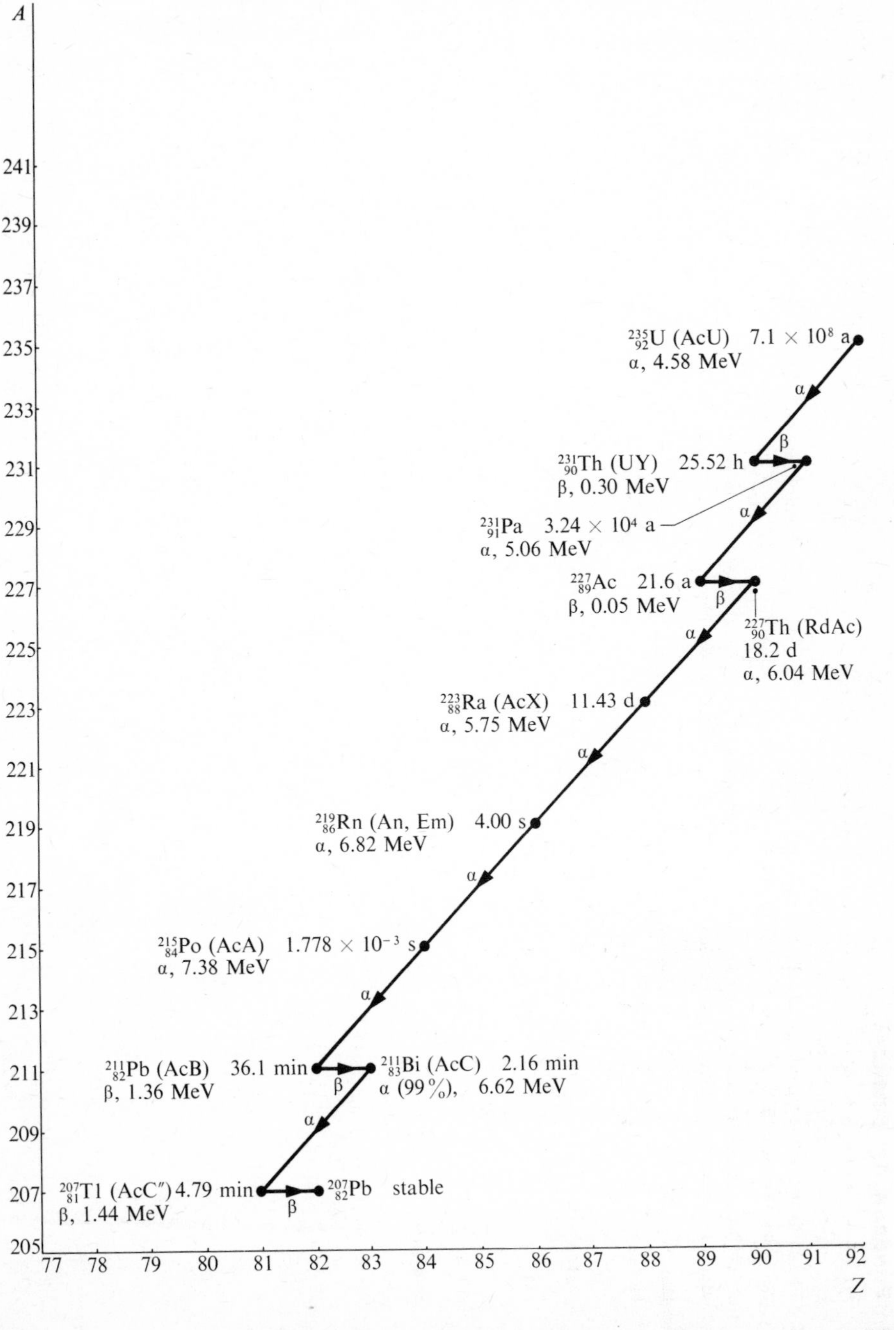

Fundamental particles

m rest mass of particle — τ mean life of particle
Q energy released on decay — R branching ratio

The suffixes give the sign of the electric charge on the particle. When no sign is given, the decay particles may assume either sign, consistent with the conservation of charge.

It has been assumed that anti-particles (same mass but opposite electrical charge) decay in an analogous manner with the same values of τ and Q, but very recent work throws some doubt on this.

Particle	m/MeV	τ/s	Principle decay modes	R/%	Q/MeV
Photon					
γ	0	stable			
Leptons					
ν	0	stable	Two types of neutrino exist, associated with electrons (ν_e) or muons (ν_μ)		
e	0.51	stable			
μ^+	105.7	2.2×10^{-6}	$e^+ + \nu_e + \bar{\nu}_\mu$	100	105.2
Mesons					
π^+	139.6	2.6×10^{-8}	$\mu^+ + \nu_\mu$	100	33.9
π^0	135.0	1.8×10^{-16}	$\gamma+\gamma$ $\gamma+e^-+e^+$	99 1	135.0 134.0
K^+	493.8	1.2×10^{-8}	$\mu^+ + \nu_\mu$ $\pi^+ + \pi^0$	63 21	388.1 219.2
K_1^0	497.8	8.6×10^{-11}	$\pi^+ + \pi^-$ $\pi^0 + \pi^0$	68 32	218.5 227.8
K_2^0	497.8	5.4×10^{-8}	$\pi^0+\pi^0+\pi^0$ $\pi^+ + \pi^- + \pi^0$ $\pi+\mu+\nu_\mu$ $\pi+e+\nu_e$	21 13 28 38	92.8 83.6 252.5 357.6
η^0	548.8	3×10^{-19}†	$\gamma+\gamma$ $3\pi^0$ $\pi^+ + \pi^- + \pi^0$	38 29 23	548.8 143.8 134.8
$\rho^{+,0}$	765	5×10^{-24}†	$\pi+\pi$	100	486
ω^0	783	5×10^{-23}†	$\pi^+ + \pi^- + \pi^0$ $\pi^0+\gamma$	88 12	369 648

Particle	m/MeV	τ/s	Principle decay modes	R/%	Q/MeV
Baryons					
p^+	938.2	stable			
n^0	939.6	1.0×10^3	$p^+ + \pi^- \rightarrow$ $p^+ + e^- + \bar{\nu}_e$	100	0.78
Λ^0	1115.6	2.5×10^{-10}	$p^+ + \pi^-$ $n+\pi^0$	65 35	37.6 40.9
Σ^+	1189.4	8.1×10^{-11}	$p^+ + \pi^0$ $n+\pi^+$	53 47	116.2 110.3
Σ^0	1192.5	$<1.0\times10^{-14}$	$\Lambda^0+\gamma$	100	77.0
Σ^-	1197.3	1.6×10^{-10}	$n+\pi^-$	100	118.1
Ξ^0	1314.7	3.0×10^{-10}	$\Lambda+\pi^0$	100	63.9
Ξ^-	1321.2	1.66×10^{-10}	$\Lambda+\pi^-$	100	65.8
Ω^-	1672.4	1.3×10^{-10}	$\Xi^+ + \pi^-$ $\Xi^- + \pi^0$ $\Lambda^0 + K^-$	8 seen 3 seen 13 seen	221 66
Δ	1236	5×10^{-24}	$N+\pi$	100	231

$\Delta^{++} \rightarrow p^+ + \pi^+(100\,\%)$; $\Delta^+ \rightarrow p^+ + \pi^0(67\,\%)$, $\rightarrow n+\pi^+(33\,\%)$;
$\Delta^0 \rightarrow n+\pi^0(67\,\%)$, $\rightarrow p^+ + \pi^-(33\,\%)$; $\Delta^- \rightarrow n+\pi^-(100\,\%)$.

† value uncertain.
Reference: R4.

Miscellaneous nuclear physics data

Range of selected α-particles

E α-particle energy at start R range

Nuclide	E/MeV	R(air, 288 K, 1 atm)/cm
^{232}Th	4.00	2.59
^{238}U	4.20	2.67
^{226}Ra	4.77	3.39
^{210}Po	5.30	3.84
^{214}Po	7.68	6.95
^{212}Po	8.78	8.57

Range of electrons in aluminium

E initial energy of electron R range

E/MeV	0.01	0.05	0.1	0.4	1.0	2.0	5.0	10.0
R/g cm^{-2}	0.16	4.0	13.5	120	420	950	2540	5200

Absorption of X-rays and γ-rays

ρ density μ_m mass absorption coefficient for energy absorption (ignoring Compton effect)
E photon energy

	E/MeV	0.01	0.05	0.1	0.4	1.0	2.0	5.0	10.0
Absorber	ρ/g cm^{-3}				μ_m/cm^2 g^{-1}				
air	0.0013^{273K}	4.55	0.203	0.155	0.095	0.064	0.044	0.027	0.020
water	1.0	4.72	0.221	0.171	0.106	0.070	0.049	0.030	0.022
aluminium	2.7	24.3	0.353	0.169	0.093	0.061	0.043	0.018	0.023
iron	7.9	169	1.90	0.37	0.094	0.060	0.042	0.031	0.030
lead	11.5	**150**^{B}	8.5	5.46^{A}	0.220	0.070	0.046	0.043	0.050
concrete	2.35*	24.6	0.35	0.17	0.095	0.063	0.045	0.029	0.023

^{A} μ_m(Pb) increases discontinuously from 0.95 to 7.2 cm^2 g^{-1} as E increases through the value 0.88 MeV.   * variable. ^{B} 0.02 MeV.

Some levels of radiation producing biological effects

Source or effect	Average dose per individual
Natural radioactivity and cosmic rays	100 mRem per year
Maximum effect of bomb testing, 1954–61	12 mRem per year
Industrial, medical, and agricultural use	20 mRem per year
Additional radiation producing no significant genetical changes in whole population	5 Rem in 30 years (=167 mRem per year)
Radiation producing slightly shortened average life span	100 Rem during working life
Radiation producing somatic damage in individual, e.g. cancer in later life	250 Rem (over a few years)
Radiation producing immediate sickness	60 Rem in a few hours
50 per cent lethal dose	400 Rem in a few hours
Maximum permissible dose rate for general public	0.75 mRem per hour

Estimation of radiation levels

ϕ dose rate at 1 m from source A activity of source
V p.d. applied to X-ray tube E photon energy

X-ray tube

V/kV	50	100	200
ϕ/Rem min^{-1} mA^{-1}	0.32	1.2	3.6

γ source

ϕ/Rem h^{-1} = 0.4(A/Ci)(E/MeV)

Reference: R4.

Properties of selected atomic nuclei

There are 1600 different nuclides (some doubtful). 238 are stable isotopes of 80 elements (see page 24 **PPE**), 49 are very slightly radioactive isotopes of elements up to ^{209}Bi, (30 have half-lives in excess of 10^{13} years), and 39 occur in naturally occurring radioactive decay chains. The remainder have been produced artificially by various forms of nuclear reaction. 102 are isotopes of transuranic elements and 41 are isotopes of Tc and Pm; none of these elements occur naturally. There are also over 200 isomeric (metastable) states of nuclides with half-lives in excess of 1 second. ^{3}H (^{3}T) and ^{14}C are produced in the atmosphere by cosmic ray bombardment.

The following table includes all known isotopes of the elements up to $_8$O (note there is no nuclide of mass 5), all members of the ^{232}Th decay chain, and other interesting or important nuclides.

Z atomic number, that is, the number of protons in the nucleus and the number of electrons in the outer part of the atom
A mass or nucleon number, that is, the number of protons and neutrons in the nucleus. (Hence $N = A - Z$ gives the number of neutrons). C shows commercial availability.
M exact mass of the nuclide including the electrons. $m_u = 1.66 \times 10^{-27}$ kg ≙ 931.5 MeV
Δ energy equivalent of the mass defect. $\Delta = \{M - ZM(^1\mathrm{H}) - NM(\mathrm{n})\}c^2$
a abundance of stable, or nearly stable, nuclides, as a percentage of the total number of atoms of the element in question on Earth
$T_{\frac{1}{2}}$ half-life of radioactive nuclide: a year, d day, h hour, min minute, s second

Decay
Only the principal modes of decay are given, with E_{max}/MeV in parentheses, where E_{max} stands for the maximum energy released in each mode. Where appropriate the percentage of nuclei in this mode is given.

α emission of alpha particle
$\beta^{\pm}$ emission of positive or negative beta particle
Ec electron capture (generally an alternative to β^+ emission—always results in γ emission)
e^- ejection of atomic electron by nuclear γ-ray (internal conversion)
γ emission of γ-ray photon
SF spontaneous fission
IT isomeric transition from an excited state to a lower state of the same nuclide by γ emission

The following symbolism is used to show the relationship of one decay mode to another.
, the first decay sometimes leaves the nucleus in an excited state which decays by the next mode
; the first decay is invariably followed by the second
: the two modes are alternative decay paths

For example, α(4.58), γ(0.19) 54 % stands for: α emission with $E_{max} = 4.58$ MeV or α emission with $E_{max} = 4.39$ (= 4.58 − 0.19) MeV followed by γ emission with $E_{max} = 0.19$ MeV in 54 per cent of decays
β^-(4.6); γ(0.197) stands for: β^-, $E_{max} = 4.6$ MeV invariably followed by γ, $E_{max} = 0.197$ MeV.
β^-(1.36)32 %: β^+(1.54) stands for: β^-, $E_{max} = 1.36$ MeV in 32 % of decays, or β^+, $E_{max} = 1.54$ MeV in 68 %.

The decay of many nuclides is quite complex and may involve several different γ-rays, or even several successive γ-rays, with consequent variations in the particle energy. Full details may be found in R24. It should also be noted that β emission is accompanied by a (virtually undetectable) neutrino, so that β-particle energy is variable with a continuous spectrum. Values quoted are the maximum possible.

Production
Only one method by which the nuclide has been produced is given. The notation is
parent nuclide (bombarding particle, outgoing particle)
d deuteron, that is, ^{2}H
t triton, that is, ^{3}H
NR natural radioactive nuclide
D daughter product of following nuclide
fiss occurs as a result of ^{235}U fission

σ absorption cross-section for thermal neutrons, that is, a measure of how readily neutrons are absorbed by the nuclide. In general, absorption of a neutron results in the emission of a γ-ray and the formation of a heavier (and possibly radioactive) isotope of the same element – the (n, γ) reaction. It may, however, cause the emission of one or more charged particles, or fission. σ gives the total absorption cross-section unless a specific reaction is noted.

Reference: R24.

Z		A		M/m_u	Δ/MeV	a/%	$T_{\frac{1}{2}}$	Decay	Production	$\sigma/10^{-28}\ m^2$
−1	**e**	0		0.000549	0.51^	—	—	stable	—	—
0	**n**	1		1.008665	8.071	—	11.7 min	$\beta^-(0.78)$	$^9Be(\alpha, n)$	0
1	**p**	1		1.007276	6.777	—	—	stable	—	0.332
1	**H**	1		1.007825	7.289	99.985*	—	stable	—	0.332
		2		2.014102	13.136	0.015*	—	stable	—	0.0005
		3	C	3.016050	14.950	—	12.6 a	$\beta^-(0.0186)$ no γ	$^6Li(n, \alpha)$	$<7\times10^{-6}$
2	**He**	3		3.016030	14.931	0.00013	—	stable	$^3H(\beta^-)$	5330
		4		4.002603	2.425	99.99987	—	stable		0
		6		6.018893	17.598	—	0.8 s	$\beta^-(5)$	$^7Li(\gamma, p)$	
		8		8.034032	31.699	—	0.12 s	$\beta^-(9.7), \gamma(0.98)98\%$; n	$^{12}C(p, ?)$	
3	**Li**	6		6.015124	14.088	7.42	—	stable	—	953
		7		7.016004	14.907	92.58	—	stable	—	0.037
		8		8.022487	20.946	—	0.85 s	$\beta^-(13), \alpha(1.6)$	$^7Li(n, \gamma)$	
		9		9.026807	24.969	—	0.17 s	$\beta^-(13.6)$, n(0.76)75 %	$^9Be(n, p)$	
4	**Be**	6		6.019721	18.370	—	0.4 s	'particle unstable'	$^9Be(p, ?)$	
		7	C	7.016929	15.769	—	53.6 d	Ec(0.477)10 %	$^{10}B(p, \alpha)$	54 000
		9		9.012186	11.351	100	—	stable	—	0.009
		10		10.013534	12.606	—	2.5×10^6 a	$\beta^-(0.555)$ no γ	$^9Be(d, p)$	
		11		11.021664	20.179	—	13.6 s	$\beta^-(11.5), \gamma(2.14)32\%$	$^{11}B(n, p)$	
		12		12.026839	24.999	—	0.0114 s	$\beta^-(12), \gamma$	$^{18}O(p, ?)$	
5	**B**	8		8.024609	22.922	—	0.78 s	$\beta^+(14.0):\alpha(1.6)$	$^6Li(^3He, n)$	
		10		10.012938	12.051	19.6	—	stable	—	3837 (n, α)
		11		11.009305	8.667	80.4	—	stable	—	0.005
		12		12.014353	13.369	—	0.020 s	$\beta^-(13.37), \gamma(4.43)1.3\%:\alpha$	$^{11}B(d, p)$	
		13		13.017780	16.561	—	0.0186 s	$\beta^-(13.44), \gamma(3.68)7\%$	$^{11}B(t, p)$	

* natural variation (<1 %).
^ energy equivalent of total mass of particle.

Properties of selected atomic nuclei

Z		A		M/m_u	Δ/MeV	a/%	$T_{\frac{1}{2}}$	Decay	Production	$\sigma/10^{-28}\ m^2$
6	**C**	9		9.031133	28.999	—	0.127 s	p(8.2); α(0.05)	^{10}B(p, 2n)	
		10		10.016811	15.659	—	19.3 s	β^+(1.87); γ(0.72)	^{10}B(p, n)	
		11		11.011431	10.647	—	20.5 min	β^+(0.97)	^{10}B(d, n)	
		12		**12.000000**	**0 (Def)**	98.89*	—	stable		0.0033
		13		13.003354	3.125	1.11*	—	stable		0.0009
		14	C	14.003241	3.020	—	5730 a	β^-(0.156) no γ	^{14}N(n, p)	
		15		15.010599	9.873	—	2.5 s	β^-(9.82), γ(5.3)68 %	^{14}C(d, p)	
		16		16.014697	13.690	—	0.74 s	β^-; n	^{14}C(t, p)	
7	**N**	12		12.018637	17.360	—	0.011 s	β^+(16.4), 3α(0.195)3 %	^{12}C(p, n)	
		13		13.005738	5.345	—	10.0 min	β^+(1.2)	^{10}B(α, n)	
		14		14.003074	2.864	99.63	—	stable	—	1.81
		15		15.000107	0.100	0.37	—	stable	—	2.4×10^{-5}
		16		16.006103	5.685	—	7.14 s	β^-(10.4), γ(6.13)68 %	^{15}N(n, γ)	
		17		17.008448	7.870	—	4.16 s	β^-(8.68), n(1.21)95 %	^{14}C(α, p)	
		18		18.014063	13.099	—	0.63 s	β^-(9.4); γ(1.98)	^{18}O(n, p)	
8	**O**	13		13.024799	23.099	—	0.0087 s	β^+; p(6.97)	^{14}N(p, 2n)	
		14		14.008597	8.008	—	71 s	β^+(4.12), γ(2.31)99 %	^{14}N(p, n)	
		15		15.003070	2.860	—	2.06 min	β^+(1.74)	^{14}N(d, n)	
		16		15.994915	−4.737	99.759*	—	stable	—	0.0002
		17		16.999133	−0.807	0.037*	—	stable	—	0.24 (n, α)
		18		17.999161	−0.782	0.204*	—	stable	—	0.0002
		19		19.003578	3.333	—	29.1 s	β^-(4.6); γ(0.197)97 %	^{18}O(n, γ)	
		20		20.004079	3.799	—	14 s	β^-(2.75); γ(1.06)	^{18}O(t, p)	
11	**Na**	22	C	21.994437	−5.181	—	2.62 a	β^+(1.82), (1.27) 99.95 %	^{19}F(α, n)	
		23		22.989772	−9.526	100	—	stable	—	0.53
		24	C	23.990963	−8.417	—	14.96 h	β^-(1.39); γ(2.75); γ(1.37)	^{23}Na(n, γ)	
13	**Al**	27		26.981540	−17.194	100	—	stable	—	0.235
15	**P**	30		29.978315	−20.198	—	2.5 min	β^+(3.24), γ(2.23) 0.5 %	^{27}Al(α, n)	
		32	C	31.973910	−24.301	—	14.3 d	β^-(1.71) no γ	^{31}P(n, γ)	

* natural variation (< 1 %). Def = definition.

Z		A		M/m_u	Δ/MeV	a/%	$T_{\frac{1}{2}}$	Decay	Production	$\sigma/10^{-28}$ m²
16	**S**	35	C	34.969031	−28.845	—	87.9 d	$\beta^-(0.17)$ no γ	^{34}S(n, γ)	
17	**Cl**	36	C	35.968309	−29.518	—	3×10^5 a	$\beta^-(0.71)$: Ec(1.14) 1.9 %: β^+	^{35}Cl(n, γ)	100
19	**K**	40		39.964001	−33.531	0.118	1.3×10^9 a	$\beta^-(1.31)$: Ec(1.51) 11 %: β^+	NR	70
26	**Fe**	54		53.939617	−56.243	5.84	—	stable	—	2.9
		55	C	54.938299	−57.471	—	2.60 a	Ec(0.23)	^{54}Fe(n, γ)	
		56		55.934937	−60.602	91.68	—	stable	—	2.7
		57	C	56.935398	−60.173	2.17	—	stable	—	2.5
		58		57.933282	−62.144	0.31	—	stable	Mössbauer resonance γ absorption (from ^{57}Co)	1.1
		59	C	58.934878	−60.657	—	45 d	$\beta^-(1.57)$ 0.3 %, $\gamma(1.1)$ 56 %	^{58}Fe(n, γ)	
27	**Co**	56	C	55.939849	−56.027	—	77d	$\beta^+(1.49)$: Ec 80 %; $\gamma(0.84)$	^{56}Fe(p, n)	
		57	C	56.936296	−59.337	—	270 d	Ec(0.84); γ, e$^-$	^{55}Mn(α, 2n) Mössbauer source	
		59		58.933189	−62.231	100	—	stable	—	18
		60	C	59.933814	−61.648	—	5.27 a	$\beta^-(0.31)$; $\gamma(1.33)$; $\gamma(1.17)$	^{59}Co(n, γ)	6
28	**Ni**	64		63.927954	−67.107	1.16	—	stable	—	1.5
29	**Cu**	64	C	63.929759	−65.426		12.8 h	$\beta^-(0.57)$ 38 %: $\beta^+(0.66)$ 19 %, e$^-$(1.33)	^{63}Cu(n, γ)	
30	**Zn**	64		63.927954	−67.107	48.89	—	stable		0.46
		65	C	64.929231	−65.917		245 d	$\beta^+(0.327)$, Ec 98 %, e$^-$(1.11)	^{64}Zn(n, γ)	
47	**Ag**	107		106.905100	−88.394	51.35	—	stable	—	35
		108		107.905950	−87.603	—	2.4 min	$\beta^-(1.64)$ 97 %; $\beta^+(0.9)$	D ^{108m}Ag	
		108^m		107.906070	−87.491	—	5 a	$\gamma(0.722)$ Ec 90 %: IT	^{107}Ag(n, γ)	
		109		108.904770	−88.702	48.65	—	stable		89 (to ^{110}Ag) 3 (to ^{110m}Ag)
		110		109.906100	−87.463		24.4 s	$\beta^-(2.87)$, $\gamma(0.66)$ 4.5 %	^{109}Ag(n, γ)	
		110^m		109.906230	−87.342		255 d	$\beta^-(1.5)$; $\gamma(0.89)$ 71 %; $\gamma(0.66)$ 96 %	^{109}Ag(n, γ)	80

^{m} metastable isomer.

Properties of selected atomic nuclei

Z		A		M/m_u	Δ/MeV	a/%	$T_{\frac{1}{2}}$	Decay	Production	$\sigma/10^{-28}$ m^2
48	**Cd**	113		112.904410	−89.037	12.26	3×10^{15} a	stable	(NR)	20 000
49	**In**	115		114.903880	−89.531	95.77	6×10^{14} a	$\beta^-(0.48)$ no γ	(NR)	45
		116		115.905320	−88.200	—	14 s	$\beta^-(3.3)$	^{115}In(n, γ)	
		116^m		115.905380	−88.134	—	54 min	$\beta^-(1.0)$; γ; $\gamma(1.3)$	Two isomeric states exist	
53	**I**	131	C	130.906130	−87.435	—	8.05 d	$\beta^-(0.81)$, $\gamma(0.36)$ 82 %	fiss	
		135		134.909830	−83.989	—	6.7 h	$\beta^-(1.4)$; γ	fiss	
54	**Xe**	135		134.907030	−86.597		9.14 h	$\beta^-(0.42)$; $\gamma(0.25)$: $e^-(0.2)$	fiss, D ^{135}I	2.7×10^6
55	**Cs**	130		129.906720	−86.885	—	30.7 min	$\beta^+(1.97)$: $\beta^-(0.44)$ 2 %	^{127}I(α, 2n)	
		133(C)		132.905360	−88.152	100	—	stable	Mössbauer resonance γ absorption (from ^{133}Ba)	28
		135		134.905750	−87.789	—	2×10^6 a	$\beta^-(0.21)$ no γ	fiss, D ^{135}Xe	8.7
		137	C	136.906710	−86.895	—	30.0 a	$\beta^-(1.18)$, $\gamma(0.66)$ 85 %	fiss	0.11
81	**Tl**	208		207.982010	−16.756		3.1 min	$\beta^-(1.80)$; $\gamma(2.61)$	D ^{232}Th	
82	**Pb**	206		205.974460	−23.788	23.6	—	stable	D ^{238}U	0.03
		207		206.975900	−22.447	22.6	—	stable	D ^{235}U	0.73
		208		207.976660	−21.739	52.3	—	stable	D ^{232}Th	0.0005
		210	C	209.984190	−14.725	—	22.7 a	$\beta^-(0.06)$, $\gamma(0.05)$ 81 %	D ^{238}U	
		212		211.988870	−10.366	—	10.6 h	$\beta^-(0.58)$, $\gamma(0.24)$ 81 %	D ^{232}Th	
		214		213.999840	−0.148	—	26.8 min	$\beta^-(1.03)$, $\gamma(0.35)$ 47 %		
83	**Bi**	212		211.991280	−8.121	—	60.6 min	$\beta^-(2.25)$: $\alpha(6.09)$ 36 %	D ^{232}Th	
84	**Po**	212		211.988870	−10.366	—	3×10^{-7} s	$\alpha(8.78)$	D ^{232}Th	
		216		216.001910	1.779	—	0.145 s	$\alpha(6.78)$	D ^{232}Th	
86	**Rn**	220		220.011390	10.609	—	55.5 s	$\alpha(6.29)$	D ^{232}Th	0.2
		222		222.017590	16.384	—	3.82 d	$\alpha(5.49)$	D ^{238}U	0.7
88	**Ra**	224		224.020200	18.815		3.64 d	$\alpha(5.68)$, $\gamma(0.24)$ 5.5 %	D ^{232}Th	12
		226		226.025430	23.687		1622 a	$\alpha(4.78)$, $\gamma(0.19)$ 5.4 %	D ^{238}U	20
		228		228.031090	28.959		6.7 a	$\beta^-(0.05)$ no γ	D ^{232}Th	36

^{m} metastable isomer.

Z		A		M/m_u	Δ/MeV	a/%	$T_{\frac{1}{2}}$	Decay	Production	$\sigma/10^{-28}$ m^2
89	**Ac**	228		228.031030	28.903		6.13 h	$\beta^-(2.11); \gamma$	D ^{232}Th	
90	**Th**	228	C	228.028730	26.761		1.91 a	$\alpha(5.43), \gamma(0.08)$ 28 %	D ^{232}Th	123
		230	C	230.033140	30.869		80 000 a	$\alpha(4.68) : \alpha(4.62)$ 24 %	D ^{238}U	
		232	C	232.038070	35.470	100	1.4×10^{10}a	$\alpha(4.01) : \alpha(3.95)$ 23 %	NR	7.4
		234		234.043620	40.630		24.1 d	β^-, γ	D ^{238}U	
91	**Pa**	234^m		234.043420	40.444		1.18 min	$\beta^-(2.29)$	D ^{238}U	
92	**U**	233	C	233.039650	36.932		1.6×10^5 a	$\alpha(4.82), \gamma(0.04)$ 15 %	^{232}Th(n, γ 2β^-)	581
		234		234.040960	38.153	0.00572	2.48×10^5 a	$\alpha(4.77), \gamma(0.05)$ 28 %	D ^{234}Pa	95
		235	C	235.043940	40.928	0.72	7.13×10^8 a	$\alpha(4.58)$ 8 % : $\alpha(4.4)$ 54 %, γ	NR	694
		236		236.045580	42.456		2.39×10^7 a	$\alpha(4.49), \gamma(0.05)$ 26 %	^{235}U (n, γ)	6
		238		238.050810	47.327	99.27	4.51×10^9 a	$\alpha(4.20), \gamma(0.05)$ 23 %	NR	2.73
		239		239.054320	50.597		23.5 min	$\beta^-(1.29), \gamma(0.07)$ 74 %	^{238}U (n, γ)	22
93	**Np**	239		239.052940	49.311		2.35 d	$\beta^-(0.71); \gamma$	D ^{239}U	25
94	**Pu**	239		239.052170	48.594		24360 a	$\alpha(5.16); \gamma$	D ^{239}Np	1025
		240		240.053820	50.131		65807 a	$\alpha(5.17), \gamma(0.05)$ 24 %	^{239}Pu (n, γ)	286
		241		241.056870	52.972		13.27 a	$\beta^-(0.02); \alpha(4.9)$ 0.002 %	^{240}Pu (n, γ)	1400
95	**Am**	239		239.053040	49.405		12 h	Ec; $\gamma(0.23); \gamma(0.29)$	^{239}Pu (p, n)	
		241	C	241.056850	52.953		458 a	$\alpha(5.49), \gamma(0.06)$ 81 %	D ^{241}Pu	700
100	**Fm**	249		249.079220	73.790		2.5 min	$\alpha(7.9)$	^{238}U (^{16}O, 5n)	
		251					7h	$\alpha(0.89)$	^{249}Cf (α, 3n)	
104	**Ku**	260		Heaviest nuclide yet claimed			0.3 s	SF	^{242}Pu (^{22}Ne, 4n)	

^{m} metastable isomer.

The electromagnetic spectrum

λ	ν	E	E	T	Radiation type	Fundamental process	Generation and detection	Applications	Notes	Absorption[a]
10^5 m	10^3 Hz	10^{-30} J	10^{-11} eV		Audio and power frequencies	Whistlers from lightning	Rotating generators and microphones	Telephones, power	A.c. mains 50 Hz (audio: 30 Hz to 30 kHz)	
10^4 m	10^4 Hz	10^{-29} J	10^{-10} eV		Very low frequency (v.l.f.)	Electrical oscillations	Electronic valves and semiconductor devices	(High audio frequencies) Navigation	Inductive heating	
10^3 m	10^5 Hz	10^{-28} J	10^{-9} eV		Low frequency (l.f.)	,, ,,	,, ,,	Maritime; long wave broadcasting (BBC Radio 2 1500 m); navigation	Inductive heating	
10^2 m	10^6 Hz	10^{-27} J	10^{-8} eV		Medium frequency (m.f.)	,, ,,	,, ,,	Distress (500 kHz); medium wave a.m. broadcasting; maritime; navigation	Inductive heating NBS std. freq. 2.5 MHz	
10 m	10^7 Hz	10^{-26} J	10^{-7} eV		High frequency (h.f.)	,, ,,	,, ,,	Short wave a.m. broadcasting; amateur bands; aeronautical; maritime; navigation; frequency stds	Dielectric heating NBS stds. 5, 10, 15, 20, 25 MHz; ionospheric reflection of radio waves	
1 m	10^8 Hz	10^{-25} J	10^{-6} eV		Very high frequency (v.h.f.)	Hyperfine structure	,, ,,	TV; f.m. radio; police; ambulance; aeronautical; navigation; radio astronomy	Dielectric heating; some frequencies reflected by ionosphere	

λ	ν	E	E	T
10^{-1} m	10^{9} Hz	10^{-24} J	10^{-5} eV	
10^{-2} m	10^{10} Hz	10^{-23} J	10^{-4} eV	1 K
10^{-3} m	10^{11} Hz	10^{-22} J	10^{-3} eV	10 K
10^{-4} m	10^{12} Hz	10^{-21} J	10^{-2} eV	100 K
10^{-5} m	10^{13} Hz	10^{-20} J	10^{-1} eV	10^{3} K
	10^{14} Hz			

Radiation type	Fundamental process	Generation and detection	Applications	Notes	Absorption[a]
Ultra high frequency (u.h.f)	Hyperfine structure	Magnetrons; klystrons; travelling wave tubes; special valves up to 10^{9} Hz	Radar; TV; radio astronomy	Dielectric heating Deuterium–2 327 MHz Hydrogen–1 1420 MHz	
Centimetre waves	Hyperfine structure. Molecular inversion and rotation	Magnetrons; klystrons; travelling wave tubes	Radar; microwave relay frequencies; telemetry; radio astronomy	Rubidium–85[b] 3036 MHz Caesium–133 9193 MHz Ammonia 23 870 MHz	
Millimetre waves	Molecular inversion and rotation	Harmonic generators and masers	Radar, amateur and experimental	Attenuation by rain and fog; O_2 and H_2O absorption bands in Earth's atmosphere	
Sub millimetre waves	" "	Masers		Water vapour absorption in atmosphere	
Far infra-red	Molecular inversion and rotation Molecular vibration	Quartz mercury lamps and Welsbach mantles Detector; thermocouple	Research	Water vapour, CO_2 and O_3 absorption in atmosphere	
Intermediate infra-red					

Notes

λ = wavelength
E = quantum energy
ν = frequency
T = corresponding temperature = E/k

[a] ‖ quartz opaque ⁞ glass opaque | atmosphere opaque
[b] frequencies used for masers and atomic clocks.

The electromagnetic spectrum

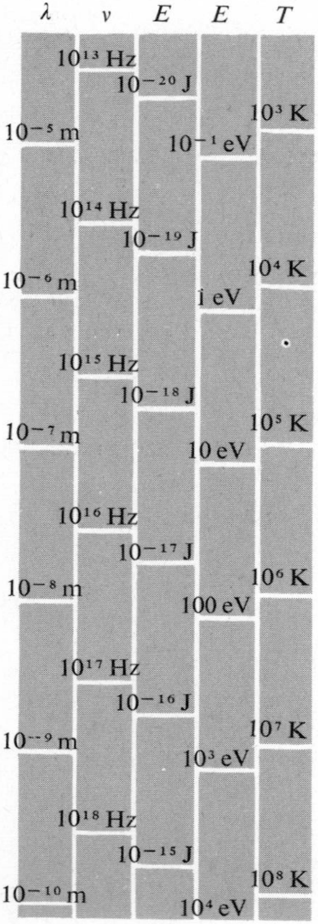

Radiation type	Fundamental process	Generation and detection	Applications	Notes	Absorption[a]
	Far infra-red				
Intermediate infra-red	Molecular vibration	Incandescent and fluorescent lamps, sparks, arcs, discharge tubes and lasers. Detectors; I.R. by thermocouple, light by eye and photocell, U.V. by fluorescent chemicals and photocell	Heating	O_3, H_2O and O_2 absorption in atmosphere	
Near infra-red			Spectroscopy		
Visible			Illumination; spectroscopy, astronomy	Eye-peak response at 5.5×10^{-7} m	
Near ultra-violet	Atomic transitions		Spectroscopy Activation of chemical reactions	O_3 and O_2 photodissociation	
Vacuum ultra-violet	Atomic transitions			O_2, O and N_2, N photoionization	
	Atomic transitions	X-ray tubes: electron and ion types		X-ray emission spectra and absorption edges, light elements	
Soft X-rays	Bremsstrahlung or "braking radiation"	Detectors: photographic plate, ionization chamber, scintillation counter, G.M. tube, etc.	X-ray spectrographic analysis. Superficial therapy; X-ray crystallography	X-ray emission spectra and absorption edges, medium elements	

λ	ν	E	E	T	Radiation type	Fundamental process	Generation and detection	Applications	Notes	Absorption[a]
10^{-11} m	10^{19} Hz	10^{-14} J	10^{5} eV	10^{9} K	Hard X-rays and soft gamma[d] rays.	Atomic transitions induced by electron bombardment	" " X-ray tubes	Superficial therapy Diagnostic X-rays X-ray spectrographic analysis	X-ray emission spectra and absorption edges, heavy elements. ^{57}Fe Mössbauer effect 14.4 keV	‖ ¦
10^{-12} m	10^{20} Hz	10^{-13} J	10^{6} eV	10^{10} K		Nuclear processes, radioactive decay[c]	Radioactive isotopes, high-voltage d.c. generators	Deep therapy, examinations of welds and heavy castings	Emission from radioactive isotopes Positron annihilation, 511 keV	
10^{-13} m	10^{21} Hz	10^{-12} J	10^{7} eV	10^{11} K		Neutron capture, nuclear reaction		Research	Emission from radioactive isotopes Neutron binding energies	
10^{-14} m	10^{22} Hz	10^{-11} J	10^{8} eV	10^{12} K	Secondary cosmic rays (gamma rays produced by cosmic rays)	Elementary particle reactions and disintegrations	Linear accelerators, betatrons and synchrotrons	Deep therapy	π° meson 68 MeV (emission by elementary particles)	
10^{-15} m	10^{23} Hz	10^{-10} J	10^{9} eV	10^{13} K			Detection: bubble chambers	Research	Antiproton annihilation 938 MeV	

Notes

[a] ‖ quartz opaque. | atmosphere opaque. ¦ glass opaque.
[c] limit of natural radioactive processes ~6 MeV.
[d] x-rays are produced by electron bombardment or deceleration. γ-rays originate in nuclear processes.

Selected spectra

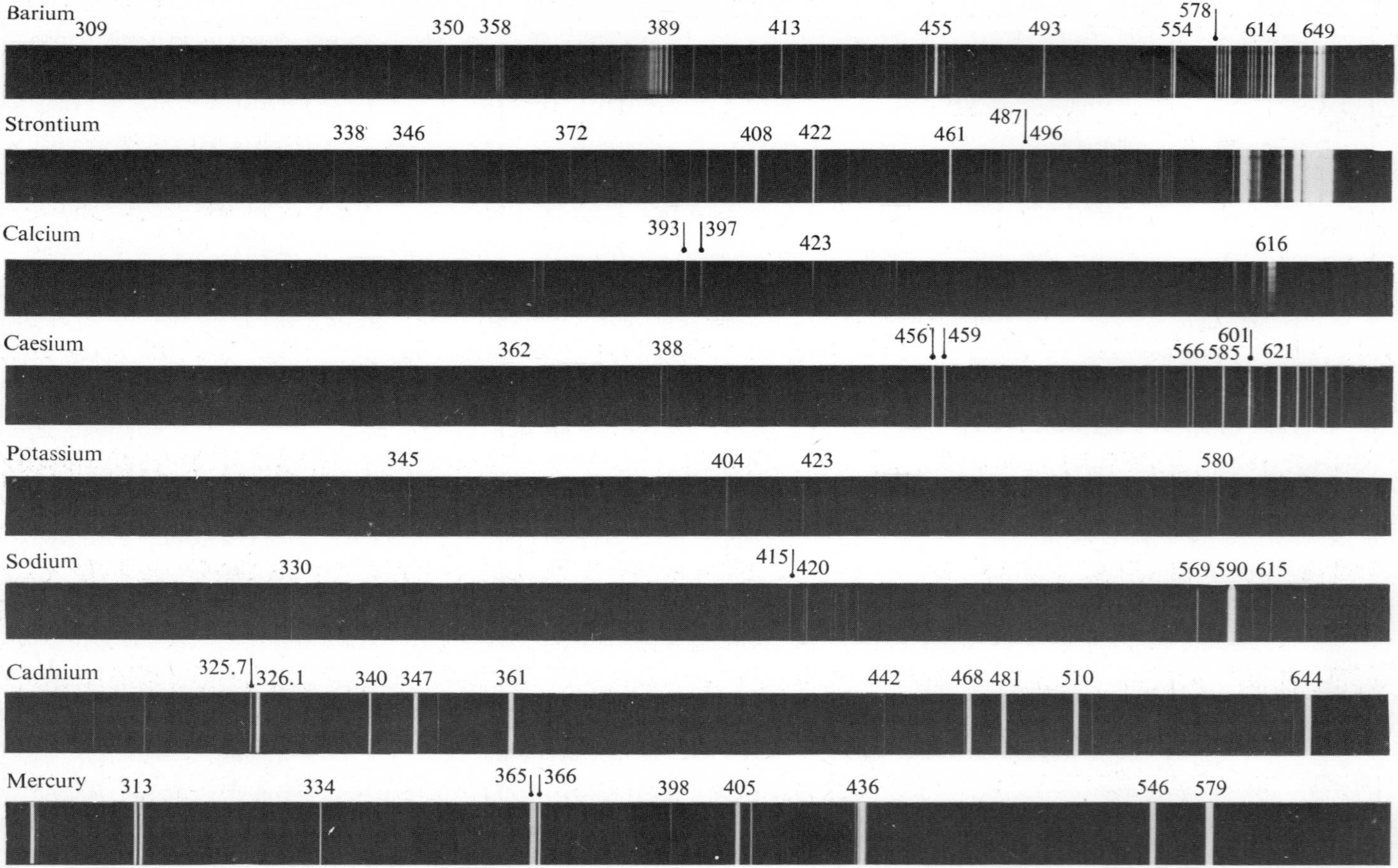
Barium
309 350 358 389 413 455 493 554 578 614 649
Strontium
338 346 372 408 422 461 487 496
Calcium
393 397 423 616
Caesium
362 388 456 459 566 585 601 621
Potassium
345 404 423 580
Sodium
330 415 420 569 590 615
Cadmium
325.7 326.1 340 347 361 442 468 481 510 644
Mercury
313 334 365 366 398 405 436 546 579

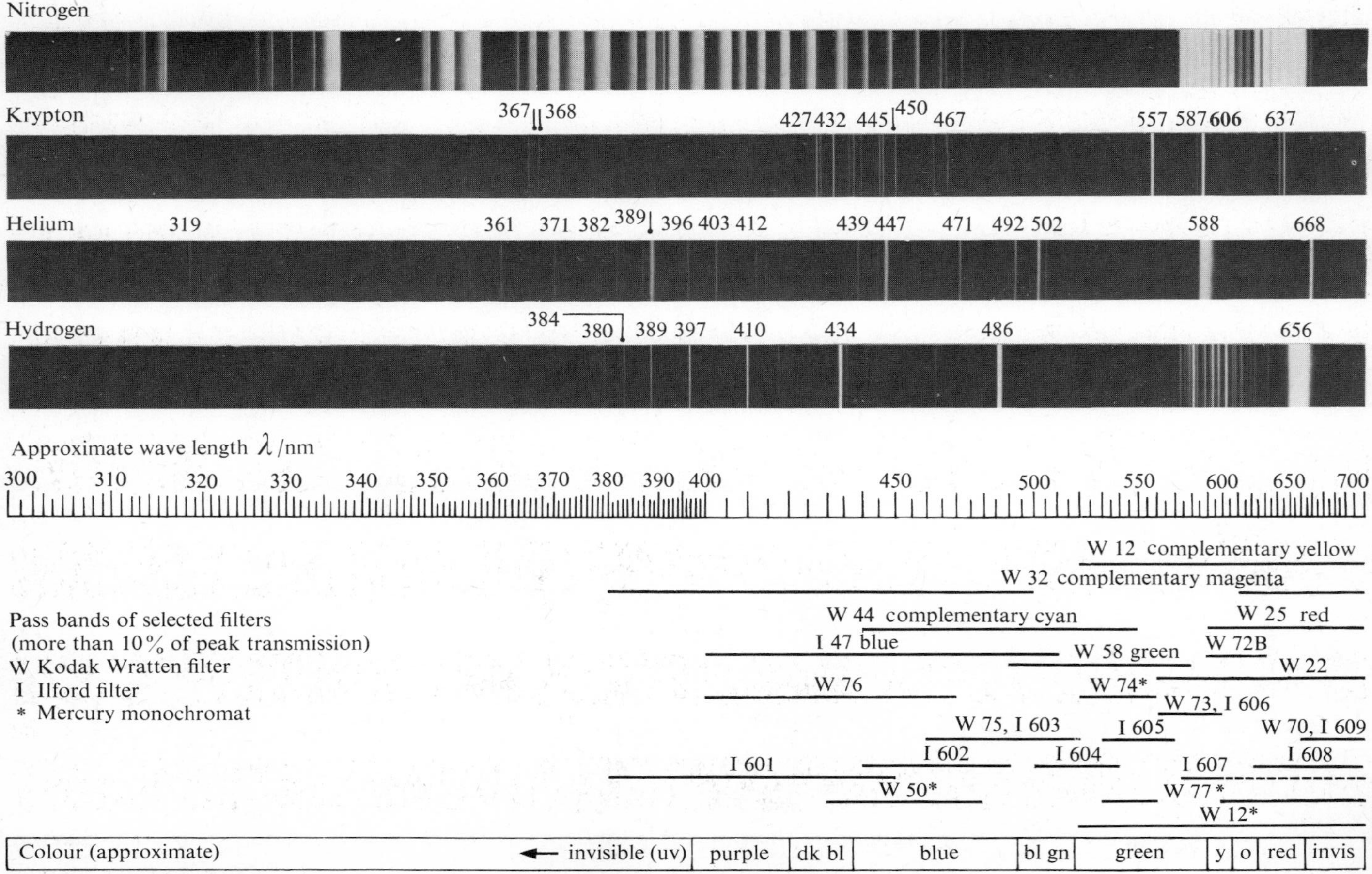
Nitrogen
Krypton
367 368 427 432 445 450 467 557 587 606 637
Helium
319 361 371 382 389 396 403 412 439 447 471 492 502 588 668
Hydrogen
384 380 389 397 410 434 486 656
Approximate wave length λ/nm
300 310 320 330 340 350 360 370 380 390 400 450 500 550 600 650 700
Pass bands of selected filters
(more than 10% of peak transmission)
W Kodak Wratten filter
I Ilford filter
* Mercury monochromat
W 12 complementary yellow
W 32 complementary magenta
W 44 complementary cyan
W 25 red
I 47 blue
W 58 green
W 72B
W 22
W 76
W 74*
W 73, I 606
W 75, I 603
I 605
W 70, I 609
I 601
I 602
I 604
I 607
I 608
W 50*
W 77*
W 12*
Colour (approximate)
← invisible (uv)
purple
dk bl
blue
bl gn
green
y
o
red
invis

References: R14, manufacturers' data.

Successive molar ionization energies of the elements (excluding lanthanides)

Z		j = 1	2	3	4	5	6	7	8	9	10	11
1	**H**	1310										
2	**He**	2370	5200									
3	**Li**	520	7300	11 800								
4	**Be**	900	1800	14 800	21 000							
5	**B**	800	2400	3700	25 000	32 800						
6	**C**	1090	2400	4600	6200	37 800	47 300					
7	**N**	1400	2900	4600	7500	9400	53 300	64 300				
8	**O**	1310	3400	5300	7500	11 000	13 300	71 300	84 100			
9	**F**	1680	3400	6000	8400	11 000	15 200	17 900	92 000	106 100		
10	**Ne**	2080	4000	6100	9400	12 200	15 200				131 200	
11	**Na**	500	4600	6900	9500	13 400	16 600	20 100	25 500	28 900	141 000	158 700
12	**Mg**	740	1500	7700	10 500	13 600	18 000	21 700	25 700	31 600	35 400	169 900
13	**Al**	580	1800	2700	11 600	14 800	18 400	23 300	27 500	31 900	38 500	42 600
14	**Si**	790	1600	3200	4400	16 100	19 800	23 800	29 200	33 900	38 700	45 900
15	**P**	1010	1900	2900	5000	6300	21 300	25 400	29 800	35 800	40 900	46 300
16	**S**	1000	2300	3400	4600	7000	8500	27 100	31 700	36 600	43 100	
17	**Cl**	1260	2300	3800	5200	6500	9300	11 000	33 600	38 700	43 900	51 200
18	**Ar**	1520	2700	3900	5800	7200	8800	12 000	13 800	40 800		
19	**K**	420	3100	4400	5900	8000	9600	11 400	14 900	17 000	48 600	
20	**Ca**	590	1100	4900	6500	8100	10 500	12 300	13 800	18 200	20 400	57 100
21	**Sc**	630	1200	2400	7100	8900	10 700	13 400	15 300	17 400	21 800	24 100
22	**Ti**	660	1300	2700	4200	9600	11 600	13 600	16 600	18 700	20 900	25 600
23	**V**	650	1400	2800	4700	6300	12 400	14 500	16 800			
24	**Cr**	650	1600	3000	4800	7100	8700	15 500	17 800	20 200		
25	**Mn**	720	1500	3300		7300		11 500	19 000	21 400	24 000	
26	**Fe**	760	1600	3000					14 600	22 600	25 300	28 000
27	**Co**	760	1600	3200								29 400
28	**Ni**	740	1800	3400								
29	**Cu**	750	2000	3600								
30	**Zn**	910	1700	3800								
31	**Ga**	580	2000	3000	6200							
32	**Ge**	760	1500	3300	4400	9000						
33	**As**	950	1800	2700	4800	6000	12 300					
34	**Se**	940	2100	3100	4100	7100	7900	15 000				
35	**Br**	1140	2100	3500	4800	5800	8500	9900	18 600			
36	**Kr**	1350	2400	3600								
37	**Rb**	400	2700	3800							26 700	

Definition

This table gives values of $E_{mj}/\text{kJ mol}^{-1}$, where E_{mj} denotes the minimum molar energy to remove the jth successive electron from the atom or ion. Z denotes atomic number.

Atomic as opposed to molar ionization energies are given by:

$E_j/\text{J} = (10^3/L)E_{mj}/\text{kJ mol}^{-1}$, where $L = 6.03 \times 10^{23}\ \text{mol}^{-1}$.

$E_j/\text{eV} = (10^3/Le)E_{mj}/\text{kJ mol}^{-1} = 0.01035 E_{mj}/\text{kJ mol}^{-1}$.

Corresponding frequencies are:

$\nu/\text{Hz} = E_j/(h\ \text{Hz}) = 2.51 \times 10^{12} E_{mj}/\text{kJ mol}^{-1}$

Corresponding wave numbers are:

$\tilde{\nu}/\text{m}^{-1} = E_j/(ch\ \text{m}^{-1}) = 8.36 \times 10^5 E_{mj}/\text{kJ mol}^{-1}$

Z		j = 1	2	3	4	5	6	7	8	9	10	11
38	**Sr**	550	1100	4200	5500							31 300
39	**Y**	620	1200	2000	6000	7400						
40	**Zr**	660	1300	2200	3300		9500					
41	**Nb**	660	1400	2400	3700	4900	9900	12 000				
42	**Mo**	680	1600	2600	4500	5900	6600	12 200	14 800			
43	**Tc**	700	1500	2800								
44	**Ru**	710	1600	2700								
45	**Rh**	720	1700	3000								
46	**Pd**	800	1900	3200								
47	**Ag**	730	2100	3400								
48	**Cd**	870	1600	3600								
49	**In**	560	1800	2700	5200							
50	**Sn**	710	1400	2900	3900	7000						
51	**Sb**	830	1600	2400	4300	5400	10 400					
52	**Te**	870	1800	3000	3600	5800	7000	13 200				
53	**I**	1010	1800	3000					16 400			
54	**Xe**	1170	2000	3100								
55	**Cs**	380	2400	3300								
56	**Ba**	500	1000									
57	**La**	540	1100	1800								
63	**Eu**	550	1100									
72	**Hf**	680	1400									
73	**Ta**	760	1600									
74	**W**	770	1700									
75	**Re**	760	1600									
76	**Os**	840	1600									
77	**Ir**	880										
78	**Pt**	860	1800									
79	**Au**	890	1900									
80	**Hg**	1010	1800	3300								
81	**Tl**	590	2000	2900	4900							
82	**Pb**	720	1500	3100	4100	6600						
83	**Bi**	700	1600	2500	4400	5400	8500					
84	**Po**	810										
86	**Rn**	1040										

Note

Values given here have been rounded off to the nearest 100 kJ mol^{-1} (except for the first column). The two final zeros do not imply 4 or 5 figure accuracy.

Reference: R75.

Electronic configurations of the elements (in the ground state)

Shell		K	L		M			N				O					
subshell		1s	2s	2p	3s	3p	3d	4s	4p	4d	4f	5s	5p	5d	5f	5g	
1	H	1															
2	He	2															
3	Li	2	1														
4	Be	2	2														
5	B	2	2	1													
6	C	2	2	2													
7	N	2	2	3													
8	O	2	2	4													
9	F	2	2	5													
10	Ne	2	2	6													
11	Na	2	2	6	1												
12	Mg	2	2	6	2												
13	Al	2	2	6	2	1											
14	Si	2	2	6	2	2											
15	P	2	2	6	2	3											
16	S	2	2	6	2	4											
17	Cl	2	2	6	2	5											
18	Ar	2	2	6	2	6											
19	K	2	2	6	2	6		1									
20	Ca	2	2	6	2	6		2									
21	Sc	2	2	6	2	6	1	2									
22	Ti	2	2	6	2	6	2	2									
23	V	2	2	6	2	6	3	2									
24	Cr	2	2	6	2	6	5	1									
25	Mn	2	2	6	2	6	5	2									
26	Fe	2	2	6	2	6	6	2									D-block elements
27	Co	2	2	6	2	6	7	2									
28	Ni	2	2	6	2	6	8	2									
29	Cu	2	2	6	2	6	10	1									
30	Zn	2	2	6	2	6	10	2									
31	Ga	2	2	6	2	6	10	2	1								
32	Ge	2	2	6	2	6	10	2	2								
33	As	2	2	6	2	6	10	2	3								
34	Se	2	2	6	2	6	10	2	4								
35	Br	2	2	6	2	6	10	2	5								
36	Kr	2	2	6	2	6	10	2	6								
37	Rb	2	2	6	2	6	10	2	6			1					
38	Sr	2	2	6	2	6	10	2	6			2					
39	Y	2	2	6	2	6	10	2	6	1		2					
40	Zr	2	2	6	2	6	10	2	6	2		2					
41	Nb	2	2	6	2	6	10	2	6	4		1					
42	Mo	2	2	6	2	6	10	2	6	5		1					
43	Tc	2	2	6	2	6	10	2	6	5		2					
44	Ru	2	2	6	2	6	10	2	6	7		1					D-block elements
45	Rh	2	2	6	2	6	10	2	6	8		1					
46	Pd	2	2	6	2	6	10	2	6	10							
47	Ag	2	2	6	2	6	10	2	6	10		1					
48	Cd	2	2	6	2	6	10	2	6	10		2					
49	In	2	2	6	2	6	10	2	6	10		2	1				
50	Sn	2	2	6	2	6	10	2	6	10		2	2				
51	Sb	2	2	6	2	6	10	2	6	10		2	3				
52	Te	2	2	6	2	6	10	2	6	10		2	4				
53	I	2	2	6	2	6	10	2	6	10		2	5				
54	Xe	2	2	6	2	6	10	2	6	10		2	6				

Note

There is still some uncertainty about some of the configurations, especially Pt and Np.

Shell		K	L	M	N				O				P				Q	
subshell					4s	4p	4d	4f	5s	5p	5d	5f 5g	6s	6p	6d	6(f, g,h)	7s	
55	Cs	2	8	18	2	6	10		2	6			1					
56	Ba	2	8	18	2	6	10		2	6			2					
57	La	2	8	18	2	6	10		2	6	1		2					
58	Ce	2	8	18	2	6	10	2	2	6			2					
59	Pr	2	8	18	2	6	10	3	2	6			2					
60	Nd	2	8	18	2	6	10	4	2	6			2					
61	Pm	2	8	18	2	6	10	5	2	6			2					
62	Sm	2	8	18	2	6	10	6	2	6			2					
63	Eu	2	8	18	2	6	10	7	2	6			2					
64	Gd	2	8	18	2	6	10	7	2	6	1		2					Lanthanides
65	Tb	2	8	18	2	6	10	9	2	6			2					
66	Dy	2	8	18	2	6	10	10	2	6			2					
67	Ho	2	8	18	2	6	10	11	2	6			2					
68	Er	2	8	18	2	6	10	12	2	6			2					
69	Tm	2	8	18	2	6	10	13	2	6			2					
70	Yb	2	8	18	2	6	10	14	2	6			2					
71	Lu	2	8	18	2	6	10	14	2	6	1		2					
72	Hf	2	8	18	2	6	10	14	2	6	2		2					
73	Ta	2	8	18	2	6	10	14	2	6	3		2					
74	W	2	8	18	2	6	10	14	2	6	4		2					
75	Re	2	8	18	2	6	10	14	2	6	5		2					
76	Os	2	8	18	2	6	10	14	2	6	6		2					D-block elements
77	Ir	2	8	18	2	6	10	14	2	6	7		2					
78	Pt	2	8	18	2	6	10	14	2	6	9		1					
79	Au	2	8	18	2	6	10	14	2	6	10		1					
80	Hg	2	8	18	2	6	10	14	2	6	10		2					
81	Tl	2	8	18	2	6	10	14	2	6	10		2	1				
82	Pb	2	8	18	2	6	10	14	2	6	10		2	2				
83	Bi	2	8	18	2	6	10	14	2	6	10		2	3				
84	Po	2	8	18	2	6	10	14	2	6	10		2	4				
85	At	2	8	18	2	6	10	14	2	6	10		2	5				
86	Rn	2	8	18	2	6	10	14	2	6	10		2	6				
87	Fr	2	8	18	2	6	10	14	2	6	10		2	6			1	
88	Ra	2	8	18	2	6	10	14	2	6	10		2	6			2	
89	Ac	2	8	18	2	6	10	14	2	6	10		2	6	1		2	
90	Th	2	8	18	2	6	10	14	2	6	10		2	6	2		2	
91	Pa	2	8	18	2	6	10	14	2	6	10	2	2	6	1		2	
92	U	2	8	18	2	6	10	14	2	6	10	3	2	6	1		2	
93	Np	2	8	18	2	6	10	14	2	6	10	4	2	6	1		2	
94	Pu	2	8	18	2	6	10	14	2	6	10	6	2	6			2	
95	Am	2	8	18	2	6	10	14	2	6	10	7	2	6			2	
96	Cm	2	8	18	2	6	10	14	2	6	10	7	2	6	1		2	Actinides
97	Bk	2	8	18	2	6	10	14	2	6	10	8	2	6	1		2	
98	Cf	2	8	18	2	6	10	14	2	6	10	10	2	6			2	
99	Es	2	8	18	2	6	10	14	2	6	10	11	2	6			2	
100	Fm	2	8	18	2	6	10	14	2	6	10	12	2	6			2	
101	Md	2	8	18	2	6	10	14	2	6	10	13	2	6			2	
102	No	2	8	18	2	6	10	14	2	6	10	14	2	6			2	
103	Lr	2	8	18	2	6	10	14	2	6	10	14	2	6	1		2	
104		2	8	18	2	6	10	14	2	6	10	14	2	6	2		2	

Beyond $_{94}$Pu, the assignments are conjectural.

Energy levels of selected elements

This table gives *some* of the energy levels available to elements with one or two outer electrons. The ground state is printed in bold. Transitions between the levels give rise to infra-red, optical, and ultra-violet spectrum lines. Except in the case of hydrogen, transitions normally take place only between a level printed in upright type and a level printed in sloping type. In the case of the elements with two outer electrons, the energy levels occur in two sets marked S and T. Transitions do not normally take place between the levels in these two sets except between the lowest S and the lowest T levels.

Figures give the value of $E/\text{aJ} = E/10^{-18}$ J, where E is the difference between the energy of an electron in the quantized state and the energy of an electron at rest well away from the atom. Values are known to an accuracy of 1 in 10^5, but they are given here to three significant figures only.

Hydrogen	Lithium	Sodium	Potassium	Rubidium
−0.022	−0.087	*−0.082*[D]	−0.079[D]	−0.068
−0.027	*−0.095*	−0.088	−0.095	−0.099
−0.034	−0.103	−0.101	−0.096	*−0.117*[D]
−0.044	−0.136	*−0.127*[D]	*−0.119*[D]	−0.147
−0.061	*−0.139*	−0.137	−0.150	−0.158[D]
−0.087	−0.168	−0.164	−0.151[D]	*−0.198*[D]
−0.136	−0.242	*−0.222*[D]	*−0.205*[D]	−0.269
−0.242	*−0.250*	−0.244	−0.268[D]	−0.285
−0.545	−0.323	−0.312	−0.278	*−0.419*[D]
−2.180	*−0.568*	*−0.487*[D]	*−0.437*[D]	**−0.669**
	−0.864	**−0.823**	**−0.695**	

Helium S	Helium T	Beryllium S	Beryllium T	Magnesium S	Magnesium T
−0.136	−0.136	−0.127	−0.144	−0.106	−0.093
−0.136	*−0.141*	−0.214	−0.212	*−0.138*	−0.115
−0.146	−0.159	−0.407	−0.261	−0.169	*−0.147*
−0.240	−0.243	*−0.648*	−0.459	−0.181	−0.149
−0.243	*−0.254*	**−1.494**	*−1.057*[T]	*−0.245*	−0.195
−0.267	−0.300			−0.303	−0.272
−0.540	*−0.580*			−0.361	*−0.275*[T]
−0.636	−0.764			*−0.529*	−0.407
−1.953				**−1.225**	*−0.791*[T]

[D] This level is the lower of the two closely spaced levels (giving rise to spectral doublets on transition).

Calcium S	Calcium T	Strontium S	Strontium T	Barium S	Barium T
−0.149	−0.106[T]	*−0.139*	−0.103	*−0.100*	−0.098
−0.151	*−0.135*	−0.149	−0.169	*−0.188*	−0.161
−0.238	−0.175	−0.221	−0.217[T]	−0.274	*−0.224*[T]
−0.250	−0.230[T]	*−0.235*	*−0.241*[T]	−0.326	−0.225[T]
−0.318	*−0.253*[T]	−0.305	−0.336	*−0.476*	−0.315
−0.509	−0.353	*−0.481*	−0.552[T]	−0.609	*−0.591*[T]
−0.545	−0.575[T]	−0.512	*−0.628*[T]	**−0.835**	−0.655[T]
−0.979	*−0.678*[T]	**−0.912**			

Zinc S	Zinc T	Cadmium S	Cadmium T	Mercury S	Mercury T
−0.193	−0.205	−0.188	−0.198	−0.194	−0.203
−0.255	−0.258[T]	*−0.251*	−0.259[T]	−0.255	−0.255[T]
−0.264	*−0.288*[T]	−0.265	*−0.281*[T]	*−0.256*	*−0.291*[T]
−0.396	−0.439	−0.381	−0.418	−0.402	−0.434
−0.576	*−0.863*[T]	*−0.573*	*−0.842*[T]	*−0.598*	*−0.924*[T]
−1.505		**−1.440**		**−1.672**	

Note

For those familiar with spectroscopic notation, the S and T sets are singlet and triplet states. Levels in sloping type are P states, those in upright type S or D states. No F states and no 'displaced' states have been included, so that a number of prominent spectral lines cannot be obtained from this table.

[T] This level is the lower of three closely spaced levels (giving rise to spectral triplets on transition).

Reference: R61.

X-ray spectra of selected elements

$K_{\alpha 2}$ emission line for electron transition from L shell to K shell
$K_{\beta 3}$ emission line for electron transition from M shell to K shell
L_1 emission line for electron transition from M shell to L shell
A absorption edge for electron removal from K shell
Z atomic number
λ wavelength

Z	Element	$K_{\alpha 2}$ λ/pm	$K_{\beta 3}$ λ/pm	L_1 λ/pm	A λ/pm
19	K	374.5	345.4		344.3
20	Ca	336.2	309.0		307.6
21	Sc	303.5	278.0		276.3
22	Ti	275.2	251.4		250.2
23	V	250.7	228.4		227.4
24	Cr	229.4	208.5		207.4
25	Mn	210.6	191.0		190.0
26	Fe	194.0	175.7	2016.1	174.7
27	Co	179.3	162.1	1823.7	161.1
28	Ni	166.2	150.0	1658.3	149.1
29	Cu	154.4	139.2	1522.1	138.3
30	Zn	143.9	129.5	1397.8	128.6
31	Ga	134.4	120.8	1291.6	119.7
32	Ge	125.8	112.9	1194.4	111.8
33	As	118.0	105.7	1107.0	104.6
34	Se	110.9	99.2	1029.3	98.1
35	Br	104.4	93.3	958.3	92.2
36	Kr	98.6	88.0		86.7
37	Rb	93.0	82.9		81.7
38	Sr	87.9	78.3	783.8	77.1
39	Y	83.3	74.1		72.9
40	Zr	79.0	70.2	691.3	69.0
41	Nb	75.0	66.6	652.3	65.4
42	Mo	71.4	63.2		62.1
74	W	21.4	18.4	167.8	
79	Au	18.5	15.9	146.0	
82	Pb	17.0	14.6	135.0	

Reference: R57.

Selected atomic and ionic radii (periodic groups): electronegativity values

- G number of group in Periodic Table
- R_V van der Waals radius of atom
- R_{cov} covalent radius of atom
- $R_{\pm}$ other important ionic radii – figures in brackets give charge state
- R_m radius of atom in metal or non-ionic solid
- R_i radius of ion in inert gas configuration—figures in brackets give charge state
- N_P Pauling electronegativity index[C]

G		R_V/nm	R_m/nm	R_{cov}/nm	R_i/nm	$R_{\pm}$/nm		N_P
I	Li		0.152	0.123	0.068(1+)[A]			1.0
	Na		0.186	0.157	0.098(1+)[A]			0.9
	K		0.227	0.203	0.133(1+)[A]			0.8
	Rb		0.248	0.216	0.148(1+)[A]			0.8
	Cs		0.263	0.235	0.167(1+)[A]			0.7
	NH_4^+		—	—	0.148(1+)			
II	Be		0.112	0.106	0.030(2+)[A]			1.5
	Mg		0.160	0.140	0.065(2+)[A]			1.2
	Ca		0.197	0.174	0.094(2+)[A]			1.0
	Sr		0.215	0.191	0.110(2+)[A]			1.0
	Ba		0.221	0.198	0.134(2+)[A]			0.9
III	B	0.217	0.079	0.088	0.016(3+)[A]			2.0
	Al	0.253	0.143	0.126	0.045(3+)[A]			1.5
	Ga		0.122	0.126	0.062(3+)	0.113(1+)		1.6
D block	Sc		0.161	0.144	0.081(3+)[A,†]			1.3
	Ti		0.145	0.132	0.068(4+)[A,†]	0.090(2+)		1.5
	V		0.132	0.122	0.059(5+)	0.088(2+)	0.074(3+)	1.6
	Mn		0.137	0.117	0.046(7+)	0.080(2+)	0.066(3+)	1.6
	Cr		0.137	0.117	0.052(6+)	0.088(2+)	0.063(3+)[B]	1.5
	Fe		0.124	0.116		0.076(2+)	0.064(3+)	1.8
	Co		0.125	0.116		0.074(2+)	0.063(3+)	1.8
	Ni		0.125	0.115		0.072(2+)	0.062(3+)	1.8
	Cu		0.128	0.135	0.096(1+)	0.069(2+)		1.9
	Zn		0.133	0.131	0.074(2+)			1.6
	Mo		0.136	0.129	0.062(6+)	0.068(4+)		1.8
	Ag		0.144	0.152	0.126(1+)	0.089(2+)		1.9

G		R_V/nm	R_m/nm	R_{cov}/nm	R_i/nm	$R_{\pm}$/nm		N_P
	Cd		0.149	0.148	0.097(2+)			1.7
	Au		0.144	0.134	0.137(1+)	0.085(2+)		2.4
	Hg	0.150	0.152	0.148	0.110(2+)			1.9
IV	C	0.185	—	0.077	0.016(4+)	0.260(4−)		2.5
	Si	0.224[T]	0.118	0.117	0.038(4+)	0.271(4−)		1.8
	Ge	0.202	—	0.122	0.053(4+)	0.272(4−)	0.093(2+)	1.8
	Sn		0.162	0.140	0.071(4+)	0.294(4−)	0.112(2+)	1.8
	Pb		0.175	0.154	0.084(4+)	0.120(2+)		1.8
V	N	0.150	—	0.070	0.171(3−)	0.013(5+)		3.0
	P	0.19	—	0.110	0.212(3−)	0.035(5+)		2.1
	As	0.20	0.125	0.118	0.222(3−)	0.046(5+)		2.0
	Sb	0.220	0.145	0.136	0.245(3−)	0.062(5+)		1.9
	Bi		0.170	0.152	0.074(5+)	0.120(3+)		1.9
VI	O	0.140	0.060	0.066	0.146(2−)[A]	0.009(6+)		3.5
	S	0.185	0.095	0.104	0.190(2−)[A]	0.029(6+)		2.5
	Se	0.200		0.114	0.202(2−)[A]	0.042(6+)		2.4
	Te	0.220	0.143	0.132	0.222(2−)[A]	0.056(6+)		2.1
VII	H	0.12	—	0.037	0.154(1−)[A]			2.1
	F	0.135	—	0.064	0.133(1−)[A]	0.008(7+)		4.0
	Cl	0.180	—	0.099	0.181(1−)[A]	0.027(7+)		3.0
	Br	0.195	0.115	0.111	0.196(1−)[A]	0.039(7+)		2.8
	I	0.215	0.133	0.128	0.219(1−)[A]	0.050(7+)		2.5

VIII	He	Ne	Ar	Kr	Xe	CH_3	C_6H_6
R_V/nm	0.099†	0.160	0.192	0.197	0.217	0.20	0.185

Notes

[A] The distance, D, between anion and cation is given by $D = R_i(+) + R_i(-) + \Delta(N)$, where the correction term $\Delta(N)$ depends on the co-ordination number, N, as follows:

N	1	2	3	4	5	6
$\Delta(N)$/nm	−0.050	−0.031	−0.019	−0.011	−0.005	0.0

N	7	8	9	10	11	12
$\Delta(N)$/nm	+0.004	+0.008	+0.011	+0.014	+0.017	+0.019

[B] Also 0.081(1+). [T] Theoretical. † discrepancy between references.

[C] N_P is a measure of how strongly the atom attracts electrons. The percentage of ionic bonding, P, in a bond depends on the difference, ΔN_P, in the N_P values of the atoms as follows:

ΔN_P	0.1	0.3	0.5	0.7	1.0	1.3	1.5	1.7	2.0	2.5	3.0	3.2
P/%	0.5	2	6	12	22	34	43	51	63	79	89	92

References: R72, R67, R65, R22, R67, R67 – this gives references in order for R_V to N_P.

Activation energies

E activation energy

	Reaction	Conditions	E/kJ mol^{-1}
1	$2H_2O_2 \rightarrow 2H_2O + O_2$	enzyme catalysed	23[A]
2	$H_2 + Cl_2 \rightarrow 2HCl$	photochemical	25
3	$(C_2H_5)_3N + C_2H_5Br \rightarrow (C_2H_5)_4NBr$	solution	47
4	$C_6H_5N(CH_3)_2 + CH_3I \rightarrow C_6H_5N(CH_3)_3I$	solution	49
5	$2NOBr \rightarrow 2NO + Br_2$		58
6	$2HI \rightarrow H_2 + I_2$	Pt catalysed	59[B]
7	$F_2O_2 \rightarrow F_2 + O_2$		72
8	$2H_2O_2 \rightarrow 2H_2O + O_2$	uncatalysed	79[A]
9	$C_6H_5CH_2ONa + C_3H_7I \rightarrow C_6H_5CH_2OC_3H_7 + NaI$	solution	89
10	$C_2H_5Br + OH^- \rightarrow C_2H_5OH + Br^-$	solution	90
11	$C_6H_2\begin{smallmatrix}(NO_2)_3 \\ CO_2H\end{smallmatrix} \rightarrow C_6H_3(NO_2)_3 + CO_2$		96
12	$2NOCl \rightarrow 2NO + Cl_2$		100
13	$2HI \rightarrow H_2 + I_2$	Au catalysed	105[B]
14	$(C_2H_5)_3N + C_2H_5I \rightarrow (C_2H_5)_4NI$	solution	107
15	$2NO_2 \rightarrow 2NO + O_2$		112
16	$2N_2O \rightarrow 2N_2 + O_2$	Au catalysed	121[C]
17	$2N_2O \rightarrow 2N_2 + O_2$	Pt catalysed	136[C]
18	$C_2H_5OC_2H_5 \rightarrow C_2H_6 + CO + CH_4$	I_2 vapour	144[D]
19	$2NH_3 \rightarrow N_2 + 3H_2$	W catalysed	162[E]
20	$H_2 + I_2 \rightarrow 2HI$	uncatalysed	164[B]
21	$C_3H_7{-}N{=}N{-}C_3H_7 \rightarrow C_6H_{14} + N_2$		172
22	$C_2H_4 + H_2 \rightarrow C_2H_6$		180
23	terpene → pinene		182
24	$2HI \rightarrow H_2 + I_2$	uncatalysed	185[B]
25	$CH_3CHO \rightarrow CH_4 + CO$		190
26	di-ester of maleic acid to fumaric acid that is, $CH_3O_2CCH{=}CHCO_2CH_3$ *cis* to *trans*		213
27	$\underset{\diagdown O \diagup}{CH_2{-}CH_2} \rightarrow C_2H_4 + \frac{1}{2}O_2$		218
28	$C_2H_5Br \rightarrow C_2H_4 + HBr$		221
29	$C_2H_5OC_2H_5 \rightarrow C_2H_6 + CO + CH_4$	uncatalysed	224[D]
30	$2N_2O \rightarrow 2N_2 + O_2$	uncatalysed	245[C]
31	$C_2H_5Cl \rightarrow C_2H_4 + HCl$		254
32	$2NH_3 \rightarrow N_2 + 3H_2$	uncatalysed	335[E]

Note
Compare values carrying the same suffix.

Selected bond lengths and mean bond energies: Dipole moments of inorganic molecules in the vapour phase

L bond length E mean bond energy

	Bond Inorganic	In	L/nm	E/kJ mol^{-1}
1	Br—Br	Br_2	0.228	193
2	Br—H	HBr	0.141	366
3	Cl—Cl	Cl_2	0.199	242
4	Cl—H	HCl	0.127	431
5	F—F	F_2	0.142	158
6	H—H	H_2	0.074	436
7	H—I	HI	0.160	299
8	H—O	H_2O	0.096	464
9	H—N	NH_3	0.101	389[†]
10	H—P	PH_3	0.142	322[†]
11	H—S	H_2S	0.135	347
12	H—Si	SiH_4	0.148	318[D]
13	I—I	I_2	0.267	151
14	K—K	K_2	0.392	53[†]
15	N—N	N_2H_4	0.147	163
16	N=N	$C_6H_{14}N_2$	0.120	410
17	N≡N	N_2	0.110	945
18	N—O	NO_2	0.119	305[D]
19	N=O	HNO_3	0.121	626
20	N≡P	PN	0.149	582
21	Na—Na	Na_2	0.308	72
22	O—O	H_2O_2	0.149	146
23	O—O	O_3	0.128	—
24	O=O	O_2	0.121	497
25	O—S	SO_3	0.143	435
26	O—Si	SiO_2	0.151	368[†]
27	P—P	P_4	0.221	201
28	P≡P	P_2	0.189	488

	Bond Organic	In	L/nm	E/kJ mol^{-1}
1	C—Br	CBr_4	0.194	209[†D]
2	C—C	general	0.154	346
3	C=C	C_2H_4	0.134	598[†]
4	C=C	general	0.135	611
5	C≡C	C_2H_2	0.121	837[†]
6	C≡C	general	0.121	835
7	C—Cl	CCl_4	0.177	327
8	C—Cl	general	0.177	339
9	C⋯Cl	C_6H_5Cl	0.169	
10	C—F	CH_3F	0.138	452[D]
11	C—F	CF_4	0.132[†]	485
12	C—H	CH_4	0.109	435
13	C—H	C_2H_2	0.106	506[†]
14	C—H	general	0.108	413
15	C—I	CH_3I	0.214	218[†]
16	C—N	CH_3NH_2	0.147	305[G]
17	C=N	CH_2N_2	0.132	615[G]
18	C≡N	HCN	0.116	891[†]
19	C≡N	general	0.116	890
20	C⋯N	aniline	0.135	—
21	C—O	CH_3OH	0.143	336
22	C—O	general	0.143	358
23	C=O	CO_2	0.116	803[†]
24	C=O	HCHO	0.122	695
25	C=O	aldehydes	0.122	736
26	C=O	ketones	0.122	745
27	C=O	$CaCO_3$	0.129	—
28	C—Si	$(CH_3)_4Si$	0.193	301

[†] Discrepancy between sources [D] Bond dissociation energy [G] General value

References: R65, R66.

Dipole moments of inorganic molecules in the vapour phase

p dipole moment $p^{\ominus}$ 3.34×10^{-30} C m ≙ 1 debye

	Compound	$p/p^{\ominus}$		Compound	$p/p^{\ominus}$		Compound	$p/p^{\ominus}$
1	AsH_3	0.16	10	HI	0.42	19	$Ni(CO)_4$	0
2	CH_4	0	11	H_2O	1.84	20	NO	0.16
3	CO	0.10	12	H_2O_2	2.13	21	NO_2	0.40
4	CO_2	0	13	H_2S	0.92	22	N_2O	0.17
5	CS_2	0	14	H_2Se	0.40	23	PCl_3	0.78
6	HBr	0.80	15	H_2Te	0.20	24	PH_3	0.55
7	HCl	1.05	16	NF_3	0.22	25	SbH_3	0.12
8	HCN	2.80	17	NH_3	1.48	26	SiH_4	0
9	HF	1.91	18	N_2H_4	1.84	27	SO_2	1.63

Reference: R2.

Bond lengths and angles

Compound	Sequence	Angle	Length/nm	
CCl_4	Cl—C—Cl	109.5°	0.177	Cl—C
CH_4	H—C—H	109.5°	0.109	H—C
CH_3Cl	H—C—H	110.5°	0.110	H—C
	Cl—C—H	108.0°	0.178	Cl—C
CH_2Cl_2	H—C—H	113.0°	0.107	H—C
	Cl—C—Cl	111.8°	0.177	Cl—C
$CHCl_3$	Cl—C—Cl	110.9°	0.107	C—H
			0.176	Cl—C
C_2H_4	H—C—H	117.3°	0.109	H—C
			0.134	C—C
C_3H_6 cyclopropane	H—C—H	120.0°	0.134	C—C
	H—C—C	120.0°	0.107	C—H
C_6H_6 benzene	C—C—C	120.0°	0.1084	C—H
			0.1397	C—C
CH_3OH	C—O—H	109.0°	0.143	C—O
			0.096	O—H
$CH_3C(=O')OH$	O—C—O′	122.0°	0.125	C—O
	C—C—O′	119.5°	0.131	C—O
	C—C—O	116.0°	0.095	O—H
	H—C—H	106.8°	0.108	H—C
CH_3CHO	C—C—O	123.6°	0.109	H—C
	H—C—H	108.3°	0.150	C—C
			0.122	C—O
$(CH_3)_2O$	C—O—C	115.5°	0.142	C—O
CH_3NH_2	H—C—H	109.5°	Methyl axis makes angle 3.5° with C—N axis	
	H—N—C	112.2°	0.096	H—C
	H—N—N	105.8°		
$(CH_3)_2NH$	C—N—C	111.0°	0.108	H—C
			0.146	C—N
$(CH_3)_3N$	C—N—C	108.7°	0.147	C—N
	H—C—H	107.1°	0.109	H—C
CO_3^{2-}	O—C—O	120.0°	0.145	O—C
$COCl_2$	Cl—C—Cl	111.3°	0.175	Cl—C
H_2O	H—O—H	104.5°	0.096	H—O
H_2S	H—S—H	93.0°	0.134	H—S
H_2Se	H—Se—H	91.0°	0.147	H—Se
H_2Te	H—Te—H	89.5°	0.170	H—Te
NH_3	H—N—H	107.0°	0.101	H—N
NO_2	O—N—O	134.0°	0.119	N—O
NO_3^-	O—N—O	120.0°	0.124	N—O
PCl_3	Cl—P—Cl	100.1°	0.204	Cl—P
PCl_5	Cl—P—Cl	120.0°	0.204	Cl—P
	Cl—P—Cl	90.0°	0.219	Cl—P
SF_6	F—S—F	90.0°	0.158	F—S
SO_3	O—S—O	120.0°	0.143	S—O

References: R65, R66.

General introduction to tables of physical and thermochemical and other properties of elements and compounds

The following notes and abbreviations apply generally to pages 59–95.

1 **State.** The normal physical state of the material at 298 K is indicated as follows: S solid; L liquid; G gas; aq aqueous solution.

2 **Crystal System.** The crystal system for the material at 298 K, or close to the melting temperature in the case of liquids and gases, is indicated as follows:

CUB cubic	TRG trigonal (not RBL)	HEX hexagonal
TET tetragonal	RBL rhombohedral	MCL monoclinic
ORH orthorhombic	(special case of TRG)	TCL triclinic

In the following cases, the structure type is indicated instead: this implies the system.

For the cubic system	BCC	body-centred cubic
	FCC	face-centred cubic (cubic close-packed)
	DIA	diamond structure
for the hexagonal system	HCP	hexagonal close-packed.

Non-crystalline solids are indicated by AMS amorphous; POW powder; VIT vitreous.

3 **Density.** Values given are measured densities and may in some cases be significantly less than the theoretical densities derived from X-ray measurements, if the crystal contains a high concentration of imperfections.

4 **Melting and boiling temperatures.** These relate to a pressure of 101 325 Pa (1 atm) unless otherwise indicated. ^{sub} indicates sublimation. ^{dec} indicates decomposition. $^{dhd(n)}$ loses (n molecules of) water of crystallization. ^{tr} phase transitions.

5 **Thermochemical data.** These relate to 298 K when the $^{\ominus}$ symbol is used. Note that $\Delta H_f^{\ominus}$ and $\Delta G_f^{\ominus}$ are zero by definition for elements in their standard state. Values given for aqueous solutions are for a molality of 1 mol kg^{-1}.

6 **Notes.** These give miscellaneous items of information as follows:
POI poisonous substance; **SK POI** poison absorbed through skin;
POI VAP poisonous vapour (with maximum permissible concentration in air in parts per million);
CUM POI cumulative poison (with max. permissible body burden);
RAD radioactive material; **COR** corrosive material.
(N.B. almost all chemical substances are poisonous and should be treated with respect. Those marked here are those requiring special precautions in laboratory or industrial practice.)

EXP explosive substance; **INF** highly inflammable;
PYR pyrophoric substance (burns spontaneously if finely divided);
VR violent reaction with H_2O; OX oxidizes in air; hyg hygroscopic; dlq deliquescent; eff efflorescent.

Colours – other than white or none – are indicated as follows.

bl: blue	bk: black	br: brown	gn: green	gr: grey
or: orange	rd: red	yl: yellow	dk: dark	pa: pale
pu: purple	vi: violet			

Solid state transitions for elements are denoted by figures in brackets: $[T_{tr}/\text{K}, \Delta H_{tr}/\text{J mol}^{-1}]$. C indicates Curie point.

Standard densities of gaseous elements (at 273.15 K and 1 atm) may be calculated from the formula $\rho = kM/V_m^{\ominus}$ where M denotes the molar mass and $V_m^{\ominus}$ the standard molar volume (22.41 dm^3 mol^{-1}). k is a correction factor given in the notes in braces. Thus {0.099940} for $k(H_2)$.

References: Crystal structure: R4 (9–4), R48. **ρ**: R1 (p 118), R2 (B and C), R45, R46, R47, R48. **ρ**(gas): R1 (p 149). ***n***: R1 (p 133), R2 (B and C), R45, R46, R47. T_m, T_b and thermochemical data: R19, R7, R46, R47 (organic), R45, R44, m_{sat}: R50, R1 (p 123), R2, R49. p, ε_r: R1, R2, R45. Phase transitions: R19, R4 (4–172). Notes: R2, R51, R52.

Thermochemical properties of elements excluding lanthanides

Z	atomic number
N	number of atoms per molecule in the most stable gaseous state at T_b
A	molar mass of element
ρ	density (at 298 K *or density of liquid at* T_b *for gases*)
T_m	normal melting temperature
T_b	normal boiling temperature
$\Delta H_m^\ominus$	molar enthalpy change on melting at T_m
$\Delta H_b^\ominus$	molar enthalpy change on evaporation at T_b
$S^\ominus$	standard molar entropy at 298 K
$\Delta H_a^\ominus$	molar enthalpy change on atomization (energy required to produce one mole of monatomic gas at 298 K from the standard state)

For this table, the mole consists of single atoms. Care may be needed in interpreting the results when $N \neq 1$. See p. 58 for general notes and abbreviations.

Z	*Element*		N	State		A / g mol^{-1}	ρ (298K) / g cm^{-3}	T_m / K	T_b / K	$\Delta H_m^\ominus$ / kJ mol^{-1}	$\Delta H_b^\ominus$ / kJ mol^{-1}	$S^\ominus$ / J mol^{-1}K^{-1}	$\Delta H_a^\ominus$ / kJ mol^{-1}	Z	Notes
1	Hydrogen	H	2	**G**	HCP	1.0	**0.07**^{20K}	14	20	0.06	0.5	65.3	218.0	1	**EXP**;{0.99940}
2	Helium	He	1	**G**	HCP‡	4.0	**0.12**^{4K}	**4**$^{103\,atm}$	4	**0.02**^{103atm}	0.1	126.0	—	2	[2.18, 0]; {0.9984}
3	Lithium	Li	1	S	BCC	6.9	0.53	454	1604	3.01†	134.7†	28.0	160.8	3	**COR**; OX; [77,]
4	Beryllium	Be	1	S	HCP	9.0	1.85	1556	2750†	11.72	294.6†	9.5	325.9	4	**POI**(0.001 in air)
5	Boron	B	1	S	TET	10.8	2.55†	2300	4200	22.18†	538.9	5.9†	589.9	5	
6	Carbon (graphite)	C	1‡	S	HEX	12.0	2.25*	**4000**^{‡SUB}			**716.7**^{SUB}	5.7	715.0	6	bk
6	Carbon (diamond)	C	1‡	S	DIA	12.0	3.53	3823	5100†	**1.87**$^{\Delta H_f^\ominus}$	**2.8**$^{\Delta G_f^\ominus}$	2.4	713.1	6	
7	Nitrogen	N	2	**G**	HCP	14.0	**0.81**^{†77K}	63	77	0.36	2.8	95.7	472.8	7	[36, 23]
8	Oxygen	O	2	**G**	CUB	16.0	**1.14**^{†90K}	54	90	0.22	3.4†	102.5	249.2	8	[24, 94]; [44, 743] dk bl liq
9	Fluorine	F	2	**G**		19.0	**1.11**^{†73K}	53	85	0.26	3.3†	101.4	79.1	9	**COR POI** (0.0001); pa yl [460, 728]
10	Neon	Ne	1	**G**	FCC	20.2	**1.21**^{27K}	25	27	0.33	1.8†	146.2†	—	10	{0.99941}
11	Sodium	Na	1	S	BCC	23.0	0.97	371	1163	2.60†	89.0†	51.0	108.4	11	**PYR**; **VR**; OX
12	Magnesium	Mg	1	S	HCP	24.3	1.74	923	1390	8.95	128.7	32.7	149.0	12	**PYR**
13	Aluminium	Al	1	S	FCC	27.0	2.70	932	2720	10.75	293.7	28.3	324.3	13	
14	Silicon	Si	1	S	DIA	28.1	2.33†	1683	2950†	46.44†	376.8†	19.0	439.7	14	
15	Phosphorus (red)	P	4	S	MCL†	31.0	2.20†	**870**^{143atm}	**704**^{SUB}	**4.71**^{143atm}	**30.1**^{SUB}	22.8	333.9	15	**POI**
15	Phosphorus (white)	P	4	S	CUB	31.0	1.82	317	554	0.63	12.4†	41.0	316.3	15	**POI**; **PYR**
15	Phosphorus (black)	P	4	S	MCL	31.0	2.70*			**−38.86**$^{\Delta H_f^\ominus}$			756.8	15	**POI**

† uncertain ‡ highly uncertain * variable

TCE

Thermochemical properties of elements excluding lanthanides – *(continued)*

Z	*Element*		*N*	State		*A* g mol^{-1}	ρ (298K) g cm^{-3}	T_m K	T_b K	$\Delta H_m^\ominus$ kJ mol^{-1}	$\Delta H_b^\ominus$ kJ mol^{-1}	$S^\ominus$ J mol^{-1}K^{-1}	$\Delta H_a^\ominus$ kJ mol^{-1}	*Z*	Notes
16	Sulphur (rhombic)	S	8	S	ORH	32.1	2.07	**369**$^{\text{tr to MCL}}$		**0.38**$^{\text{tr to MCL}}$		31.9	238.1	16	
16	Sulphur (monoclinic)	S	8	S	MCL	32.1	1.96	392†	718	1.41	9.6	32.6	237.8	16	sol in CS_2
17	Chlorine	Cl	2	**G**	TET	35.5	**1.56**$^{239\text{K}}$	172	239	3.20	10.2	111.5	121.1	17	**POI VAP** (1.0); {1.0160}; yl-gn
18	Argon	Ar	1	**G**	FCC	39.9	**1.40**$^{85\text{K}}$	84	87	1.18	6.5	154.7	—	18	{1.000 9}
19	Potassium	K	1	S	BCC	39.1	0.86	336	1039	2.30	77.5	64.4	89.5	19	**PYR**; **VR**; OX
20	Calcium	Ca	1	S	FCC	40.1	1.55	1123	1765	8.66	149.8	41.6	176.6	20	OX; [713†, 1130]
21	Scandium	Sc	1	S	HCP	45.0	2.99	1673‡	2750‡	16.11‡	304.8‡	37.7	343.1	21	
22	Titanium	Ti	1	S	HCP	47.9	4.54	1950	3550	15.48‡	428.9	30.7	471.1	22	[1155, 3975]
23	Vanadium	V	1	S	BCC	50.9	6.11†	2190	3650	17.57‡	458.6	29.3	513.8	23	**POI**
24	Chromium	Cr	1	S	BCC	52.0	7.19†	2176	2915	13.81	348.9	23.8	397.5	24	[2113, 1464]
25	Manganese	Mn	1	S	CUB	54.9	7.42*	1517	2314	14.64	219.7	32.0	279.2	25	[1000, 2238]; [1374, 2280]; [1410, 1799]
26	Iron	Fe	1	S	BCC	55.9	7.86*	1812	3160	15.36	351.0†	27.2	417.7	26	[1033, 0 C]; [1183, 900]; [1673, 690]
27	Cobalt	Co	1	S	FCC	58.9	8.90	1768	3150	15.23	382.4†	30.0†	425.1	27	[720, 251]; [1395, 544 C]
28	Nickel	Ni	1	S	FCC	58.7	8.90	1728	3110	17.61	371.8†	29.9	423.8	28	[680, 377 C]
29	Copper	Cu	1	S	FCC	63.5	8.94	1356	2855	13.05	304.6	33.3	339.3	29	yl-rd
30	Zinc	Zn	1	S	HCP^{A}	65.4	7.13†	693	1181	7.38†	115.3	41.6	130.5	30	
31	Gallium	Ga	1	S	ORH	69.7	**5.91**^{B}	303	2510†	5.59	256.1†	41.1†	272.0	31	
32	Germanium	Ge	1	S	DIA	72.6	5.32*†	1210	3100‡	31.80†	334.3	31.1†	376.6	32	
33	Arsenic (grey)	As	4	S	TRG	74.9	5.73	**1090**$^{36\text{ atm}}$	**886**^{SUB}	**27.61**$^{\ddagger 36\text{ atm}}$	**129.7**^{SUB}	35.1	288.7	33	**CUM POI**
34	Selenium	Se	2	S	TRG	79.0	4.79	490	958	5.23	26.3	42.7	206.7	34	**POI**; gr, rd or bk; [398, 4393]

† uncertain ‡ highly uncertain * variable ^{A} distorted, c/a = 1.9 ^{B} ρ(liq) = 6.11 g cm^{-3} ^{tr} transition temperature

Z	Element		N	State		A g mol⁻¹	ρ (298K) g cm⁻³	T_m K	T_b K	$\Delta H_m^\ominus$ kJ mol⁻¹	$\Delta H_b^\ominus$ kJ mol⁻¹	$S^\ominus$ J mol⁻¹K⁻¹	$\Delta H_a^\ominus$ kJ mol⁻¹	Z	Notes
35	Bromine	Br	2	**L**	ORH	79.9	$\mathbf{3.12}^{266K}$	266	331	5.29	15.0	75.8	112.0	35	**COR POI**; rd-br
36	Krypton	Kr	1	**G**	FCC	83.8	$\mathbf{2.16}^{120K}$	116	120	1.64	9.0	164.0	—	36	{1.0028}
37	Rubidium	Rb	1	S	BCC	85.5	1.53	312	974	2.36	69.2	76.2†	82.0	37	**PYR**; **VR**; OX; [243,]
38	Strontium	Sr	1	S	FCC	87.6	2.58†	1043	1640	9.20†	138.9	52.3†	163.6	38	**PYR**; [486,]; [862, 837‡]
39	Yttrium	Y	1	S	HCP	88.9	4.40†	1773‡	3500‡	17.15‡	393.3‡	46.0	426.8	39	
40	Zirconium	Zr	1	S	HCP	91.2	6.53†	2125	4650	16.74‡	581.6	38.9	610.9	40	**PYR** [1135, 3828]
41	Niobium	Nb	1	S	BCC	92.9	8.55	2770	5200	26.78‡	696.6	36.5†	742.7	41	
42	Molybdenum	Mo	1	S	BCC	95.9	10.22	2890†	5100†	27.61†	594.1	28.6	659.0	42	
43	Technetium	Tc	1	S	HCP	99.0	11.50^{CALC}	2400‡	4900‡	23.01‡	577.4‡	33.5	648.5	43	**RAD**
44	Ruthenium	Ru	1	S	HCP	101.1	12.41†	2700‡	4000‡	25.52‡	569.0‡	28.9	602.5	44	[1473, 0]; [1773, 134]
45	Rhodium	Rh	1	S	FCC	102.9	12.41	2239	4000‡	21.76‡	495.4‡	31.8	556.5	45	
46	Palladium	Pd	1	S	FCC	106.4	12.02	1823	3400†	16.74	393.3	37.9	393.3	46	
47	Silver	Ag	1	S	FCC	107.9	10.50	1234	2450†	11.30	255.1	42.7	286.2	47	
48	Cadmium	Cd	1	S	HCP^D	112.4	8.65	594	1038	6.07	99.9	51.8	111.9	48	**POI VAP** (0.1)
49	Indium	In	1	S	TET^A	114.8	7.31	429	2320‡	3.26	226.4	57.8†	238.5	49	**POI**
50	Tin (white)	Sn	1	S	TET	118.7	7.31	505	2960†	7.20	290.4†	51.4	301.2	50	[476, 8]
50	Tin (grey)	Sn	1	S	DIA	118.7	5.75	**292**^tr to white		**2.26**^tr to white		44.8	303.5	50	
51	Antimony	Sb	4	S	RBL	121.8	6.68	903	1910	19.83	67.9†	45.7†	262.3	51	**POI** (0.5 in air): [368,]; [690,]
52	Tellurium	Te	2	S	TRG	127.6	6.25	723	1260	17.49	50.6	49.7	194.6	52	**POI**(0.01 in air)
53	Iodine	I	2	S	ORH	126.9	4.94	387	456	7.89	20.9†	58.4	106.6	53	**SK POI**^B;pu-bk
54	Xenon	Xe	1	**G**	FCC	131.3	$\mathbf{3.52}^{164K}$	161	165	2.29	12.6	169.6	—	54	{1.00706}
55	Caesium	Cs	1	S	BCC	132.9	1.87	302	958	2.13	65.9†	84.3	78.1	55	**EXP** in H_2O
56	Barium	Ba	1	S	BCC	137.3	3.50	983	1910	7.66	150.9	64.9†	174.6	56	**POI**; OX; [643, 586]
57	Lanthanum	La	1	S	HCP	138.9	6.19	1193	3640	11.30‡	399.6	56.9	416.7	57	[110,]; [821,]; [982,]

† uncertain ‡ highly uncertain * variable ^A distorted FCC ^B I is a skin irritant rather than a poison. ^D distorted, c/a = 1.9 ^CALC calculated, not measured ^tr transition temperature

Thermochemical properties of elements excluding lanthanides – *(continued)*

Z	*Element*		N	State		A / g mol^{-1}	ρ (298K) / g cm^{-3}	T_m / K	T_b / K	$\Delta H_m^\ominus$ / kJ mol^{-1}	$\Delta H_b^\ominus$ / kJ mol^{-1}	$S^\ominus$ / J mol^{-1}K^{-1}	$\Delta H_a^\ominus$ / kJ mol^{-1}	Z	Notes
72	Hafnium	Hf	1	S	HCP	178.5	13.30	2495†	5500†	21.76†	661.1	45.6†	702.9	72	
73	Tantalum	Ta	1	S	BCC	181.0	16.60†	3270	5700‡	31.38‡	753.1	41.4	781.6	73	gr
74	Tungsten	W	1	S	BCC	183.9	19.35†	3650	5800‡	35.23‡	799.1	33.6	836.8	74	
75	Rhenium	Re	1	S	HCP	186.2	21.02	3453	5900‡	33.05‡	707.1	37.2†	777.0	75	
76	Osmium	Os	1	S	HCP	190.2	22.57†	3000‡	4500‡	29.29‡	627.6‡	32.6	669.4	76	
77	Iridium	Ir	1	S	FCC	192.2	22.42†	2727	4400‡	26.36‡	563.6‡	36.4	627.6	77	
78	Platinum	Pt	1	S	FCC	195.1	21.45	2043	4100‡	19.66†	510.4	41.8	564.0	78	
79	Gold	Au	1	S	FCC	197.0	19.32	1336	2980†	12.38	324.3	47.4	354.4	79	yl
80	Mercury	Hg	1	**L**	RBL	200.6	13.53	234	630	2.30	59.2	76.1	61.3	80	**CUM SK POI VAP** (0.1)
81	Thallium	Tl	1	S	HCP	204.4	11.85	577	1740	4.27	162.1	64.6	179.9	81	**SK POI**; [507, 377]
82	Lead	Pb	1	S	FCC	207.2	11.35	601	2024	4.77	179.5	64.8	195.8	82	**CUM POI**
83	Bismuth	Bi	1	S	TRG	209.0	9.75ᶜ	545	1832	10.88	151.5	56.9	198.7	83	
84	Polonium	Po	2	S	RBL	210.0	9.32	527	1235	12.55‡	60.2	62.8†	144.1	84	**RAD POI** (7 pg in body); [370,]
85	Astatine	At	2	S		210.0		575‡	650†	11.92‡	45.2‡	60.7†	90.4	85	**RAD**
86	Radon	Rn	1	**G**		222.0	**4.4**†211K	202‡	211‡	2.89‡	16.4‡	176.1		86	**RAD POI VAP**
87	Francium	Fr	1	S		223.0		300‡	950‡	2.09‡	63.6‡	94.1†	72.8	87	**RAD**
88	Radium	Ra	1	S		226.0	5.00‡	973	1800‡	8.37‡	136.8‡	71.1	161.9	88	**RAD CUM POI VAP**
89	Actinium	Ac		S		227.0	10.07CALC	1470‡	3600‡	14.23‡	397.5‡	62.8†		89	**RAD**
90	Thorium	Th	1	S	FCC	232.0	11.66	1968	4500‡	15.65‡	543.9	53.4†		90	**RAD**; [498,]; [1673, 2803‡]

† uncertain ‡ highly uncertain *variable ᶜcontracts on melting CALC calculated, not measured

Z	*Element*		N	State		A / g mol^{-1}	ρ (298K) / g cm^{-3}	T_m / K	T_b / K	$\Delta H_m^\ominus$ / kJ mol^{-1}	$\Delta H_b^\ominus$ / kJ mol^{-1}	$S^\ominus$ / J mol^{-1}K^{-1}	$\Delta H_a^\ominus$ / kJ mol^{-1}	Z	Notes
91	Protactinium	Pa	1	S	TET	231.0	15.37	1500	4300	14.64	460.2	51.9		91	**RAD**
92	Uranium	U	1	S	BCC	238.1	18.95	1406	4200	15.48	422.6	50.3	490.4	92	**RAD CUM**
											POI (0.2 μCi in body); **PYR**; [941, 2820]; [1047, 4531‡]				
94	Plutonium	Pu	1	S	MCL	239.1	19.84	913	3500	2.09†	317.1			94	**RAD CUM**
							POI (0.5 ng in body); Danger of criticality; [394, 3975]; [480, 586]; [590, 669]; [726,]; [750, 1966]								

† uncertain ‡ highly uncertain

Electron affinities of selected elements

Element	H	C	N	O	O$^-$	F	P	S	S$^-$	Cl	Br	I
ΔH_e/kJ mol^{-1}	−72.0	−120.5	≈0	−141.4	+790.8	−332.6	−66.9	−199.5	+648.5	−364	−342	−295.4

Composition of the Earth

x mass fraction of given element in the Earth

Element	O	Si	Al	Fe	Ca	Na	K	Mg	Ti	P	Mn	All other elements together
x/%	46.6	27.7	8.1	5.0	3.6	2.8	2.6	2.1	0.4	0.1	0.1	<1

Composition of the Earth's atmosphere

V_p partial volume of constituent gas in dry air

Gas	N_2	O_2	Ar	CO_2	Ne	He	CH_4	Kr	Xe
V_p/%	78.09	20.95	0.93	0.03	0.0018	0.0005	0.0002	0.0001	0.00001

Composition of sea water

x mass fraction of element in sea water

Element	O	H	Cl	Na	Mg	S	Ca	K	Br	C
x/%	85.7	10.8	1.90	1.1	0.14	0.09	0.04	0.04	0.007	0.003

Reference: R1 (for above four tables).

Physical, thermochemical and other properties of inorganic compounds

A	molar mass of element	$\Delta H_f^\ominus$	standard molar enthalpy change on formation at 298 K
M	molar mass (including water of crystallization)	$\Delta G_f^\ominus$	standard molar Gibbs free energy change on formation at 298 K
ρ	density (at 298 K or at T_b for gases)	$S^\ominus$	standard molar entropy at 298 K
T_m	normal melting temperature	m_{sat}	solubility in water
T_b	normal boiling temperature	$m^\ominus$	1 mol per 100 g of H_2O

This table includes certain elements not in the standard state given in bold type
All acids are grouped under hydrogen

	Compound	State	Crystal	$\frac{M}{\text{g mol}^{-1}}$	$\frac{\rho(298\text{ K})}{\text{g cm}^{-3}}$	$\frac{T_m}{\text{K}}$	$\frac{T_b}{\text{K}}$
	Aluminium $A = 27.0\ \text{g mol}^{-1}$, $S^\ominus = 28.3\ \text{J mol}^{-1}\text{K}^{-1}$						
1	**Al**	G		**27.0**		**932**	**2720**
2	AlF_3	S		83.9	2.88		**1530**^{sub}
3	$AlCl_3$	S	HEX	133.3	2.44	**453**$^{2.5\ atm}$	696
4	$AlBr_3$	S	ORH	266.7	3.01	371	530
5	Al_2O_3(corundum)	S	ORH	101.9	3.97	2313	3253
6	$Al(OH)_3$	S	MCL	78.0	2.42	573	dec
7	Al_2S_3	S	HEX	150.1	2.03	1373	1773
8	$Al_2(SO_4)_3$	S	POW	342.1	2.71	1043	dec
9	$Al_2(SO_4)_3{\cdot}6H_2O$	S		450.2		dec	dec
10	$Al_2(SO_4)_3{\cdot}18H_2O^\dagger$	S	MCL	666.4	1.69	360	dec
	Antimony $A = 121.8\ \text{g mol}^{-1}$, $S^\ominus = 45.7\ \text{J mol}^{-1}\text{K}^{-1}$						
11	SbH_3 (stibine)	G		124.7	**2.26**^{liq}	185	256
12	$SbCl_3$	S	ORH	228.1	3.14	347	556
13	$SbCl_5$	L		299.0	2.35	276	413
14	Sb_4O_6	S	CUB	583.0	5.20	929	**1698**^{sub}
15	Sb_2S_3 (black)	S		339.6	4.64	823	1423
	Arsenic $A = 74.9\ \text{g mol}^{-1}$, $S^\ominus = 35.1\ \text{J mol}^{-1}\text{K}^{-1}$						
16	AsH_3 (arsine)	G		77.9	**2.69**^{liq}	157	218
17	$AsCl_3$	L		181.2	2.16	265	403
18	$AsBr_3$	S		314.6	3.54	306	494
19	As_2O_3	S	AMS	197.8	3.74	588‡	630‡
20	As_2O_5	S	AMS	229.8	4.32	**588**^{dec}	
21	As_2S_3 (orpiment)	S	RBL	246.0	3.43	573	980
	Barium $A = 137.3\ \text{g mol}^{-1}$, $S^\ominus = 64.9\ \text{J mol}^{-1}\text{K}^{-1}$						
22	BaH_2	S		139.3	4.21	948	1673
23	BaF_2	S	CUB	175.3	4.83	1563	2498
24	$BaCl_2$	S	ORH	208.2	3.86	1236	1833
25	$BaCl_2{\cdot}2H_2O$	S	MCL	244.2	3.10	**386**^{dhd}	
26	$Ba(ClO_3)_2{\cdot}H_2O$	S	MCL	322.2	3.18	687	dec
27	$Ba(ClO_4)_2$	S	HCP	336.2	3.20	778	dec
28	$BaBr_2$	S	ORH	297.1	4.79	1123	dec
29	$BaBr_2{\cdot}2H_2O$	S	MCL	333.1	3.58	**345**^{dhd1}	**393**^{dhd}
30	$Ba(BrO_3)_2{\cdot}H_2O$	S	MCL	411.1	3.99	**443**^{dhd}	**533**^{dec}
31	BaI_2	S	ORH	391.1	4.92	1013	

† uncertain ‡ highly uncertain ^{dec} decomposes $^{dhd(n)}$ dehydrates (loses n molecules of H_2O)

All information relates to the state indicated on the left unless indicated by a superscript and bold type.
Crystal structures for materials normally liquid or gaseous relate to just below T_m.
Densities for gases relate to the liquid just below T_b.
A figure in brackets after the solubility gives the concentration of the saturated solution in moles per 100 cm^3 of solution for cases where the solution density is known to be significantly different from 1.0 g cm^{-3}. This information is not available for many compounds for which it would be relevant. A superscript gives water of crystallization of solid phase when different from standard state.

See page 58 for general notes and abbreviations

$\Delta H_f^\ominus$(298K) / kJ mol^{-1}	$\Delta G_f^\ominus$(298K) / kJ mol^{-1}	$S^\ominus$(298K) / J mol^{-1} K^{-1}	m_{sat}(298K) / $m^\ominus$	Notes	
324.3	**283.7**	**164.4**	—		1
$-1504.1^\dagger$	$-1425.1^\dagger$	$66.4^\dagger$	$6.71 \times 10^{-3\ 3H_2O}$		2
-704.2	-628.9	110.7	$3.46 \times 10^{-1\ 6H_2O}$	**COR POI** dec in H_2O dlq	3
-527.2	-505.0	184.1	dec **VR**	**COR POI** dec in H_2O dlq	4
-1675.7	-1582.4	50.9	$1.00 \times 10^{-10\ddagger}$		5
-1276.1			$1.28 \times 10^{-6\ddagger 291K}$		6
$-508.8^\dagger$	-492.5	96.2	dec	yl	7
-3440.8	-3100.1	239.3	9.15×10^{-2}		8
-5311.7	-4622.6	469.0	—		9
-8878.9			$1.13 \times 10^{-1\dagger ?16H_2O}$		10
				All Sb compounds POI	
145.1	147.7	232.6	8.92×10^{-4}	**POI** (0.1) **INF**	11
-382.0	-324.7	186.2	$4.33^\dagger$	dlq	12
-438.5			dec	rd	13
-1409.2	-1213.4	246.0	slightly soluble		14
-174.9	-173.6	182.0	2.06×10^{-6}	bk (or yl–rd)	15
				All As compounds CUM SK POI	
66.4	68.9	22.5	8.92×10^{-4}	**POI** (0.1)	16
-335.6	-295.0	233.5	dec		17
-195.0			dec		18
-1312.1	-1152.3	214.2	1.04×10^{-2}		19
-915.9	-772.4	105.4	$2.97 \times 10^{-1\ 4H_2O}$	dlq	20
-169.0	-168.6	163.6	$2.03 \times 10^{-7\ 291K}$	yl–rd	21
				All soluble Ba compounds POI	
-171.1			dec gives H_2	gr	22
-1200.4	-1148.5	96.2	$9.24 \times 10^{-4\dagger}$		23
-860.2	-810.9	125.5	1.46×10^{-1}		24
-1461.9	-1295.8	202.9	$1.78 \times 10^{-1\dagger}$		25
-1066.5			$1.25 \times 10^{-1\dagger}$ (0.114 mol/100 cm^3)		26
-806.7			$8.60 \times 10^{-1\ddagger 8H_2O,293K}$ (0.423 mol/100 cm^3)		27
-754.8			$3.30 \times 10^{-1\dagger}$		28
-1365.2			3.56×10^{-1}		29
			2.02×10^{-3}		30
-602.5			5.64×10^{-1} (0.401 mol/100 cm^3)^{15H_2O}		31

^{sub} sublimes. See p. 58.

Physical, thermochemical and other properties of inorganic compounds – *(continued)*

	Compound	State	Crystal	$\frac{M}{\text{g mol}^{-1}}$	$\frac{\rho(298\text{ K})}{\text{g cm}^{-3}}$	$\frac{T_m}{\text{K}}$	$\frac{T_b}{\text{K}}$
	Barium—*(continued)* $A = 137.3$ g mol^{-1}, $S^{\ominus} = 64.9$ J mol^{-1} K^{-1}						
32	$Ba(IO_3)_2$	S	MCL	487.1	5.00	dec	
33	BaO	S	CUB	153.3	5.72	2196	2273
34	BaO_2	S	POW	169.3	4.96	723	**1073**^{dec}
35	$Ba(OH)_2$	S	ORH	171.3	4.50	681	dec
36	$BaCO_3$	S	ORH	197.3	4.43	**1723**^{dec}	
37	$Ba(HCO_3)_2$	aq		259.3			
38	BaS	S	CUB	169.4	4.25	2473	
39	$BaSO_4$	S	ORH	233.4	4.50	1623	
40	$Ba(NO_3)_2$	S	CUB	261.3	3.24	865	dec
41	$BaC_2O_4{\cdot}2H_2O$ (oxalate)	S		261.4	3.17	dec	
42	$BaCrO_4$	S	ORH	253.3	4.50		
	Beryllium $A = 9.0$ g mol^{-1}, $S^{\ominus} = 9.5$ J mol^{-1} K^{-1}						
43	BeF_2	S	HEX	47.0	1.99	1073	1603
44	$BeCl_2$	S		79.9	1.90	683	820
45	$BeBr_2$	S	HEX	168.8	3.47	761	793
46	BeO	S	HEX	25.0	3.01	2823	4393
47	$Be(OH)_2$(alpha)	S		43.0			
48	$BeSO_4{\cdot}4H_2O$	S	TET	177.1	1.71	**673**^{dhd}	**823**^{T_m}
49	$Be(NO_3)_2{\cdot}3H_2O$	S		187.0	1.56	333	415
	Bismuth $A = 209.0$ g mol^{-1}, $S^{\ominus} = 56.9$ J mol^{-1} K^{-1}						
50	$BiCl_3$	S	CUB	315.3	4.75	505	714
51	BiOCl	S	TET	260.4	7.72		
52	Bi_2O_3	S	BCC	495.9	8.55	1090	2163
53	Bi_2S_3	S	RBL	514.1	7.39	**958**^{dec}	
54	$Bi(NO_3)_3{\cdot}5H_2O$	S	TCL	485.0	2.83	**303**^{dec}	
	Boron $A = 10.8$ g mol^{-1}, $S^{\ominus} = 5.9^{\dagger}$ J mol^{-1} K^{-1}						
55	B_2H_6 (diborane)	G		27.6	0.45	108	181
56	BF_3	G		67.8	2.99	144	174
57	BCl_3	L		117.1	1.35	166	286
58	BCl_3	G		117.1		166	286
59	B_2O_3	S	ORH	69.6	2.46	733	2133
60	B_2O_3	S	VIT	69.6	1.81	723	2133
	Bromine $A = 79.9$ g mol^{-1}, $S^{\ominus}(Br_2(l)) = 151.6$ J mol^{-1} K^{-1}, $\Delta H_f^{\ominus}(Br_2^+(g)) = 1060.6$ kJ mol						
61	Br_2	G		159.8		266	332
	Cadmium $A = 112.4$ g mol^{-1}, $S^{\ominus} = 51.8$ J mol^{-1} K^{-1}						
62	$CdBr_2$	S	HEX	272.2	5.19	841	1136
63	CdO	S	FCC	128.4	8.15	**1173**^{dec}	
64	CdS	S	HEX	144.4	4.82	**2023**^{100atm}	**1253**^{sub}
65	$CdSO_4$	S	ORH	208.4	4.69	1273	
66	$CdSO_4{\cdot}2.67H_2O$	S	MCL	256.5	3.09	**315**$^{dhd?1.67}$	

† uncertain ‡ highly uncertain ^{dec} decomposes $^{dhd(n)}$ dehydrates (loses n molecules of H_2O)

$\Delta H_f^\ominus$(298K) / kJ mol^{-1}	$\Delta G_f^\ominus$(298K) / kJ mol^{-1}	$S^\ominus$(298K) / J mol^{-1} K^{-1}	m_{sat}(298K) / $m^\ominus$	Notes	
−997.5			8.11×10^{-5}		32
−558.1	−528.4	70.3	2.27×10^{-2}		33
−629.7			slightly soluble dec	gr	34
−946.4			1.50×10^{-2} ^{8H_2O}		35
−1218.8	−1138.9	112.1	9.12×10^{-6}		36
−1920.5	−1734.7	200.8	2.80×10^{-3} $^{22\ atm\ CO_2}$		37
−443.5			5.29×10^{-2}	hydrolyses in H_2O	38
−1465.2	−1353.1	132.2	9.43×10^{-7}		39
−728.0	−795.0	213.8	3.91×10^{-2} (0.038 mol/100 cm^3)		40
−1966.5	−1742.2		5.20×10^{-5}		41
−1428.0			$1.14 \times 10^{-6\dagger}$	rd	42
				All Be compounds SK POI	
−1051.9			$1.80^{\dagger}$ $^{after\ 82d}$		43
−511.7			8.96×10^{-1} ^{4H_2O}	dlq	44
−369.9			soluble	dlq	45
−610.9	−581.6	14.1	1.40×10^{-8}		46
−907.1					47
−2411.2			3.79×10^{-1} (0.353 mol/100 cm^3)		48
−787.8			8.04×10^{-1} ^{4H_2O}	dlq pa yl	49
−379.1	−318.8		dec	dlq	50
−365.3	−322.2	86.2	insoluble	yl (or gr-bk)	51
−577.0	−496.6	151.5	insoluble		52
−143.1	−140.6	200.4	3.6×10^{-8}	br-bk	53
			dec		54
35.6	86.8	233.0	dec		55
−1145.4	−1120.3	254.0	4.72×10^{-3} ^{273K}	**COR POI VAP**	56
−427.2	**−387.4**	**206.3**	dec		57
−395.4	−380.3	290.0	dec		58
−1272.8	−1193.7	54.0	1.60×10^{-2} (0.256 mol/100 g at 376 K)		59
−1245.2	−1173.2	78.7	1.58×10^{-2}		60
31.9	3.1	245.4	2.24×10^{-2} ^{293K}	**COR POI VAP** (1) (rd-br)	61
−314.6	−293.3	133.5	$4.13 \times 10^{-1\dagger}$ ^{4H_2O} (0.345 mol/100 cm^3)	yl	62
−254.8	−225.1	54.8	3.80×10^{-6}	br	63
−144.3	−140.6	71.1	1.46×10^{-11}	or-yl	64
−820.0	−926.2	137.2	3.62×10^{-1}		65
−1723.0	−1462.7	242.3	$1.58^{\dagger}$		66

^{sub} sublimes. See p. 58.

Physical, thermochemical and other properties of inorganic compounds – *(continued)*

	Compound	State	Crystal	M / g mol^{-1}	ρ(298 K) / g cm^{-3}	T_m / K	T_b / K
	Caesium $A = 132.9$ g mol^{-1}, $S^{\ominus} = 84.3$ J mol^{-1} K^{-1}						
67	CsF	S	CUB	151.9	3.59	955	1524
68	CsCl	S	CUB	168.3	3.97	918	1573
69	CsBr	S	CUB	212.8	4.44	909	1573
70	CsI	S	CUB	259.8	4.51	894	1553
71	Cs_2O	S	RBL	281.8	4.25	**763**$^{\text{in } N_2}$	**673**^{dec}
72	CsOH	S		149.9	3.68	545	
	Calcium $A = 40.1$ g mol^{-1}, $S^{\ominus} = 41.6$ J mol^{-1} K^{-1}						
73	**Ca**	G		**40.0**		**1123**	**1765**
74	CaH_2	S	ORH	42.1	1.70	1089	
75	CaF_2	S	CUB	78.0	3.18	**1691**$^{\text{in } H_2}$	2745
76	$CaCl_2$	S	ORH	110.9	2.51	1055	1873
77	$CaCl_2{\cdot}H_2O$	S		129.0		533	
78	$CaCl_2{\cdot}2H_2O$	S	TET	147.0	0.84	**473**^{dhd}	
79	$CaCl_2{\cdot}4H_2O$	S		183.0		dhd	
80	$CaCl_2{\cdot}6H_2O$	S	HEX	219.0	1.71	**303**$^{\text{dhd2}}$	
81	$CaBr_2$	S		199.9	3.35	1038	1083
82	CaI_2	S	HEX	293.8	3.96	1013	1373
83	CaO	S	CUB	56.0	3.35	2873	3123
84	$Ca(OH)_2$	S	HEX	74.0	2.24	**853**^{dhd}	
85	CaC_2 (carbide)	S	TET	64.1	2.22	720	2573
86	$CaCO_3$ (calcite)	S	HEX	100.0	2.71	**1612**$^{\text{1025 atm}}$	**1172**^{dec}
87	$CaCO_3$ (aragonite)	S	ORH	100.0	2.93	5473	**1098**^{dec}
88	CaS	S	CUB	72.1	2.18	**2673**^{dec}	
89	$CaSO_4$ (anhydrite)	S	ORH	136.1	2.96	**1723**^{dec}	1846
90	$CaSO_4{\cdot}0.5H_2O$	S	HEX	145.1		**436**^{dhd}	
91	$CaSO_4{\cdot}2H_2O$ (gypsum)	S	MCL	172.1	2.32	**401**$^{\text{dhd 1.5}}$	**436**^{dhd}
92	$Ca(NO_3)_2$	S	CUB	164.0	2.36	834	
93	$Ca(NO_3)_2{\cdot}4H_2O$	S	MCL	236.1	1.82	313	**405**^{dhd}
94	$Ca_3(PO_4)_2$ (beta)	S	HEX	310.1	3.14	2003†	
95	$CaCrO_4{\cdot}2H_2O$	S	TET	192.1		**473**^{dhd}	
96	$CaSi_2$	S		96.2	2.50		
97	$CaSiO_3$ (wollastonite)	S	MCL	116.1	2.50	1803	
98	Ca_2SiO_4	S	MCL	172.2	3.27	2393	
99	$CaC_2O_4.H_2O$ (oxalate)	S		146.1	2.20	**473**^{dhd}	dec
	Carbon $A = 12.0$ g mol^{-1}, $S^{\ominus}$ (graphite) $= 5.7$ J mol^{-1} K^{-1}. $\Delta H_f^{\ominus}$ (diamond) $= 1.87$ kJ mol^{-1}, $\Delta G_f^{\ominus}$ (diamond) $= 2.8$ kJ mol^{-1}.						
100	**C**	G		**12.0**			
101	$\mathbf{C_2}$	G		**24.0**			
102	$\mathbf{C_3}$	G		**36.0**			
103	CO	G		28.0	1.25	68	82
104	CO_2	G		44.0	1.98	217	195
105	CS_2	L		76.1	1.26	161	319
106	HCN	L		27.0		260	299
107	C_2N_2 (cyanogen)	G		52.0		245	252

† uncertain ‡ highly uncertain ^{dec} decomposes $^{\text{dhd}(n)}$ dehydrates (loses n molecules of H_2O)

$\Delta H_f^\ominus(298K)$ / kJ mol⁻¹	$\Delta G_f^\ominus(298K)$ / kJ mol⁻¹	$S^\ominus(298K)$ / J mol⁻¹ K⁻¹	$m_{sat}(298K)/m^\ominus$	Notes	
−530.9			3.84 $^{1\ H_2O}$	dlq	67
−433.0			1.13	dlq	68
−394.6	−383.3	121.3	5.80×10^{-1}	dlq	69
−336.8	−333.5	129.7	3.29×10^{-1}	dlq	70
−317.6			very soluble (dec)	or	71
−406.7			2.02^{303K}	dlq pa yl	72
176.6	**142.8**	**154.8**	—		73
−188.7	−149.8	41.8	dec		74
−1214.6	−1161.9	69.0	2.31×10^{-5}		75
−795.0	−750.2	113.8	5.36×10^{-1}	dlq	76
−1109.2			5.95×10^{-1}	dlq	77
−1403.7			6.65×10^{-1}		78
−2009.2			9.79×10^{-1}		79
−2607.5			7.46×10^{-1}	dlq	80
−674.9	−656.1	129.7	$6.25 \times 10^{-1\dagger}$	dlq	81
−534.7	−529.7	142.3	6.19×10^{-1}	dlq pa yl	82
−635.5	−604.2	39.7	2.34×10^{-3}	**VR**	83
−986.6	−896.8	76.1	1.53×10^{-3} free of CO_2		84
−62.8	−67.8	70.3	dec **VR**	**EXP** (gives ethyne in H_2O)	85
−1206.9	−1128.8	92.9	1.30×10^{-5}		86
−1207.0	−1127.7	88.7			87
−482.4	−477.4	56.5	$2.94 \times 10^{-4\ 293K}$		88
−1432.6	−1320.5	106.7	4.66×10^{-3} dec		89
−1575.3	−1435.1	130.5	$1.10 \times 10^{-3\dagger}$	plaster of Paris	90
−2021.3	−1795.8	194.1	7.00×10^{-2}	(max m_{sat} at 313 K)	91
−937.2	−741.8	193.3	$6.22 \times 10^{-1\dagger}$	hyg	92
−2131.3	−1700.8	338.9	8.41×10^{-1}	dlq	93
−4137.6	−3899.5	236.0	$6.35 \times 10^{-5*}$		94
−1379.0	−1277.4	133.9	1.07×10^{-1} (0.106 mol/100 cm^3)	dk yl	95
−150.6			dec		96
−1567.3	−1498.7	82.0	$8.18 \times 10^{-5\ 290K}$		97
−2255.2					98
−1669.8	−1508.8	156.1	$4.92 \times 10^{-6\dagger}$	**POI**	99
714.7	**669.6**	**158.0**	insoluble		100
836.8	**780.4**	**200.5**	insoluble		101
836.8	**773.1**	**230.9**	insoluble		102
−110.5	−137.3	197.9	$2.14 \times 10^{-5\dagger}$ 1 atm total pressure		103
−393.5	−394.4	213.6	$3.29 \times 10^{-3\dagger}$ 1 atm total pressure		104
87.9	63.6	151.0	2.22×10^{-3}	**INF**	105
−108.9	124.8	201.7	4.50×10^{-2}	**POI VAP**(20)	106
307.9	296.3	242.1	$2.14 \times 10^{-2*}$	**POI VAP**	107

sub sublimes. See p. 58. * variable

Physical, thermochemical and other properties of inorganic compounds – *(continued)*

	Compound	State	Crystal	$\frac{M}{\text{g mol}^{-1}}$	$\frac{\rho(298\text{ K})}{\text{g cm}^{-3}}$	$\frac{T_m}{\text{K}}$	$\frac{T_b}{\text{K}}$
	Chlorine $A = 35.5\text{ g mol}^{-1}$, $S^{\ominus}(Cl_2(g)) = 233.0\text{ J mol}^{-1}\text{ K}^{-1}$, $\Delta H_f^{\ominus}(Cl_2^+(g)) = 1114.2\text{ kJ mol}^{-1}$						
108	Cl_2O	G		86.9	**3.89**^{253K}	253	275
109	ClO_2	G		67.4	**3.01**^{214K}	214	283
	Chromium $A = 52.0\text{ g mol}^{-1}$, $S^{\ominus} = 23.8\text{ J mol}^{-1}\text{ K}^{-1}$						
110	$CrCl_3$	S	HEX	158.3	2.76	1423	1573
111	CrO_2Cl_2	L		154.9	1.91	177	390
112	Cr_2O_3	S	HEX	151.9	5.21	2538	4273
113	CrO_3	S	ORH	99.9	2.70	**469**^{dec}	
114	$Cr_2(SO_4)_3$	S	POW	392.1	3.01		
115	$Cr_2(SO_4)_3 \cdot 18H_2O$	S	CUB	716.4	1.70	**373**$^{dhd\ 12}$	
	Cobalt $A = 58.9\text{ g mol}^{-1}$, $S^{\ominus} = 30.0^{\dagger}\text{ J mol}^{-1}\text{ K}^{-1}$						
116	$CoCl_2$	S	HEX	129.8	3.36	**997**$^{in\ HCl}$	1323
117	$CoCl_2 \cdot 6H_2O$	S	MCL	237.9	2.48	359	**383**^{dhd}
118	CoO	S	CUB	74.9	6.45	2078	
119	Co_3O_4	S	CUB	240.8	6.07	**1173**^{dec}	
120	$Co(OH)_2$	S	HEX	92.9	3.60	dec	
121	$CoSO_4$	S	ORH	155.0	3.71	**1008**^{dec}	
122	$CoSO_4 \cdot 7H_2O$	S	MCL	281.1	1.95	370	**693**^{dhd}
123	$Co(NO_3)_2 \cdot 6H_2O$	S	MCL	291.0	1.87	**330**$^{dhd\ 3}$	
	Copper $A = 63.5\text{ g mol}^{-1}$, $S^{\ominus} = 33.3\text{ J mol}^{-1}\text{ K}^{-1}$						
124	**Cu**	G		**63.5**		**356**	**2855**
125	$CuCl$	S	CUB	98.9	3.53	703	1763
126	$CuCl_2$	S	POW	134.4	3.05	771	1266
127	Cu_2O	S	CUB	143.0	6.00	1502	**2073**^{dec}
128	CuO	S	MCL	79.5	6.40	1599	
129	$Cu(OH)_2$	S	ORH	97.5	3.37	dec	
130	Cu_2S	S	ORH	159.1	5.60	1400	
131	CuS	S	HEX	95.6	4.60	376	**493**^{dec}
132	$CuSO_4$	S	ORH	159.6	3.60	473	**923**^{dec}
133	$CuSO_4 \cdot 5H_2O$	S	TCL	249.6	2.28	**383**$^{dhd\ 4}$	**423**^{dhd}
	Fluorine $A = 19.0\text{ g mol}^{-1}$, $S^{\ominus}(F_2(g)) = 202.8\text{ J mol}^{-1}\text{ K}^{-1}$, $\Delta H_f^{\ominus}(F_2^+(g)) = 1533.9\text{ kJ mol}^{-1}$						
134	F_2O	G		54.0	**1.65**^{49K}	49	128
	Gallium. See page 86.						
	Germanium $A = 72.6\text{ g mol}^{-1}$, $S^{\ominus} = 31.1^{\dagger}\text{ J mol}^{-1}\text{ K}^{-1}$						
135	$GeCl_4$	L		143.5	1.88	224	356
136	GeO	S		88.5		**983**^{sub}	
137	GeO_2	S	HEX	104.5	4.23	1389	
138	GeS	S	ORH	104.6	4.01	803	1088
	Gold $A = 197.0\text{ g mol}^{-1}$, $S^{\ominus} = 47.4\text{ J mol}^{-1}\text{ K}^{-1}$						
139	Au_2O_3	S		441.9		**433**$^{dec-O}$	**523**$^{dec-3O}$
140	$AuCl_3$	S		303.3	3.90	**527**^{dec}	**538**$^{sub\ in\ Cl}$

† uncertain ‡ highly uncertain ^{dec} decomposes $^{dhd(n)}$ dehydrates (loses n molecules of H_2O)

$\Delta H_f^\ominus(298K)$ / kJ mol^{-1}	$\Delta G_f^\ominus(298K)$ / kJ mol^{-1}	$S^\ominus(298K)$ / J mol^{-1} K^{-1}	$m_{sat}(298K)$ / $m^\ominus$	Notes	
80.3	97.9	266.1	3.29×10^{-1} ^{293K}	dec **POI**(1) yl-rd	**108**
102.5	120.5	256.7	1.29×10^{-1} ^{287K}	**POI**(1) yl-rd	**109**
−563.2	−493.7	125.5	1.62	violet	**110**
−567.8	−510.9	221.3	dec	**COR POI** rd fuming	**111**
−1128.4	−1046.8	81.2	1.20×10^{-9}	gn	**112**
−589.5	−495.8†		1.69 (1.072 mol/100 cm^3)	dk rd **COR POI** (0.03)	**113**
			1.63×10^{-1}	vi-rd	**114**
−8339.5			1.67×10^{-1} ^{16H_2O}	bl-vi	**115**
−325.5	−282.4	106.3	3.39×10^{-1}	hyg bl	**116**
−2129.2			4.33×10^{-1}	rd	**117**
−239.3	−213.4	43.9	insoluble	gn-br	**118**
−878.6	−758.9		insoluble	bk	**119**
−548.9	−455.6		1.40×10^{-6}	pa rd	**120**
−868.2	−761.9	113.4	2.34×10^{-1}	dk bl	**121**
−2986.5			2.41×10^{-1}†	pa rd	**122**
−2216.3			5.57×10^{-1}†	rd	**123**
				All Cu compounds POI	
339.3	**299.1**	**166.3**	—		**124**
−136.0	−118.0	84.5	6.06×10^{-5}† ^{H_2O}		**125**
−205.9			2.00×10^{-3}	yl-br	**126**
−166.7	−146.4	100.8	insoluble	rd	**127**
−155.2	−127.2	43.5	3.00×10^{-6} †dec	bk	**128**
−448.5			insoluble (dec)	bl	**129**
−79.5	−86.2	120.9	1.20×10^{-15}	bk	**130**
−48.5	−49.0	66.5	2.60×10^{-16}	bk	**131**
−769.9	−661.9	113.4	—	white	**132**
−2278.2	−1879.9	305.4	1.39×10^{-1} (0.138 mol/100 cm^3)	blue vitriol	**133**
−21.8	−4.6	247.3	slightly soluble (dec)	**POI VAP**	**134**
−543.9			dec	bk	**135**
−212.1†	−237.2†	50.2	2.00×10^{-5}	(also an insoluble form)	**136**
−551.0	−497.1	55.3	4.51×10^{-3}		**137**
5.6			2.29×10^{-3}	yl rd	**138**
80.8	163.2	125.5	insoluble		**139**
−118.4			7.01×10^{-1}	dk rd	**140**

^{sub} sublimes. See p. 58.

Physical, thermochemical and other properties of inorganic compounds – *(continued)*

	Compound	State	Crystal	$\frac{M}{\text{g mol}^{-1}}$	$\frac{\rho(298\text{ K})}{\text{g cm}^{-3}}$	$\frac{T_m}{\text{K}}$	$\frac{T_b}{\text{K}}$
	Hydrogen (acids) $A = 1.0$ g mol^{-1}, $S^{\ominus}(H_2(g)) = 130.6$ J mol^{-1} K^{-1}, $\Delta G_f^{\ominus}(H(g)) = 203.3$ kJ mol^{-1}, $S^{\ominus}(H(g)) = 114.6$ J mol^{-1}, $\Delta H_f^{\ominus}(H_2^+(g)) = 1494.6$ kJ mol^{-1}						
141	HF	G		20.0	0.95	190	293
142	HCl	G		36.4	**1.64**^{159K}	159	188
143	HBr	G		80.9		186	206
144	HI	G		127.9		222	238
145	HIO_3	S		175.9	4.63	**383**^{dec}	
146	H_2O	L		18.0	1.00	273	373
147	H_2O	G		18.0		273	373
148	H_2O_2	L		34.0	1.40	273	323
149	H_2CO_3	aq		62.0			
150	H_2S	G		34.0	**1.54**^{188K}	188	213
151	H_2S	aq		34.0			
152	H_2S_2	G		66.1	**1.33**^{183K}	183	202
153	H_2SO_4	L		98.0	1.83	284	603
154	HNO_3	L		63.0	1.51	231	356
155	H_3PO_4	S	ORH	98.0	1.86	316	**438**^{dhd}
156	H_3BO_3 (boric, boracic)	S	TCL	61.8	1.44	458	573
	Iodine $A = 126.9$ g mol^{-1}, $S^{\ominus}(I(s)) = 58.4$ J mol^{-1} K^{-1}						
157	I_2	G		**253.8**		**387**	**456**
158	ICl	S	CUB	162.3	3.85	300	371
159	ICl_3	S	ORH	233.3	3.12	**374**^{16atm}	**350**^{dec}
160	IBr	S		206.8	4.42	315	**389**^{dec}
161	I_2O_5	S		333.8	4.98	**573**$^{\dagger dec}$	
	Iron $A = 55.9$ g mol^{-1}, $S^{\ominus} = 27.2$ J mol^{-1} K^{-1}						
162	$FeCl_2$	S	HEX	126.7	2.98	**950**^{sub}	1299
163	$FeCl_3$	S	HEX	162.2	2.80	577	**592**^{dec}
164	FeO	S	CUB	71.8	5.70*	1693	
165	Fe_2O_3 (haematite)	S	TET	159.6	5.24	1730	1838
166	Fe_3O_4 (magnetite)	S	CUB	231.5	5.18	**1807**^{dec}	
167	$Fe(OH)_2$	S	HEX	89.8	3.40	dec	
168	$Fe(OH)_3$	S		106.8			
169	$FeCO_3$ (siderite)	S	HEX	115.8	3.80	dec	
170	$Fe(CO)_5$	L		195.9	1.46	252	378
171	FeS (alpha)	S	HEX	87.9	4.74	**1468**^{dec}	
172	$FeSO_4$	S		151.9			
173	$FeSO_4{\cdot}7H_2O$	S	MCL	278.0	1.90	337	**363**$^{dhd\,6}$
174	$Fe_2(SO_4)_3$	S	ORH	399.8	3.10	**753**^{dec}	

† uncertain ‡ highly uncertain ^{dec} decomposes $^{dhd(n)}$ dehydrates (loses n molecules of H_2O)

$\Delta H_f^\ominus$(298K) / kJ mol^{-1}	$\Delta G_f^\ominus$(298K) / kJ mol^{-1}	$S^\ominus$(298K) / J mol^{-1} K^{-1}	m_{sat}(298K) / $m^\ominus$	Notes	
−271.1	−273.2	173.7	4.33×10^{-2} ^{272K}	**COR POI VAP** (1)	141
−92.3	−95.3	186.7	5.97 (2.257 mol/100 cm^3)	**COR POI VAP** (5)	142
−36.2	−53.2	198.5	2.39	**COR POI VAP** (5)	143
26.5	2.1	206.5	5.56×10^{-2} $^{0.13mmHg}$	**COR POI VAP**	144
	−238.6		1.44^{289K}		145
−285.9	−237.2	70.0	—	$\Delta H_f^\ominus(H_2O^+(g))$ = 979.9 kJ mol^{-1}; $\Delta H_f^\ominus(OH^+(g))$ = 1328.4 kJ mol^{-1}	146
−241.8	−228.6	188.7	—	$\Delta H_f^\ominus(OH^-(g))$ = −140.9 kJ mol^{-1}	147
−187.6	−118.0	109.6	∞	$\Delta H_f^\ominus(H_2O_2^+(g))$ = 923.4 kJ mol^{-1}; **COR POI EXP** with organic compounds and some metals	148
−699.6	−623.0	187.4	—		149
−20.6	−33.6	205.7	9.80×10^{-3}	**POI GAS** (20)	150
−39.3	−27.4	122.2	—	$\Delta H_f^\ominus(H_2S^+(g))$ = 995.0 kJ mol^{-1}	151
−23.1			dec		152
−814.0	−690.1	156.9	∞	**COR EXP** if H_2O added	153
−173.2	−79.9	155.6	∞	**COR POI VAP** (10)	154
−1279.0	−1119.2	110.5	6.83 $^{0.5\ H_2O}$	dlq	155
−1094.3	−969.0	88.8	4.37×10^{-2}		156
2.3	**19.4**	**260.6**	—	$\Delta H_f(I_2^+(g))$ = 967.3 kJ mol^{-1}	157
17.6^{gas}	**−5.5**^{gas}	**247.3**^{gas}	dec	or-rd	158
−88.3	−22.4	172.0	dec	**COR POI** or-rd	159
40.8^{gas}	**3.8**^{gas}	**258.6**^{gas}	dec	dk gr	160
−158.1	−177.2†		5.61×10^{-1} $^{286\ K}$	**COR POI**	161
−341.0	−302.1	119.7	6.36×10^{-1} $^{4\ H_2O}$ (0.508 mol/100 cm^3)	**EXP** dlq yl-gr	162
−399.3	−334.1	142.3	1.73 $^{3.5\ H_2O\ dec}$	**COR** dlq bk-br	163
−266.5*	−244.3*	54.0*	insoluble	bk	164
−822.2	−741.0	87.4	insoluble	rd-br	165
−1117.1	−1014.2	146.4	insoluble	bk (rd) magnetic	166
−568.2	−483.7	87.9	$6.70 \times 10^{-6\dagger}$	pa gr	167
−824.2	−706.6	106.7	3.40×10^{-7}		168
−740.7	−666.7	92.9	6.22×10^{-4} $^{291\ K,\ 1\ atm\ CO_2}$		169
−785.8			insoluble	**POI** yl	170
−100.0	−100.4	60.3	$5.01 \times 10^{-6\dagger}$ ^{291K}	bk	171
−928.4	−821.0	107.5	1.03×10^{-1}		172
−3014.6	−2510.3	309.2	1.94×10^{-1}	bl–gn 573 K$^{dhd\ 1}$	173
−2581.5			$2.18 \times 10^{-1*}$	hyg yl	174

^{sub} sublimes. See p. 58. * variable

Physical, thermochemical and other properties of inorganic compounds – *(continued)*

	Compound	State	Crystal	M / g mol^{-1}	ρ(298 K) / g cm^{-3}	T_m / K	T_b / K
	Lead $A = 207.2$ **g mol^{-1}, $S^{\ominus} = 64.8$ J mol^{-1} K^{-1}**						
175	PbF_2	S		245.1	8.24	1095	1563
176	$PbCl_2$	S	ORH	278.1	5.90	771	1227
177	$PbBr_2$	S	ORH	367.0		643	1187
178	PbI_2	S	TRG	461.0	6.16	685	1145
179	PbO (litharge)	S	TET	223.1	9.53	1159	1745
180	Pb_3O_4 (minium)	S	TET	685.5	9.10	**773**^{dec}	
181	PbO_2	S	TET	239.1	9.40	**573**^{dec}	
182	$PbCO_3$ (cerussite)	S	ORH	267.2	6.60	**588**^{dec}	
183	PbS (galena)	S	FCC	239.2	7.50	1387	1553
184	$PbSO_4$	S	ORH	303.2	6.20	1360	
185	$Pb(NO_3)_2$	S	CUB	331.2	4.53	**743**^{dec}	
186	$PbCrO_4$ (chrome yellow)	S	MCL	323.1	6.30	**1117**^{dec}	
187	$Pb(C_2H_3O_2)_2{\cdot}3H_2O$	S	MCL	325.2	3.25	553	dec
188	$Pb(C_2H_5)_4$	L		323.4	1.66	137	473
	Lithium $A = 6.9$ **g mol^{-1}, $S^{\ominus} = 28.0$ J mol^{-1} K^{-1}**						
189	LiH	S	CUB	7.9	0.78	961	
190	Li_3H_4	S		21.7	0.66	557	
191	LiF	S	CUB	25.9	2.64	1118	1953
192	LiCl	S	CUB	42.3	2.07	887	1655
193	LiBr	S	CUB	86.8	3.46	823	1583
194	LiI	S	CUB	133.8	4.06	722	1444
195	Li_2O	S	CUB	29.8	2.02	> 1973	
196	LiOH	S	TET	23.9	1.46	723	**1197**^{dec}
197	Li_2CO_3	S	MCL	73.8	2.11	996	**1583**^{dec}
198	$LiHCO_3$	aq		67.9			
199	$LiNO_3$	S	TRG	68.9	2.38	527	**873**^{dec}
200	Li_3PO_4	S	ORH	115.7	2.54	8843	
201	$LiAlH_4$	S	MCL	37.9	0.92	**398**^{dec}	
	Magnesium $A = 24.3$ **g mol^{-1}, $S^{\ominus} = 32.7$ J mol^{-1} K^{-1}**						
202	Mg	G		**24.3**		**923**	**1390**
203	$MgCl_2$	S	MCL	95.2	2.32	987	1691
204	$MgCl_2{\cdot}6H_2O$	S	MCL	203.3	1.56	**390**^{dhd}	
205	$Mg(ClO_4)_2$	S		223.2	2.60	**524**^{dec}	
206	$MgBr_2$	S	HEX	184.1	3.72	984	1503
207	MgO (periclase)	S	CUB	40.3	3.58	3173	3873
208	$Mg(OH)_2$	S	TRG	58.3	2.36	**623**^{dhd}	
209	$MgCO_3$ (magnesite)	S	TRG	84.3	2.96	**623**^{dec}	
210	MgS	S	CUB	56.3	2.84	**2273**^{dec}	
211	$MgSO_4$	S	ORH	120.3	2.65	**1400**^{dec}	
212	$MgSO_4{\cdot}7H_2O$	S	ORH	246.4	1.68	**423**$^{dhd\ 6}$	**473**^{dhd}

† uncertain ‡ highly uncertain ^{dec} decomposes $^{dhd(n)}$ dehydrates (loses n molecules of H_2O)

$\dfrac{\Delta H_f^\ominus(298K)}{kJ\ mol^{-1}}$	$\dfrac{\Delta G_f^\ominus(298K)}{kJ\ mol^{-1}}$	$\dfrac{S^\ominus(298K)}{J\ mol^{-1}\ K^{-1}}$	$\dfrac{m_{sat}(298K)}{m^\ominus}$	Notes	
				All Pb compounds CUM POI	
−664.0	−617.1	110.5	2.45×10^{-4} 333K		**175**
−359.4	−314.1	136.0	3.90×10^{-3}		**176**
−278.7	−261.9	161.5	2.65×10^{-3}		**177**
−175.5	−173.6	174.8	1.65×10^{-4}	yl	**178**
−217.3	−187.9	68.7	1.08×10^{-5} 291K	yl (massicot is ORH)	**179**
−718.4	−601.2	211.3	insoluble	red lead	**180**
−277.4	−217.4	68.6	insoluble† 293K dec		**181**
−700.0	−626.3	131.0	4.12×10^{-7}		**182**
−100.4	−98.7	91.2	2.84×10^{-7} † depends on pH	bk	**183**
−919.9	−813.2	148.6	1.48×10^{-5}		**184**
−451.9			4.47×10^{-1} (0.263 mol/100 cm^3)		**185**
			5.26×10^{-8}	yl	**186**
−1853.9			2.04×10^{-1} (0.175 mol/100 cm^3)	lead acetate	**187**
217.6				tetraethyl lead	**188**
−90.4	−70.0	24.7	dec		**189**
−186.6			dec		**190**
−612.1	−583.7	35.9	5.09×10^{-3}		**191**
−408.8			2.00 (1.402 mol/100 cm^3) $1H_2O$		**192**
−350.3			2.00×10^{-2} $2H_2O$	dlq	**193**
−271.1			1.21		**194**
−595.8			dec in cold H_2O		**195**
−487.2	−443.9	50.2	5.16×10^{-1}	**COR**	**196**
−1215.5	−1132.6	90.4	1.75×10^{-2} (0.018 mol/100 cm^3)		**197**
−969.6	−880.9	123.4	1.74×10^{-1} 291K, 1atm CO_2		**198**
−482.3			1.23 $3H_2O$		**199**
			2.57×10^{-4}		**200**
−101.3			dec **VR**	**EXP** in H_2O	**201**
149.0	**114.4**	**148.6**	—		**202**
−641.8	−592.3	89.5	5.57×10^{-1}		**203**
−2499.6	−2115.6	366.1	5.77×10^{-1}	dlq	**204**
−588.3			4.48×10^{-1}	dlq	**205**
−517.6			5.51×10^{-1} (0.453 mol/100 cm^3)	dlq	**206**
−601.7	−569.4	26.8	as $Mg(OH)_2$		**207**
−924.7	−833.7	63.1	2.00×10^{-5}		**208**
−1112.9	−1029.3	65.7	1.50×10^{-4} 291K		**209**
−347.3			dec	pa rd-br	**210**
−1278.2	−1173.6	91.6	1.83×10^{-1}		**211**
−3383.6			3.60×10^{-1} (0.281 mol/100 cm^3)	epsom salt	**212**

sub sublimes. See p. 58.

Physical, thermochemical and other properties of inorganic compounds – *(continued)*

	Compound	State	Crystal	$\frac{M}{\text{g mol}^{-1}}$	$\frac{\rho(298\text{ K})}{\text{g cm}^{-3}}$	$\frac{T_m}{\text{K}}$	$\frac{T_b}{\text{K}}$
	Magnesium—(*continued*) A = **24.3 g mol^{-1}**, $S^\ominus$ = **32.7 J mol^{-1} K^{-1}**						
213	Mg_3N_2	S	CUB	100.9	2.71	**1073**^{dec}	**973**^{sub}
214	$Mg(NO_3)_2{\cdot}6H_2O$	S	MCL	256.4	1.64	363	**603**^{dec}
215	$Mg_3(PO_4)_2{\cdot}4H_2O$	S	MCL	334.7	1.64		
216	Mg_2Si	S	CUB	76.7	1.94	1375	
217	$MgSiO_3$	S	CUB	231.8	7.16	**1746**^{dec}	
218	Mg_2SiO_2 (forsterite)	S		140.7	3.21	2158	
	Manganese A = **54.9 g mol^{-1}**, $S^\ominus$ = **32.0 J mol^{-1} K^{-1}**						
219	$MnCl_2$	S	HEX	125.8	2.98	923	1463
220	$MnCl_2{\cdot}4H_2O$	S	MCL	197.9	2.01	331	**471**^{dhd}
221	MnO	S	ORH	70.9	5.46	2058	
222	Mn_3O_4	S	CUB	228.8	4.86	1978	
223	Mn_2O_3	S	CUB	157.8	4.50	**1353**^{dec}	
224	MnO_2 (pyrolusite)	S	TET	86.9	5.03	**808**^{dec}	
225	$MnCO_3$	S	HEX	114.9	3.13	dec	
226	MnS	S	CUB	87.0	3.99	**1888**^{dec}	
227	$MnSO_4$	S	ORH	151.0	3.25	973	**1123**^{dec}
228	$MnSO_4{\cdot}H_2O$	S	MCL	169.0	2.95	**390**^{dhd}	
229	$MnSO_4{\cdot}4H_2O$	S	MCL	223.0	2.11	**300**$^{dhd\ 3}$	
230	$Mn(NO_3)_2{\cdot}6H_2O$	S	VIT	287.0	1.82	**299**^{dhd}	
	Mercury A = **200.6 g mol^{-1}**, $S^\ominus$ = **76.1 J mol^{-1} K^{-1}**						
231	**Hg**	G		**200.6**		**234**	**630**
232	Hg_2Cl_2 (calomel)	S	TET	472.0	7.15	816	**673**^{sub}
233	$HgCl_2$	S	ORH	271.5	5.44	550	577
234	Hg_2Br_2	S	TET	561.0	7.31	**680**$^{?atm}$	**618**^{sub}
235	Hg_2I_2	S	TET	654.9	7.70	**413**^{sub}	**563**^{dec}
236	HgI_2 red	S	TET	450.9	6.28	530	627
237	HgO red	S	ORH	216.5	11.10	**773**^{dec}	
238	HgS black	S	CUB	232.6	7.73	**857**^{sub}	
239	HgS red (cinnabar)	S	HEX	232.6	8.10	**659**$^{tr\ to\ bk}$	
240	Hg_2SO_4	S	MCL	497.2	7.56	dec	
241	$HgSO_4$	S	ORH	296.6	6.47	dec	
	Nickel A = **58.7 g mol^{-1}**, $S^\ominus$ = **29.9 J mol^{-1} K^{-1}**						
242	NiF_2	S	TET	96.7	4.63	**1723**†	**1273**^{sub}
243	$NiCl_2$	S	HEX	129.6	3.55	**1274**^{sub}	
244	NiO	S	CUB	74.7	6.67	2263	
245	$Ni(OH)_2$	S	HEX	92.7	4.15*	**503**^{dec}	
246	$Ni(CO)_4$	L		170.7	1.34	248	316
247	$NiSO_4{\cdot}7H_2O$	S	TET	262.8	2.07	**376**$^{dhd\ 6}$	**553**^{dhd}
248	$Ni(NO_3)_2{\cdot}6H_2O$	S	TCL	290.8	2.05	330	410

* variable † uncertain ‡ highly uncertain ^{dec} decomposes

$\Delta H_f^\ominus(298K)$ / kJ mol^{-1}	$\Delta G_f^\ominus(298K)$ / kJ mol^{-1}	$S^\ominus(298K)$ / J mol^{-1} K^{-1}	$m_{sat}(298K)$ / $m^\ominus$	Notes	
−461.2			dec	gn-yl	213
−2612.3			4.90×10^{-1} (0.394 mol/100 cm^3)		214
−4022.9			7.61×10^{-5}	bl	215
−77.8			insoluble	dec	216
−840.3	−763.5	83.3	insoluble		217
−2042.6	−1923.8	95.0	insoluble		218
−482.4	−441.4	117.2	5.04×10^{-1}	dlq pa rd	219
−1687.4	−1423.8	303.3	6.13×10^{-1} (0.518 mol/100 cm^3)	dlq pa rd	220
−384.9	−363.2	60.2	3.60×10^{-6}	gn	221
−1386.6	−1280.3	148.5	insoluble	bk	222
−971.1	−893.3	110.5	insoluble	bk	223
−520.9	−466.1	53.1	insoluble	bk	224
−895.0	−817.6	85.8	$5.92 \times 10^{-6\ 278K}$	pa rd	225
−204.2	−208.8	78.2	$6.90 \times 10^{-6\ 291K}$	gn or pa rd	226
−1063.6	−956.0	112.1	3.44×10^{-1}	rd	227
−1374.4			5.83×10^{-1}	pa rd	228
−2256.4			4.25×10^{-1}	pa rd	229
−2370.0			8.77×10^{-1}	pa rd	230
				All Hg compounds CUM POI, Hg(II) worse than Hg(I)	
61.3	**31.9**	**20.8**	—		231
−264.8	−210.9	195.8	3.75×10^{-6}		232
−224.3	−178.7	146.0	2.69×10^{-2}	**corrosive sublimate**	233
−206.7	−178.7	213.0	6.95×10^{-9}	pa yl	234
−120.9	−111.3	239.3	slightly soluble	yl	235
−105.4			1.06×10^{-5}	rd (yl above 400K)	236
−90.7	−58.5	72.0	2.37×10^{-5}	rd, yl	237
−54.0	−46.4	83.3	$5.40 \times 10^{-7\ 291K}$	bk	238
−58.2	−49.0	77.8		rd	239
−742.0	−623.9	200.7	9.45×10^{-5}	pa yl	240
−704.2			dec		241
−651.5	−604.2	176.2	$2.65 \times 10^{-2\ 293K}$	gn	242
−315.9	−272.4	107.1	5.06×10^{-1}	dlq yl	243
−244.3	−216.3	38.6	insoluble	gn–bk	244
−678.2	−453.1	79.5	1.00×10^{-5}	gn	245
−633.0	−588.3	313.4	$1.05 \times 10^{-4\ 282K}$	**INF**	246
−2976.3	−2462.4	378.9	$4.45 \times 10^{-1\ 6H_2O}$	gn	247
−2223.4			5.47×10^{-1}	dlq gn	248

$^{dhd(n)}$ dehydrates (loses n molecules of H_2O) ^{sub} sublimes. ^{tr} transition. See p. 58.

Physical, thermochemical and other properties of inorganic compounds – *(continued)*

	Compound	State	Crystal	$\frac{M}{\text{g mol}^{-1}}$	$\frac{\rho(298\text{ K})}{\text{g cm}^{-3}}$	$\frac{T_m}{\text{K}}$	$\frac{T_b}{\text{K}}$
	Nitrogen $A = 14.0\text{ g mol}^{-1}$, $S^{\ominus}(N_2(g)) = 191.4\text{ J mol}^{-1}\text{ K}^{-1}$						
249	N_2H_4 (hydrazine)	L		32.0	1.01	275	387
250	NF_3	G		71.0	**1.54**^{67K}	67	144
251	NCl_3	L		120.3	1.65	236	344
252	N_2O (laughing gas)	G		44.0	**1.98**^{182K}	182	185
253	NO	G		30.0	**1.34**^{110K}	110	121
254	N_2O_3	G		76.0	**1.45**^{171K}	171	**277**^{dec}
255	NO_2	G		46.0	**1.49**^{262K}	262	294
256	N_2O_4	G		92.0	**1.45**^{262K}	262	294
257	N_2O_5	S	RBL	108.0	1.64	305	**314**^{dec}
	Ammonia $\Delta H_f^{\ominus}(NH_3^+(g)) = 1023.1\text{ kJ mol}^{-1}$						
258	NH_3	G		17.0	**0.77**^{195K}	195	240
259	NH_4Cl (sal ammoniac)	S	CUB	53.4	1.50	**613**^{sub}	**793**$^{>1\text{ atm}}$
260	NH_4Br	S	CUB	97.9	2.43	**725**^{sub}	**669**$^{>1\text{ atm}}$
261	NH_4I	S	CUB	144.9	2.51	**824**^{sub}	**493**^{vac}
262	$(NH_4)_2SO_4$	S	ORH	132.1	1.77	**508**^{dec}	**786**$^{>1\text{ atm}}$
263	$NH_4Fe(SO_4)_2\cdot 12H_2O$	S	CUB	482.1	1.71	313	**503**^{dhd}
264	NH_4NO_3	S	ORH	80.0	1.70	443	483
	Oxygen $A = 16.0\text{ g mol}^{-1}$, $S^{\ominus}(O_2(g)) = 204.9\text{ J mol}^{-1}\text{ K}^{-1}$, $\Delta H_f(O_2^+(g)) = 1177.7\text{ kJ mol}^{-1}$						
265	O_3 (ozone)	G		48.0	**2.14**^{81K}	81	163
	Phosphorus (red) $A = 31.0\text{ g mol}^{-1}$, $S^{\ominus} = 22.8\text{ J mol}^{-1}\text{ K}^{-1}$						
266	PH_3 (phosphine)	G		34.0		140	183
267	PH_4I	S	TET	161.9	2.86	292	353
268	PF_3	G		87.9	**3.99**^{122K}	122	172
269	PF_5	G		125.9		179	189
270	PCl_3	L		137.3	1.58	181	349
271	PCl_5	S	TET	208.2	2.12	**433**^{dec}	
272	$POCl_3$	L		153.3	1.67	274	378
273	PBr_3	L		270.7	2.89	233	446
274	PBr_5	S		430.5	3.46	**373**^{dec}	
275	$POBr_3$	S		270.7	3.25	325	465
276	P_4O_6	L	MCL	219.8	2.13	297	**448**$^{\text{in } N_2}$
277	P_4O_{10}	S	MCL†	283.8	2.39	**853**$^{>1\text{ atm}}$	**573**^{sub}
278	P_2S_5	S		222.2	2.03	580	787
	Plutonium $A = 239.1\text{ g mol}^{-1}$						
279	$PuCl_3$	S	HEX	348.3	5.70	1033	
280	PuO_2	S	FCC	274.6	1.46		

† uncertain ‡ highly uncertain ^{dec} decomposes $^{dhd(n)}$ dehydrates (loses n molecules of H_2O)

$\Delta H_f^\ominus$(298K) / kJ mol^{-1}	$\Delta G_f^\ominus$(298K) / kJ mol^{-1}	$S^\ominus$(298K) / J mol^{-1} K^{-1}	m_{sat}(298K) / $m^\ominus$	Notes	
50.6	149.2	121.2	very soluble	**COR**	249
−124.7	−83.7	260.6	slightly soluble	**EXP** at 368 K yl	250
230.1			insoluble		251
82.0	104.2	219.7	2.66×10^{-3}		252
90.4	86.6	210.5	1.88×10^{-4}	**POI GAS** (25) (bl liq)	253
83.8	139.4	312.2	soluble (dec)	**POI GAS** (25) rd–br	254
33.2	51.3	240.0	soluble (dec)	**POI GAS** (25) yl–br	255
9.2	97.8	304.2	soluble (dec)	**POI GAS** (25)	256
−43.1	113.8	178.2	soluble (dec)	**POI GAS** (25)	257
−46.0	−16.7	192.5	$3.11^{291\,K}$ (1.79 mol/100 cm^3)	**COR POI** (100)	258
−315.5	−203.8	94.6	7.34×10^{-1}		259
−270.3	−175.3	113.0	7.99×10^{-1}	hyg	260
−201.4	−112.5	117.2	1.27	hyg	261
−1180.9	−901.9	220.1	5.78×10^{-1}		262
			4.62×10^{-1}	violet	263
−365.6	−184.0	151.1	2.68	**EXP** (above 484 K)	264
142.3	163.4	237.7	2.19×10^{-1}	**POI GAS** (0.1)	265
				Many P compounds POI	
5.4	13.4	210.1	8.88×10^{-4}	**POI GAS** (0.05)	266
−69.9	0.8	123.0	soluble		267
−918.8	−897.5	273.1	dec	**POI GAS**	268
−1595.8			dec	**POI GAS**	269
−319.7	−272.4	217.1	dec **VR**	**COR POI VAP** (1)	270
−443.5		**364.5**^{gas}	dec **VR**	**COR POI VAP** (0.01) pa yl	271
−597.1	−520.9	222.5	dec **VR**	**COR POI VAP**	272
−184.5	−175.7	240.2	dec **VR**	**COR POI VAP** yl	273
−269.9			dec **VR**	**COR POI VAP**	274
−458.6		**359.7**^{gas}	dec **VR**	**COR POI VAP**	275
−1640.1			dec **VR**	**COR** dlq	276
−2984.0	−2697.8	228.9	dec **VR**	**COR** dlq	277
			insoluble	**COR** yl-gr	278
				All Pu compounds RAD POI	
−962.3			soluble	gn	279
−1050.2				yl–gn	280

^{sub} sublimes. ^{vac} at very low pressure. See p. 58.

Physical, thermochemical and other properties of inorganic compounds – *(continued)*

	Compound	State	Crystal	$\frac{M}{g\ mol^{-1}}$	$\frac{\rho(298\ K)}{g\ cm^{-3}}$	$\frac{T_m}{K}$	$\frac{T_b}{K}$
	Potassium $A = 39.1\ g\ mol^{-1}$, $S^{\ominus} = 64.4\ J\ mol^{-1}\ K^{-1}$						
281	K	G		**39.1**		**336**	**1039**
282	KF	S	CUB	58.1	2.48	1130	1775
283	KCl (sylvite)	S	CUB	74.5	1.98	1045	1680
284	$KClO_3$	S	MCL	122.5	2.32	641	**673**^{dec}
285	$KClO_4$	S	ORH	138.5	2.52	**883**$^{>1\ atm}$	**673**^{dec}
286	KBr	S	CUB	119.0	2.75	1008	1708
287	$KBrO_3$	S	HEX	167.0	3.27	**707**$^{>1\ atm}$	**643**^{dec}
288	KI	S	CUB	166.0	3.12	958	1597
289	KIO_3	S	MCL	214.0	3.89	833	**373**^{dec}
290	KIO_4	S	TET	230.0	3.62	855	**573**^{dec}
291	K_2O	S	CUB	94.2	2.32	**623**^{dec}	
292	KO_2	S	TET	71.1	2.14	653	dec
293	KOH	S	RBL	56.1	2.04	673	1600
294	$KOH{\cdot}2H_2O$	S		92.1			
295	K_2CO_3	S	MCL	138.2	2.43	1169	dec
296	$KHCO_3$	S	MCL	100.1	2.17	**373**^{*dec}	
297	K_2S	S	CUB	110.2	1.81	1113	
298	K_2SO_4	S	ORH	174.2	2.66	1342	1962
299	$KHSO_4$	S	ORH	136.1	2.32	492	dec
300	$KAl(SO_4)_2{\cdot}12H_2O$	S	CUB	474.3	1.76	**364**$^{dhd\ 9}$	**473**^{dhd}
301	$KCr(SO_4)_2{\cdot}12H_2O$	S	CUB	499.4	1.83	**362**$^{dhd\ 10}$	**673**^{dhd}
302	KNO_2	S	MCl	85.1	1.92	**713**^{dec}	
303	KNO_3 (saltpetre)	S	ORH	101.1	2.11	610	**673**^{dec}
304	$KMnO_4$	S	ORH	158.0	2.70	**513**^{dec}	
305	KH_2PO_4	S	TET	136.0	2.34	**526**^{dec}	
306	K_2CrO_4	S	ORH	194.2	2.73	1253	
307	$K_2Cr_2O_7$	S	TCL	294.1	2.68	671	**773**^{dec}
308	KCN	S	CUB	65.1	1.52	883	
309	KCNS	S	RBL	97.1	1.89	450	**773**^{dec}
310	$K_3Fe(CN)_6$	S	MCL	329.2	1.85	dec	
311	$K_4Fe(CN)_6$	S		368.3		dec	
312	$K_4Fe(CN)_6{\cdot}3H_2O$	S	MCL	422.4	1.85	**343**^{dhd}	dec
	Rubidium $A = 85.5\ g\ mol^{-1}$, $S^{\ominus} = 76.2^{\dagger}\ J\ mol^{-1}\ K^{-1}$						
313	RbF	S	CUB	104.4	3.56	1048	1681
314	RbCl	S	CUB	120.9	2.76	990	1654
315	RbBr	S	CUB	165.3	3.35	953	1625
316	RbI	S	CUB	212.3	3.55	913	1577
317	RbOH	S		102.4	3.20	574	

* variable † uncertain ‡ highly uncertain dec decomposes

$\Delta H_f^\ominus$(298K) / kJ mol^{-1}	$\Delta G_f^\ominus$(298K) / kJ mol^{-1}	$S^\ominus$(298K) / J mol^{-1} K^{-1}	m_{sat}(298K) / $m^\ominus$	Notes	
89.6	**61.0**	**160.2**	—		281
−562.6	−533.1	66.6	1.75 (1.303 mol/100 cm^3)		282
−435.9	−408.3	82.7	4.81×10^{-1} (0.417 mol/100 cm^3)	dlq	283
−391.2	−289.9	143.0	7.00×10^{-2} (0.068 mol/100 cm^3)		284
−433.5	−304.2	151.0	1.29×10^{-2}		285
−392.2	−379.2	96.4	5.70×10^{-1} (0.468 mol/100 cm^3)	slightly hyg	286
−332.2	−243.5	149.2	4.88×10^{-2}		287
−327.6	−322.3	104.3	8.92×10^{-1} (0.619 mol/100 cm^3)		288
−508.4	−425.5	151.5	4.29×10^{-2}		289
−408.4			2.23×10^{-3}		290
−361.5			as KOH	hyg	291
−560.7			2.39×10^{-3} dec	yl	292
−425.8			1.71	**COR** dlq	293
−1051.0			2.12		294
−1146.0			8.11×10^{-1} (0.596 mol/100 cm^3)	dlq	295
−959.4			3.62×10^{-1} (0.316 mol/100 cm^3)		296
−418.4			soluble	dlq yl–br	297
−1433.9	−1316.3	175.7	6.91×10^{-2}		298
−1158.1			3.78×10^{-1}	**COR** dlq	299
−6057.2	−5137.1	687.4	3.02×10^{-2}		300
−5786.9			4.41×10^{-2}	dk rd	301
−370.3			$3.60^{293 K}$	pa yl	302
−492.7	−393.1	132.9	3.75×10^{-1}		303
−813.4	−713.8	171.5	4.83×10^{-2}	purple	304
			1.09×10^{-1}	dlq	305
−1382.8			3.35×10^{-1}	yl	306
−2033.0			5.10×10^{-2}	rd	307
−112.5			1.10	**POI** liberates HCN dlq	308
−203.4			2.46	dlq	309
−173.2			1.48×10^{-1} (0.118 mol/100 cm^3)	rd	310
−523.4			7.38×10^{-2}		311
−1398.7			8.57×10^{-2} (0.076 mol/100 cm^3)	pa yl	312
−549.3			$2.88^{291 K}$		313
−430.6			7.81×10^{-1} (0.597 mol/100 cm^3)		314
−389.2	−378.1	108.3	7.01×10^{-1}		315
−328.4	−325.5	118.0	7.70×10^{-1}		316
−476.6	−439.5	113.8	1.69^{303K}	dlq gr	317

dhd(*n*) dehydrates (loses *n* molecules of H_2O) sub sublimes. See p. 58.

Physical, thermochemical and other properties of inorganic compounds – *(continued)*

No.	Compound	State	Crystal	M / g mol^{-1}	ρ(298 K) / g cm^{-3}	T_m / K	T_b / K
	Rubidium—*(continued)* A = 85.5 g mol^{-1}, $S^{\ominus}$ = 76.2† J mol^{-1} K^{-1}						
318	Rb_2CO_3	S		230.9		**1108**$^{>1\ atm}$	**1013**^{dec}
319	$RbHCO_3$	S		146.4		**448**^{dec}	
320	Rb_2SO_4	S	ORH	267.0	3.61	1347	1973
321	$RbHSO_4$	S		182.5	2.89		
322	$RbNO_3$	S		147.4	3.11	434	589
	Silicon A = 28.1 g mol^{-1}, $S^{\ominus}$ = 19.0 J mol^{-1} K^{-1}						
323	**Si**	G		**28.0**		**1683**	**2960**
324	SiH_4 (silane)	G		32.1	**1.44**^{88K}	88	161
325	SiF_4	G		104.0	**4.69**^{183K}	183	178
326	$SiCl_4$	L		169.9	1.48	203	330
327	$SiCl_4$	G		169.9	**7.59**^{203K}	203	330
328	SiO_2 (quartz)	S	HEX	60.0	2.65	1883	2503
329	SiO_2 (cristobalite)	S	CUB	60.0	2.32	1986	2503
330	SiO_2 (tridymite)	S	HEX	60.0	2.26	1976	2503
331	SiC (carborundum)	S	HEX	40.1	3.22	**2973**$^{sub\ dec}$	
332	SiS_2	S	ORH	92.2	2.02	**1363**^{sub}	
	Silver A = 107.9 g mol^{-1}, $S^{\ominus}$ = 42.68 J mol^{-1} K^{-1}						
333	**Ag**	G		**107.8**		**1234**	**2450**
334	AgF	S	CUB	126.8	5.85	708	1432
335	AgCl	S	CUB	143.3	5.56	728	1830
336	AgBr	S	CUB	187.7	6.48	703	1806
337	AgI	S	HEX	234.7	5.48	831	1777
338	Ag_2O	S	CUB	231.7	7.14	**573**^{dec}	
339	Ag_2CO_3	S	MCL	275.7	6.08	**491**^{dec}	
340	Ag_2S (alpha)	S	BCC	247.8	7.32	1115	dec
341	Ag_2S (beta)	S	CUB	247.8	7.32	1098	dec
342	$AgNO_3$	S	ORH	169.8	4.35	483	**717**^{dec}
343	Ag_2CrO_4	S	MCL	331.7	5.63		
344	AgCN	S	HEX	133.8	3.94	**623**$^{\dagger dec}$	
	Sodium A = 23.0 g mol^{-1}, $S^{\ominus}$ = 51.0 J mol^{-1} K^{-1}						
345	**Na**	G		**22.9**		**371**	**1163**
346	NaH	S	FCC	24.0	0.92	**1073**^{dec}	
347	NaF	S	CUB	41.9	2.79	1268	1977
348	NaCl	S	CUB	58.4	2.17	1081	1738
349	NaBr	S	CUB	102.9	3.20	1023	1665
350	NaI	S	CUB	149.8	3.67	935	1577
351	Na_2O	S	CUB	61.9	2.27	1193	**1548**^{sub}
352	Na_2O_2	S	POW	77.9	2.81	**733**^{dec}	
353	NaOH	S	ORH	40.0	2.13	592	1663
354	$NaOH \cdot H_2O$	S	ORH	58.0		337	

† uncertain ‡ highly uncertain ^{dec} decomposes $^{dhd(n)}$ dehydrates (loses n molecules of H_2O)

$\Delta H_f^\ominus(298K)$ / kJ mol^{-1}	$\Delta G_f^\ominus(298K)$ / kJ mol^{-1}	$S^\ominus(298K)$ / J mol^{-1} K^{-1}	$m_{sat}(298K)$ / $m^\ominus$	Notes	
−1128.0			1.95	dlq	318
−956.0			7.88×10^{-1} ^{293K}		319
−1424.7			1.90×10^{-1} (0.168 mol/100 cm^3)		320
−1145.2			soluble		321
−454.0	−392.7	270.7	4.45×10^{-1} (0.340 mol/100 cm^3)	dlq	322
43932	**3949.2**	**167.9**	—		323
34.3†	56.9	204.5	insoluble		324
−1548.1	−1506.2	284.5	dec		325
−640.2	−572.8	239.3	dec **VR**	**COR POI VAP**	326
−609.6	−569.9	331.4	dec		327
−910.9†	−856.7†	41.8	}	**Dangerous dusts**	328
−909.5†	−855.9†	42.7	2.00×10^{-4} }	**esp asbestos**	329
−909.1†	−855.3†	43.5	}		330
−65.3†	−62.8†	16.6	insoluble	gr–bk	331
−145.2			dec		332
286.2	**247.4**	**172.9**			333
−202.9	−184.9	83.7	1.42	dlq yl	334
−127.0	−109.6	95.8	1.35×10^{-6}		335
−99.5	−95.9	107.1	7.19×10^{-8}	pa yl	336
−62.4	−66.3	114.2	1.11×10^{-8}	yl(α), or(β) (T_{tr} = 419 K)	337
−30.6	−10.8	121.8	2.00×10^{-5}	br–bk	338
−505.8	−437.2	167.4	1.20×10^{-5}	yl	339
−31.8	−40.3	145.6	2.48×10^{-16}	gr–bk	340
−29.3	−39.2	150.2	2.48×10^{-16}		341
−123.1	−32.2	140.9	1.42	**COR**	342
−712.1	−621.7	216.7	9.92×10^{-5}	rd	343
146.2	164.0	83.7	5.25×10^{-5}		344
108.3	**77.8**	**153.6**	—		345
−57.3			dec		346
−569.0	−541.0	58.6	9.87×10^{-2} (0.098 mol/100 cm^3)	**POI**	347
−411.0	−384.0	72.4	6.15×10^{-1} (0.542 mol/100 cm^3)	hyg	348
−359.9			9.19×10^{-1} (0.728 mol/100 cm^3)	hyg	349
−288.0			1.23 (0.829 mol/100 cm^3)		350
−415.9	−376.6	72.8	dec	**COR** dlq yl	351
−504.6			dec	pa yl	352
−426.8			1.05	**COR**	353
−732.9	−623.4	84.5	1.97		354

^{sub} sublimes. See p. 58.

	Compound	State	Crystal	M / g mol^{-1}	ρ(298 K) / g cm^{-3}	T_m / K	T_b / K
	Sodium—*(continued)* A = 23.0 g mol^{-1}, $S^{\ominus}$ = 51.0 J mol^{-1} K^{-1}						
355	Na_2CO_3	S	POW	105.9	2.51	1131	dec
356	$Na_2CO_3 \cdot 10H_2O$	S	MCL	286.1	1.44	**306**^{dhd}	
357	$NaHCO_3$	S	MCL	84.0	2.16	**543**^{dec}	
358	Na_2S	S	CUB	78.0	1.86	1223	
359	Na_2SO_4	S	ORH	142.0	2.66	1163	
360	$Na_2SO_4 \cdot 10H_2O$	S	MCL	322.1	1.46	306	**373**^{dhd}
361	$NaHSO_4$	S	TCL	120.0	2.47	6588	
362	$Na_2S_2O_3$	S	MCL	158.1	1.67		
363	$Na_2S_2O_3 \cdot 5H_2O$	S	MCL	248.1	1.69	322	**373**^{dhd}
364	$NaNO_2$	S	ORH	69.0	2.17	544	**593**^{dec}
365	$NaNO_3$ (nitre)	S	HEX	84.9	2.62	583	**653**^{dec}
366	$Na_2B_4O_7 \cdot 10H_2O$	S	MCL	381.3	1.73	348	**593**^{dhd}
367	Na_2SiO_3 (water glass)	S	HEX	122.0	2.40	1361	
368	$NaCN$	S	CUB	49.0		837	1769
369	$NaNH_2$ (amide)	S		39.0		481	673
	Strontium A = 87.6 g mol^{-1}, $S^{\ominus}$ = 52.3† J mol^{-1} K^{-1}						
370	SrF_2	S	FCC	125.6	4.24	1723	2762
371	$SrCl_2$	S	CUB	158.5	3.05	1148	1523
372	$SrBr_2$	S		247.4	4.22	916	dec
373	SrO	S	FCC	103.6	4.70	2703	3273
374	$Sr(OH)_2$	S		121.6	3.63	648	
375	$Sr(OH)_2 \cdot 8H_2O$	S	TET	265.7	1.90		**373**^{dhd}
376	$SrCO_3$	S	ORH	147.6	3.70	**1770**^{dec}	
377	$Sr(HCO_3)_2$	aq	—	209.6			
378	SrS	S	CUB	119.6	3.70	2273	
379	$SrSO_4$	S	ORH	183.6	3.96	1878	
380	$Sr(NO_3)_2$	S	CUB	211.6	2.99	918	1373
	Sulphur A = 32.1 g mol^{-1}, $S^{\ominus}$ = 31.9 J mol^{-1} K^{-1}						
381	S	G		**32.1**		393	717
382	S_2	G		**64.2**		393	717
383	S_8	G		**256.8**		393	717
384	SF_4	G		108.0		149	233
385	SF_6	G		146.0	**6.50**^{233K}	223	337
386	S_2Cl_2	L		135.0	1.68	193	409
387	$SOCl_2$	L		118.9	1.66	168	352
388	SO_2Cl_2	L		134.9	1.67	227	342
389	SO_2	G		64.0	**2.93**^{198K}	198	263
390	SO_3	L		80.0	1.92	290	318

† uncertain ‡ highly uncertain ^{dec} decomposes $^{dhd(n)}$ dehydrates (loses n molecules of H_2O)

$\Delta H_f^\ominus(298K)$ / kJ mol^{-1}	$\Delta G_f^\ominus(298K)$ / kJ mol^{-1}	$S^\ominus(298K)$ / J mol^{-1} K^{-1}	$m_{sat}(298K)$ / $m^\ominus$	Notes	
−1130.9	−1047.7	136.0	6.60×10^{-2}	hyg	355
−4081.9			1.03×10^{-1} (0.099 mol/100 cm^3)	washing soda	356
−947.7	−851.9	102.1	1.22×10^{-1}	baking soda	357
−373.2			2.53×10^{-1}	**COR** dlq releases H_2S	358
−1384.5	−1266.8	149.5	3.03×10^{-2}		359
−4324.1	−3644.0	591.9	1.97×10^{-1}	eff Glaubers salt	360
−1126.3			2.38×10^{-1}	**COR**	361
−1117.1			3.16×10^{-1}		362
−2602.0			4.80×10^{-1}	eff hypo	363
−359.4	−365.9	120.5	1.23 (0.898 mol/100 cm^3)	pa yl	364
−466.7	−365.9	116.3	1.08		365
−6264.3			1.60×10^{-2}	borax	366
−1518.8	−1426.7	113.8	8.39×10^{-1}	dlq	367
−90.0			1.29	**POI liberates HCN** dlq	368
−118.8			dec **VR**	**COR**	369
				All Sr compounds POI	
−1214.6			9.50×10^{-5}		370
−828.4	−781.2	117.2	1.00×10^{-2}		371
−715.9			4.33×10^{-1} (0.355 mol/100 cm^3)		372
−590.4	−559.8	54.4	8.27×10^{-3}		373
−959.4			3.37×10^{-3}	dlq	374
−3352.2			6.55×10^{-3}	dlq	375
−1218.4	−1137.6	97.1	7.38×10^{-6}		376
−1927.6	−1731.3	150.6	5.68×10^{-4}		377
−452.3			insoluble (dec)		378
−1444.7	−1334.3	121.8	7.11×10^{-5}		379
−975.9			1.55×10^{-1} ^{353K} (0.186 mol/100 cm^3)		380
238.1	**197.6**	**167.7**	—		381
1290.3	**800.4**	**228.1**	—		382
1018.8	**497.1**	**429.9**	—		383
−774.9	−731.4	291.9	dec		384
−1209.2	−1105.0	291.7	3.70×10^{-3}		385
−60.2			dec	**COR POI VAP** (1) yl–br fuming	386
−245.6			dec	**COR POI VAP** rd–br	387
−389.1			dec	**COR POI VAP** rd–br	388
−296.9	−300.4	248.5	1.66×10^{-1} ^{293K}	**COR POI GAS** (10) rd–br	389
−395.4	−370.3	256.1	∞	dlq	390

^{sub} sublimes. See p. 58.

	Compound	State	Crystal	M / g mol^{-1}	ρ(298 K) / g cm^{-3}	T_m / K	T_b / K
	Tin (white) $A = 118.7$ g mol^{-1}, $S^\ominus = 51.4$ J mol^{-1} K^{-1}						
391	SnH_4 (stannane)	G		122.7		123	221
392	$SnCl_2$	S	ORH	189.6	3.95	520	896
393	$SnCl_2{\cdot}2H_2O$	S	MCL	225.6	2.71	**311**^{dhd}	
394	$SnCl_4$	L		260.5	2.23	240	386
395	$SnBr_4$	S	RBL	438.3	3.34	303	478
396	SnO	S	TET	134.6	6.45	**1353**^{dec}	
397	SnO_2 (cassiterite)	S	TET	150.6	6.95	1400	2073
398	SnS	S	ORH	150.7	5.22	1155	1503
	Tungsten $A = 183.9$ g mol^{-1}, $S^\ominus = 33.6$ J mol^{-1} K^{-1}						
399	WO_3 (wolframite)	S	MCL	100.4	3.19	1830	
400	WCl_6	S	RBL	396.5	3.52	557	610
401	WC	S	HEX	195.8	15.65	3143	6273
402	WS_2	S	HCP	247.9	7.50	**1523**^{dec}	
	Uranium $A = 238.1$ g mol^{-1}, $S^\ominus = 50.3$ J mol^{-1} K^{-1}						
403	UF_6	G		352.0	4.68	**338**$^{>1\,atm}$	**329**^{sub}
404	UO_2	S	CUB	270.0	10.96	2779	
405	UO_3	S		286.0	7.29	dec	
406	$UO_2(NO_3)_2$	S		394.0			
407	$UO_2(NO_3)_2{\cdot}6H_2O$	S		502.1	2.81	333	391
	Xenon $A = 131.3$ g mol^{-1}, $S^\ominus = 169.6$ J mol^{-1} K^{-1}						
408	XeF_2	S		169.3			
409	XeF_4	S		207.2			
410	XeF_6	S		245.3			
411	XeO_3	S		179.3			
	Zinc $A = 65.4$ g mol^{-1}, $S^\ominus = 41.6$ J mol^{-1} K^{-1}						
412	$ZnCl_2$	S	HEX	136.2	2.91	548	1038
413	$ZnBr_2$	S	RBL	225.1	4.20	667	943
414	ZnO (zincite)	S	HEX	81.3	5.68	2248	
415	$ZnCO_3$	S	TRG	125.3	4.44	**573**^{dec}	
416	ZnS (wurtzite)	S	HEX	97.4	3.98	**2123**$^{150\,atm}$	**1458**^{sub}
417	ZnS (blende)	S	CUB	97.4	4.10	**1293**^{tr}	
418	$ZnSO_4$	S	ORH	161.4	3.54	1013	**873**^{dec}
419	$ZnSO_4{\cdot}7H_2O$	S	ORH	287.5	1.97	373	**553**^{dhd}
	Gallium $A = 69.7$ g mol^{-1}, $S^\ominus = 40.9$ J mol^{-1} K^{-1}						
420	GaF_3	S	POW	126.7	4.47	**1073**^{sub}	
421	$GaCl_2$	S		140.6		437	808
422	$GaCl_3$	S		176.3	2.47	361	475
423	$GaBr_2$	S		309.5	3.69	395	552
424	GaI_3	S		450.4	4.15	485	**618**^{sub}
425	$Ga_2O_3(\beta)$	S	MCL	187.4	6.44	**2173**^{tr}	

† uncertain ‡ highly uncertain ^{dec} decomposes $^{dhd(n)}$ dehydrates (loses n molecules of H_2O)

$\Delta H_f^\ominus$(298K) / kJ mol^{-1}	$\Delta G_f^\ominus$(298K) / kJ mol^{-1}	$S^\ominus$(298K) / J mol^{-1} K^{-1}	m_{sat}(298K) / $m^\ominus$	Notes	
				All Sn compounds POI	
162.8	188.3	226.3			391
−325.1†			1.42^{228K} (0.703 mol/100 cm^3)		392
−921.3			dec		393
−511.3	−440.2	258.6	soluble (dec)		394
−377.4	−350.2	264.4	dec	dlq	395
−285.8	−256.9	56.5	5.00×10^{-7}	bk	396
−580.7	−519.7	52.3	1.40×10^{-11}		397
−100.4†	−98.3†	77.0†	1.3×10^{-8}	gn–bk	398
−842.9	−764.1	75.9	insoluble	yl	399
−602.5			(dec)	dk bl	400
−40.6			insoluble	bk	401
−209.2	−193.3†	96.2†	insoluble	dk gr, br	402
				All U compounds RAD POI	
−2112.9	−2029.2	379.7	dec	dlq	403
−1129.7	−1075.3	77.8	3.00×10^{-7}	br–bk	404
−1263.6	−1184.1	98.6	3.95×10^{-6}	yl–rd	405
−1377.4	−1142.7	276.1			406
−3197.8	−2615.0	505.6	3.22×10^{-1}	dlq yl	407
−133.9	−62.8	133.9			408
−261.5	−121.3	146.4			409
−380.7					410
401.7					411
−415.9	−369.4	108.4	3.03	hyg	412
−327.2	−310.0	137.2	2.09	dlq	413
−348.0	−318.2	43.9	1.23×10^{-5}		414
−812.5	−731.4	82.4	1.64×10^{-4}		415
−189.5			1.47×10^{-10}		416
−206.4	−205.4	57.7			417
−978.6	−871.5	124.7			418
−3075.7	−2560.2	386.6	3.56×10^{-1}	eff	419
−1163.2	−1085.4	83.7	1.58×10^{-5}		420
			dec	dlq	421
−524.7	−454.8	142.3	v. soluble		422
−386.6	−359.8	179.9	soluble		423
−238.1			dec	yl	424
−1089.1	−998.3	85.0	insoluble		425

sub sublimes. See p. 58.

Physical, thermochemical and other properties of organic compounds

M molar mass
ρ density (at 298 K or at T_b for substances which are gases at 298 K)
T_m normal melting temperature
T_b normal boiling temperature

See page 58 for general notes and abbreviations.

	Compound	Formula	State	M / g mol^{-1}	ρ / g cm^{-3}	T_m / K	T_b / K
	Miscellaneous						
1	Water	H_2O	L	18.0	0.997	273.15	373.15
2	Water (steam)	H_2O	G	18.0		273.15	373.15
3	Carbon monoxide	CO	G	28.0	**1.25**[A]	**68.10**[115mmHg]	81.66
4	Carbon dioxide	CO_2	G	44.0	**1.98**[A]	**216.6**[Sub]	—
5	Furan	$(CH)_4O$	L	68.1	0.938	187.50	304.51
6	Phenol	C_6H_5OH	S	94.1	1.076	314.05	454.98
7	Nitrobenzene	$C_6H_5NO_2$	L	124.1	1.203	278.85	484.00
8	Pyridine	$(CH)_5N$	L	79.1	0.983	231.48	388.35
	Straight chain alkanes						
9	Methane	CH_4	G	16.0	**0.424**	90.67	111.66
10	Ethane	CH_3CH_3	G	30.1	**0.546**	89.88	184.52
11	Propane	$CH_3CH_2CH_3$	G	44.1	**0.582**	85.46	231.08
12	Butane	$CH_3(CH_2)_2CH_3$	G	58.1	**0.579**	134.80	272.65
13	Pentane	$CH_3(CH_2)_3CH_3$	L	72.2	0.626	143.43	309.22
14	Hexane	$CH_3(CH_2)_4CH_3$	L	86.2	0.659	177.80	341.89
15	Heptane	$CH_3(CH_2)_5CH_3$	L	100.2	0.684	182.54	371.57
16	Octane	$CH_3(CH_2)_6CH_3$	L	114.2	0.703	216.35	398.81
17	Nonane	$CH_3(CH_2)_7CH_3$	L	128.3	0.718	219.63	423.94
18	Decane	$CH_3(CH_2)_8CH_3$	L	142.3	0.730	243.49	447.27
19	Eicosane	$CH_3(CH_2)_{18}CH_3$	S	282.6	0.785	309.59	616.95
	Branched alkanes						
20	2-Methylpropane	$(CH_3)_2CHCH_3$	G	58.1	**0.557**	113.55	261.42
21	2-Methylbutane (isopentane)	$(CH_3)_2CHCH_2CH_3$	L	72.2	0.620	113.25	301.00
22	2,2-Dimethylpropane (neopentane)	$C(CH_3)_4$	G	72.2	**0.591**	256.60	282.65
	Cyclo-alkanes						
23	Cyclopropane	$(CH_2)_3$	G	42.1		145.73	240.35
24	Cyclobutane	$(CH_2)_4$	G	56.1	**0.694**	182.42	285.66
25	Cyclopentane	$CH_2(CH_2)_3CH_2$	L	70.1	0.745	179.27	322.41
26	Cyclohexane	$CH_2(CH_2)_4CH_2$	L	84.2	0.779	279.70	353.89
	Alkenes (olefins)						
27	Ethene (ethylene)	$CH_2{=}CH_2$	G	28.1	**0.610**	104.00	169.44
28	Propene	$CH_2{=}CHCH_3$	G	42.1	**0.514**	87.90	225.45
29	But-1-ene	$CH_2{=}CHCH_2CH_3$	G	56.1	**0.595**	87.80	266.89
30	*trans*-But-2-ene	$CH_3CH{=}CHCH_3$	G	56.1	**0.604**	167.60	274.03
31	*cis*-But-2-ene	$CH_3CH{=}CHCH_3$	G	56.1	**0.621**	134.24	276.87
32	Hex-1-ene	$CH_2{=}CH(CH_2)_3CH_3$	L	84.2	0.673	134.33	336.64
33	Buta-1,2-diene	$CH_2{=}C{=}CHCH_3$	G	54.1	**0.652**	136.25	284.00
34	Buta-1,3-diene	$CH_2{=}CHCH{=}CH_2$	G	54.1	**0.621**	164.23	268.74
35	Cyclohexene	$CH_2(CH_2)_3CH{=}CH$	L	81.2	0.811	169.45	356.35

[sub] sublimes. See p. 58. [A] measured in g dm^{-3}.

PTO

$\Delta H_c^\ominus$ standard molar enthalpy change on combustion[A]
$\Delta H_f^\ominus$ standard molar enthalpy change on formation at 298 K
$\Delta G_f^\ominus$ standard molar Gibbs free energy change on formation at 298 K
$S^\ominus$ standard molar entropy at 298 K
n refractive index
p dipole moment
$p^\ominus$ 3.34×10^{-30} C m ≙ 1 debye[B]
ε_r relative permittivity (static, 298 K)

$\frac{\Delta H_c^\ominus}{\text{kJ mol}^{-1}}$	$\frac{\Delta H_f^\ominus}{\text{kJ mol}^{-1}}$	$\frac{\Delta G_f^\ominus}{\text{kJ mol}^{-1}}$	$\frac{S^\ominus}{\text{J mol}^{-1}\text{K}^{-1}}$	n	$\frac{p}{p^\ominus}$	ε_r	Notes (see p. 58) Synonyms	
—	−285.9	−237.2	70.0	1.3325	1.85	78.54		1
—	−241.8	−228.6	188.7	—	1.85	—		2
−283.0	−110.5	−137.3	197.9	—		—	POI GAS (100)	3
—	−393.7	−394.6	213.8	—		—		4
−2083.5				1.4214	0.66	2.95	Furfuran	5
−3055.8	−165.0	−50.9	146.0	1.5521	1.45	**9.78**^{333K}	COR SK POI VAP (5)	6
−3067.7	−21.3			1.5523	4.22	34.9	SK POI VAP (1)	7
				1.5102	2.20	12.3	POI VAP (10) INF	8

Ion (g)	CO^+	CO^{2+}	CO_2^+	CH^+	CH_2^+	CH_3^+	CH_4^+
$\Delta H_f^\ominus$/kJ mol^{-1}	1247.5	3956.0	942.4	1675.3	1401.2	1095.0	1157.7

$\frac{\Delta H_c^\ominus}{\text{kJ mol}^{-1}}$	$\frac{\Delta H_f^\ominus}{\text{kJ mol}^{-1}}$	$\frac{\Delta G_f^\ominus}{\text{kJ mol}^{-1}}$	$\frac{S^\ominus}{\text{J mol}^{-1}\text{K}^{-1}}$	n	$\frac{p}{p^\ominus}$	ε_r	Notes (see p. 58) Synonyms	
							All alkanes INF	
−890.4	−74.8	−50.8	186.2	—	0	—		9
−1559.8	−84.6	−32.8	229.5	—	0	—		10
−2220.0	−103.8	−23.5	269.9	—	0	**1.66**^{Liq}		11
−2877.1	−126.1	−17.1	310.1	1.3326	0	**1.78**^{Liq}		12
−3509.4	−173.2	−9.6	261.2	1.3575	0	1.84		13
−4194.7	−198.8	−4.4†	295.9	1.3749	0	1.89		14
−4853.5	−224.4	+1.0†	328.5	1.3876	0	1.92		15
−5512.5	−249.9	+6.4†	361.1†	1.3974	0	1.95		16
−6124.5	−275.5	+11.8†	393.7	1.4054	0	1.97		17
−6778.3	−301.0	+17.2†	425.9	1.4119	0			18
−13316.3^{Liq}	**−556.6**^{Liq}	**+71.6**^{Liq}	**751.7**^{Liq}	1.4405	0	2.08	Entries marked ^{Liq} relate to the undercooled liquid	19
−2868.7	−134.5	−20.9	294.6	—	0	1.73		20
−3502.9	−179.7†	−15.1†	260.4	1.3537		1.84		21
−3516.6	−165.9	−15.2	306.4	1.3420		1.80		22
−1966.0	+55.2				0	—	EXP	23
	−7.1			1.3650		—		24
−3290.9	−105.9	+36.4	204.3	1.4070	0	**1.97**^{293K}		25
−3919.8	−156.2	+26.7	204.4	1.4260		2.02		26
−1411.0	+52.3	+68.1	219.5	—	0			27
−2058.5	+20.4	+62.7	266.9	—	0.35	1.86		28
−2717.3	−0.1	+71.5	305.6	—	0.38			29
−2702.2	−11.9	+62.9	296.4	—	0			30
−2710.4	−7.0	+65.9	300.8	—				31
−4003.7	**−41.7**^{Vap}	**+87.6**^{Vap}	**384.6**^{Vap}	1.3880			Entries marked ^{Vap} relate to the vapour phase	32
−2593.8	+162.2	+198.4	293.0					33
−2541.7	+110.1	+150.6	278.7	1.4290	0			34
−4128.0†				1.4467	0.55	2.22		35

[A] Enthalpy changes of combustion are measured with any water formed in the liquid state at 298 K.
[B] Dipole moments have not been converted to SI units because debye units have been used so frequently in the past and conversion is rarely needed.

† Other values may be found elsewhere.

Physical, thermochemical and other properties of organic compounds

	Compound	Formula	State	M/g mol^{-1}	ρ/g cm^{-3}	T_m/K	T_b/K
	Alkynes						
36	Ethyne (acetylene)	$CH{\equiv}CH$	G	26.0	**0.618**	193.15	189.75
37	Propyne (methylacetylene)	$CH_3C{\equiv}CH$	G	40.1	**0.671**	170.45	249.93
	Arenes						
38	Benzene	C_6H_6	L	78.1	0.879	278.68	353.25
39	Naphthalene	$C_{10}H_8$	S	128.2	1.101	353.44	491.10
40	Methyl benzene (toluene)	$C_6H_5CH_3$	L	92.1	0.867	178.16	383.78
41	Ethylbenzene	$C_6H_5CH_2CH_3$	L	106.2	0.867	178.17	409.34
42	Propylbenzene	$C_6H_5(CH_2)_2CH_3$	L	120.2	0.862	173.65	432.37
43	1,2-Dimethylbenzene	$C_6H_4(CH_3)_2$	L	106.2	0.880	247.97	417.56
44	1,3-Dimethylbenzene	$C_6H_4(CH_3)_2$	L	106.2	0.864	225.28	412.25
45	1,4-Dimethylbenzene	$C_6H_4(CH_3)_2$	L	106.2	0.861	286.41	411.50
46	Ethenylbenzene (styrene)	$C_6H_5CH{=}CH_2$	L	104.1	0.906	242.52	418.35
47	Cyclooctatetraene	C_8H_8	L	104.2	0.921	268.47	413.71
	Amines (aminoalkanes, etc.)						
48	Methylamine	CH_3NH_2	G	31.1	**0.660**	179.66	266.82
49	Dimethylamine	$(CH_3)_2NH$	G	45.1	**0.656**	180.96	280.03
50	Trimethylamine	$(CH_3)_3N$	G	59.1	**0.633**	155.85	276.02
51	Ethylamine	$CH_3CH_2NH_2$	G	45.1	**0.683**	192.15	289.73
52	1-Aminopropane (propylamine)	$CH_3CH_2CH_2NH_2$	L	59.1	0.717	190.15	321.65
53	2-Aminopropane	$CH_3CHNH_2CH_3$	L	59.1	0.688	177.95	305.55
54	1-Aminobutane (butylamine)	$CH_3(CH_2)_3NH_2$	L	73.1	0.739	224.05	350.55
55	2-Aminobutane	$CH_3CH_2CHNH_2CH_3$	L	73.1	0.734	188.55	340.88
56	Triethylamine	$(C_2H_5)_3N$	L	101.2	0.728	158.45	362.65
57	Phenylamine (aniline)	$C_6H_5NH_2$	L	93.1	1.022	266.85	457.28
	Organic halogen compounds						
58	Chloromethane	CH_3Cl	G	50.5	**0.916**	175.43	248.93
59	Bromomethane	CH_3Br	G	95.0	**1.676**	179.55	276.71
60	Iodomethane	CH_3I	L	141.9	2.279	206.70	315.58
61	Dichloromethane	CH_2Cl_2	L	85.0	1.316	178.01	412.90
62	Trichloromethane	$CHCl_3$	L	119.4	1.479	209.66	334.88
63	Tetrachloromethane	CCl_4	L	153.8	1.594	250.16	349.69
64	Tetrabromomethane	CBr_4	S	331.6	3.420	365.15	463.15
65	Tetraiodomethane	CI_4	S	519.6	4.320	444.15	408.15
66	Chloroethane	CH_3CH_2Cl	G	64.5	**0.898**	136.75	285.42
67	Bromoethane	CH_3CH_2Br	L	109.0	1.461	154.55	311.50
68	Iodoethane	CH_3CH_2I	L	156.0	1.936	162.05	345.45
69	1,2-Dibromoethane	CH_2BrCH_2Br	G L	187.9	**2.179**	282.94	286.51
70	1-Chloropropane	$CH_3CH_2CH_2Cl$	L	78.5	0.891	150.35	319.75
71	2-Chloropropane	$CH_3CHClCH_3$	L	78.5	0.863	155.97	308.89
72	1-Bromopropane	$CH_3CH_2CH_2Br$	L	123.0	1.354	163.15	344.15
73	2-Bromopropane	$CH_3CHBrCH_3$	L	123.0	1.314	184.15	332.53
74	1-Iodopropane	$CH_3CH_2CH_2I$	L	170.0	1.748	171.85	375.60
75	2-Iodopropane	CH_3CHICH_3	L	170.0	1.703	182.15	362.55
76	1-Chlorobutane	$CH_3(CH_2)_3Cl$	L	92.6	0.886	150.05	351.59
77	1-Bromobutane	$CH_3(CH_2)_3Br$	L	137.0	1.276	160.75	374.75
78	2-Bromobutane	$CH_3CH_2CHBrCH_3$	L	137.0	1.259	161.25	364.37
79	1-Iodobutane	$CH_3(CH_2)_3I$	L	184.0	1.615	142.62	403.68
80	2-Chloro-2-methylpropane	$(CH_3)_2CClCH_3$	L	92.6	0.842	247.75	323.85
81	2-Bromo-2-methylpropane	$(CH_3)_2CBrCH_3$	L	137.0	1.221	256.95	346.40
82	2-Iodo-2-methylpropane	$(CH_3)_2CICH_3$	L	184.0	1.571	234.95	376.15

PTO

$\frac{\Delta H_c^\ominus}{\text{kJ mol}^{-1}}$	$\frac{\Delta H_f^\ominus}{\text{kJ mol}^{-1}}$	$\frac{\Delta G_f^\ominus}{\text{kJ mol}^{-1}}$	$\frac{S^\ominus}{\text{J mol}^{-1}\text{K}^{-1}}$	n	$\frac{p}{p^\ominus}$	ε_r	Notes (see p. 58) Synonyms	
−1299.6	+226.8	+209.2	200.8		0		EXP	36
−1937.7	+185.4	+193.8	248.1		0.75		EXP	37
−3267.6†	+49.0†	+124.5†	172.8†	1.5010	0	2.28	SK POI VAP (25) INF	38
−5149.2				1.5898		2.54		39
−3909.9	+12.1	+115.5	319.7	1.4970	0.36	2.38		40
−4564.9	−12.5†	+119.7†	255.2†	1.4960	0.35	2.24		41
−5218.2	−34.4†	+123.8	290.5†	1.4920		2.27		42
−4552.9	−24.4	+110.3	246.5	1.5060	0.62	2.27	*o*-xylene	43
−4551.9	−25.4	+107.6	252.1	1.4970		2.24	*m*-xylene	44
−4552.9	−24.4	+110.1	247.4	1.4960	0	2.24	*p*-xylene	45
−4395.3	**+103.9**^{gas}	**+213.8**^{gas}	345.1	1.5470	0	2.43	vinyl benzene	46
				1.5379				47
−1079.9	−23.0	+32.1	247.1	1.3527	1.30	9.4	INF	48
−1759.8	−18.5	+68.4	280.5	1.3597	0.93	5.26	INF	49
−2418.8	−24.3	+98.9	287.0	1.3476	0.71	$5.5^{360\text{MHz}}$	INF	50
−1738.9	−47.2			1.3663	0.99	5.26	INF	51
−2335.9	−68.8			1.3882	1.35	2.44	COR POI VAP (5) INF	52
				1.3742			COR POI VAP (5) INF	53
−2973.2	−173.2†	−81.8		1.4014	1.32			54
−2985.7	−160.7†			1.3972				55
−134.3				1.4010	0.82	2.42		56
−3396.2				1.5863	1.53	6.89	SK POI VAP (5)	57
−687.0	−80.8	−57.4	234.3	1.3390	1.86	$12.6^{253\text{K}}$	Methyl chloride	58
−769.9	−35.2	−25.9	246.2	1.4218	1.79	$9.82^{273\text{K}}$	SK POI GAS (20)	59
−814.6	−15.5	+13.4	163.2	1.5308	1.64	7.00	SK POI VAP	60
−447	−121.4	−67.3	177.8	1.4211	1.54	9.08	methylene chloride	61
−373	−134.5	−73.7	201.8	1.4429	1.02	4.81	Chloroform POI VAP	62
−156.1	−135.5	−69.3	216.4	1.4601	0	2.24	Carbon tetrachloride	63
	+18.4	+47.2	212.5		0		Carbon tetrabromide	64
			391.8^{gas}		0		Carbon tetraiodide	65
−1325.1	−136.5	−59.4	190.8	1.3676	1.98	—	SK POI GAS (25)	66
−1424.7	−92.0	−27.8	198.7	1.4239	2.02		SK POI VAP (200)	67
−1489.5	−31.0			1.5133	1.90		Ethyl iodide	68
	−80.7			1.5387	1.40		SK POI ~~GAS~~ VAP (25)	69
−2001.2				1.3879	2.10		*n*-Propyl chloride	70
				1.3777	2.04		Isopropyl chloride	71
−2056.6				1.4343	1.93†		*n*-Propyl bromide	72
				1.4250	2.04†		Isopropyl bromide	73
−2151.8				1.5058	1.74		*n*-Propyl iodide	74
					1.95		Isopropyl iodide	75
				1.4021	2.16		*n*-Butyl chloride	76
−2716.1				1.4401	1.93		*n*-Butyl bromide	77
				1.4367	2.12		sec-Butyl bromide	78
				1.5001	1.88		*n*-Butyl iodide	79
				1.3857	2.13		*tert*-Butyl chloride	80
				1.4278			*tert*-Butyl bromide	81
							tert-Butyl iodide	82

† Other values may be found elsewhere.

Physical, thermochemical and other properties of organic compounds

	Compound	Formula	State	$\frac{M}{g\,mol^{-1}}$	$\frac{\rho}{g\text{-}cm^{-1}}$	$\frac{T_m}{K}$	$\frac{T_b}{K}$
83	Chlorobenzene	C_6H_5Cl	L	112.6	1.106	227.57	404.85
84	Bromobenzene	C_6H_5Br	L	157.0	1.495	242.33	429.21
85	Iodobenzene	C_6H_5I	L	104.1	0.901	242.52	418.35
86	Benzyl chloride	$C_6H_5CH_2Cl$	L	126.6	1.102	234.15	452.15
	Alcohols						
87	Methanol	CH_3OH	L	32.0	0.793	175.47	337.66
88	Ethanol	CH_3CH_2OH	L	46.1	0.789	159.05	351.47
89	Propan-1-ol	$CH_3CH_2CH_2OH$	L	60.1	0.804	146.95	370.35
90	Propan-2-ol	$CH_3CHOHCH_3$	L	60.1	0.787	184.65	355.65
91	Butan-1-ol	$CH_3(CH_2)_2CH_2OH$	L	74.1	0.810	183.85	390.88
92	Pentan-1-ol	$CH_3(CH_2)_3CH_2OH$	L	88.2	0.815	194.95	411.15
93	Hexan-1-ol	$CH_3(CH_2)_4CH_2OH$	L	102.2	0.820	228.55	430.23
94	Heptan-1-ol	$CH_3(CH_2)_5CH_2OH$	L	116.2	0.822	239.15	449.40
95	Octan-1-ol	$CH_3(CH_2)_6CH_2OH$	L	130.2	0.826	256.65	468.35
96	Ethane-1,2-diol	CH_2OHCH_2OH	L	62.1	1.114	259.59	470.45
97	Propane-1,2,3-triol	$CH_2OHCHOCH_2OH$	L	92.1	1.260	291.75	563.15
98	Cyclohexanol	$CH_2(CH_2)_4CHOH$	S	100.2	0.962	298.30	434.65
	Ethers						
99	Methoxymethane	CH_3OCH_3	G	46.1	0.669	131.66	248.31
100	Ethoxyethane	$CH_3CH_2OCH_2CH_3$	L	74.1	0.713	156.85	307.70
101	Methoxybenzene	$C_6H_5OCH_3$	L	108.1	0.994	235.85	427.15
	Aldehydes						
102	Methanal (formaldehyde)	$HCHO$	G	30.0	0.815	181.15	254.05
103	Ethanal (acetaldehyde)	CH_3CHO	G	44.1	0.778	150.15	293.55
104	Propanal (proprionaldehyde)	CH_3CH_2CHO	L	58.1	0.797	193.15	321.15
105	Butanal (butyraldehyde)	$CH_3CH_2CH_2CHO$	L	72.1	0.801	176.75	347.95
106	2-Methylpropanal	$(CH_3)_2CHCH_2CHO$	L	72.1	0.789	208.15	337.25
107	Benzenal (benzaldehyde)	C_6H_5CHO	L	106.1	1.050	247.15	451.15
	Ketones						
108	Propan-2-one (acetone)	CH_3COCH_3	L	58.1	0.789	178.45	329.44
109	Butan-2-one	$CH_3CH_2COCH_3$	L	72.1	0.805	186.46	352.79
110	Pentan-2-one	$CH_3CH_2COCH_2CH_3$	L	86.1	0.814	234.18	375.14
111	Methylphenyl ketone	$C_6H_5COCH_3$	L	120.2	1.028	292.80	475.15
112	Methanoic acid (formic)	HCO_2H	L	46.0	1.220	281.55	373.71
113	Ethanoid acid (acetic)	CH_3CO_2H	L	60.1	1.049	289.78	391.05
114	Propanoic acid (proprionic)	$CH_3CH_2CO_2H$	L	74.1	0.993	252.35	414.14
115	Butanoic acid (butyric)	$CH_3CH_2CH_2CO_2H$	L	88.1	0.958	268.89	436.68
116	2-Methylpropanoic acid	$(CH_3)_2CHCO_2H$	L	88.1	0.950	226.15	427.45
117	Chloroethanoic acid	$ClCH_2CO_2H$	S	94.5	1.404	336.15	462.65
118	Dichloroethanoic acid	Cl_2CHCO_2H	L	128.9	1.563	283.95	465.65
119	Trichloroethanoic acid	Cl_3CCO_2H	S	163.4	1.617	329.45	470.70
120	1-Aminoethanoic acid	$NH_2CH_2CO_2H$	S	75.1	1.595	507.15	559.15
121	2-Hydroxypropanoic acid	$CH_3CHOHCO_2H$	L	90.1	1.206	291.15	329.15
122	Ethandioic acid (oxalic)	CO_2HCO_2H	S	90.0	1.653	430.15	462.65
123	Hexandioic acid (adipic)	$CO_2H(CH_2)_4CO_2H$	S	146.2	1.360	425.15	540.15
124	Benzenesulphonic acid	$C_6H_5SO_3H$	S	158.2		798.15	273.15
125	Benzoic acid	$C_6H_5CO_2H$	S	122.1	1.321	394.85	522.15

PTO

$\Delta H_c^\ominus$ / kJ mol^{-1}	$\Delta H_f^\ominus$ / kJ mol^{-1}	$\Delta G_f^\ominus$ / kJ mol^{-1}	$S^\ominus$ / J mol^{-1}K^{-1}	n	$p/p^\ominus$	ε_r	Notes (see p. 58) Synonyms	
				1.5241	1.67	5.62	POI VAP (75) INF	83
				1.5597	1.77	5.40	Phenyl bromide	84
				1.5439	1.70		Phenyl iodide	85
−3708.7							COR POI VAP (1) INF	86
−726.3	−238.9	−166.7	127.2	1.3280	1.70	32.6	POI	87
−1366.7	−277.7	−174.9	160.7	1.3610	1.69	24.3		88
−2017.3	−304.0	−171.3	196.6	1.3860	1.66	20.1		89
−1986.6	−317.9	−180.3	180.5	1.3772	1.68	18.1		90
−2674.9	−327.1	−168.9	228.0	1.3990	1.66	—	POI VAP (100)	91
−3322.9	−357.1	−161.6	259.0	1.4100		13.9		92
−3976.1	−379.5	−152.3	289.5	1.4180	1.60	13.3		93
−4622.9	−398.7	−141.8	325.9	1.4240	1.71	—		94
−5280.2	−425.1	−136.4	354.4	1.4295	1.68	10.3		95
−1179.5	−454.8	−323.2	166.9	1.4318	2.00†	37.7	Ethylene glycol	96
−1661.0				1.4746		42.5	Glycerol, glycerine	97
−3726.7	−358.2			1.4650		15.0	POI VAP (100)	98
−1454.4	−184.1	−112.8	266.7	1.3018	1.32	5.02	INF Dimethyl ether	99
−2761.4	−279.6	−122.7	251.9	1.3524	1.14	4.34	INF (Diethyl) ether	100
−3786.9					1.38	—	Methyl phenyl ether, anisole	101
−549.8	−117.2	−113.0	218.7		2.27†	—	POI GAS (5)	102
−1167.3	−192.3	−128.2	160.2	1.3311	2.49†	$21.8^{283K, 400MHz}$	INF	103
−1816.7	−221.3	−142.1		1.3619	2.54†	$18.5^{290K, 400MHz}$		104
−2497.0	−219.2	−306.4		1.3791	2.57†	13.4		105
−2497.0	−220.5			1.3727	2.58	—		106
−3520.0					2.96	17.4		107
−1821.4	−216.7	−152.4		1.3587	2.95	20.7		108
−2438.4	−279.0			1.3788		18.5	Methyl ethyl ketone	109
−3077.8	−308.8			1.3923		15.5	Diethyl ketone	110
−4137.6				1.5342	2.96	17.4	Acetophenone	111
−270.3	−422.7	−361.4	129.0	1.3714	1.52	58.5^{400MHz}	COR POI VAP (10)	112
−873.2	−484.5	−389.9	159.8	1.3719	1.74	6.2	INF	113
−1574.0	−509.2	−383.5		1.3865	1.74	3.3^{283K}		114
−2193.7	−538.9			1.3980		2.97		115
−2343.9						2.71^{283K}	Isobutyric acid	116
−715.5						12.3^{333K}	COR Chloracetic acid	117
						8.2	COR Dichloracetic acid	118
−388.3	−513.8					4.6^{333K}	COR Trichloracetic acid	119
−981.1	−528.6					28.1	Glycine	120
−1364.0						22.0^{290K}	Lactic acid	121
−246.4	−826.8						occurs in rhubarb leaves	122
−2799.1								123
								124
−3228.4	−394.1				1.71		Standard for bomb calorimetry	125

† Other values may be found elsewhere.

Physical, thermochemical and other properties of organic compounds

	Compound	Formula	State	$\frac{M}{\text{g mol}^{-1}}$	$\frac{\rho}{\text{g cm}^{-3}}$	$\frac{T_m}{\text{K}}$	$\frac{T_b}{\text{K}}$
	Carboxylic acid derivatives						
126	Ethanoyl (acetyl) chloride	CH_3COCl	L	78.5	1.104	161.15	324.15
127	Ethanoyl (acetyl) bromide	CH_3COBr	L	123.0	1.663	177.15	349.85
128	Ethanoyl (acetyl) iodide	CH_3COI	L	170.0	1.980	273.15	381.15
129	Ethanamide (acetamide)	CH_3CONH_2	S	59.1	1.159	355.30	494.25
130	Phenylethanamide	$CH_3CONHC_6H_5$	S	135.2	1.211	388.15	577.15
131	Methyl methanoate (formate)	HCO_2CH_3	L	60.1	0.974	174.15	305.15
132	Methyl ethanoate (acetate)	$CH_3CO_2CH_3$	L	74.1	0.972	175.10	330.05
133	Methyl propanoate (propionate)	$CH_3CH_2CO_2CH_3$	L	88.1	0.915	185.65	352.91
134	Ethyl ethanoate (acetate)	$CH_3CO_2CH_2CH_3$	L	88.1	0.901	233.65	350.25
135	Ethyl propanoate (propionate)	$CH_3CH_2CO_2CH_2CH_3$	L	102.1	0.890	199.20	372.25
136	Ethyl 3-oxo-butanoate	$CH_3COCH_2O_2C_2H_5$	L	129.1	1.027	193.15	454.15
137	Ethanoic anhydride	$(CH_3CO)_2O$	L	102.1	1.082	200.10	413.15
	Miscellaneous						
138	Carbonyl diamide (urea)	NH_2CONH_2	S	60.1	1.32	405.9	dec

PTO

$\Delta H_c^\ominus$ / kJ mol^{-1}	$\Delta H_f^\ominus$ / kJ mol^{-1}	$\Delta G_f^\ominus$ / kJ mol^{-1}	$S^\ominus$ / J mol^{-1}K^{-1}	n	$p/p^\ominus$	ε_r	Notes (see p. 58) Synonyms	
	−273.8	−208.0	200.8		2.45	15.8	**COR SK POI** (1) **INF** dec in H_2O	**126**
	−223.4					—	**COR SK POI**	**127**
	−164.3					—		**128**
−1182.4					3.44	$59^{356K, 400MHz}$		**129**
−4227.5	−318.0					—		**130**
−975.3						8.5		**131**
−1592.8				1.3614	1.72	6.68		**132**
−2245.6						5.5		**133**
−2238.0	−485.8			1.3728	1.78	6.02		**134**
−2890.3				1.3793		—		**135**
−2890.3						—	**Ethyl acetoacetate**	**136**
−1807.1	−637.2				2.8‡	20.7^{292K}	**Acetic anhydride**	**137**
	−332.8	−205.2	104.6	1.484				**138**

‡ Value uncertain.

Standard thermochemical data for ions in aqueous solution

$\Delta H_f^\ominus$ standard molar enthalpy change on formation
$\Delta G_f^\ominus$ standard molar Gibbs free energy change on formation
$S^\ominus$ standard molar entropy
$\Delta H_h^\ominus$ standard enthalpy change on hydration

The values given relate to the internationally accepted standard state for ions in aqueous solution at 298 K, which involves extrapolation to infinite dilution and other adjustments to measured data. The standard state is generally described as a hypothetical ideal solution of molality 1 mol kg^{-1}. $\Delta H_f^\ominus$, $\Delta G_f^\ominus$, and $S^\ominus$ are all zero for H^+ by convention.

	Ion	$\Delta H_f^\ominus$ / kJ mol^{-1}	$\Delta G_f^\ominus$ / kJ mol^{-1}	$S^\ominus$ / J mol^{-1} K^{-1}	$\Delta H_h^\ominus$ / kJ mol^{-1}
1	Ag^+	105.6	77.1	72.8	−464.4
2	$Ag(NH_3)_2^+$	−111.7	−16.9		—
3	Ag^{2+}		264.2		
4	$Ag(CN)_2^-$	269.9	301.5	205.0	—
5	Al^{3+}	−524.6	−481.1	−313.3	−4613.3
6	AlF_6^{3-}	−2522.4	−2267.6		—
7	$Al(OH)_4^-$	−1490.2	−1308.2		—
8	Au^+		161.9		
9	Au^{3+}		410.9		
10	$AuCl_4^-$	−325.4	653.5	255.2	—
11	$Au(CN)_2^-$	244.3	215.5	414.2	—
12	Ba^{2+}	−538.3	−559.7	12.6	−1272.8
13	Be^{2+}	−389.0	−329.2		
14	Br^-	−121.4	−103.9	82.4	−351.0
15	Br_3^-	−125.7	−107.0	215.5	
16	Br_5^-	−142.2	−103.7	316.7	
17	Br_2Cl^-	−170.2	−128.3	123.4	—
18	BrO^-	−94.0	−33.4	41.8	—
19	BrO_3^-	−83.6	1.7	163.2	—
20	CO_3^{2-}	−677.0	−527.8	−56.8	—
21	HCO_3^-	−587.0	−690.6	95.0	—
22	CN^-	150.6	171.5	94.1	—
23	CNO^-	−145.9	−97.4	106.7	—
24	CNS^-	76.4	92.7	144.3	—
25	HCO_2^- [A]	−409.9	−334.6	91.6	—
26	$C_2H_3O_2^-$ [B]	−488.8			—
27	$C_2O_4^{2-}$	−824.1	−674.8	51.0	—
28	$HC_2O_4^-$	−817.9	−699.0	153.6	—
29	Ca^{2+}	−543.0	−553.0	−55.1	−1561.5
30	Cd^{2+}	−72.3	−77.6	−61.0	−1774.8
31	$Cd(NH_3)_4^{2+}$		−220.8		—
32	Cl^-	−167.1	−131.2	56.5	−384.1
33	ClO^-	−107.0	−36.7	41.8	—
34	ClO_2^-	−66.4	17.2	101.3	—
35	ClO_3^-	−99.1	−3.2	162.3	—
36	ClO_4^-	−129.2	−8.5	182.0	—
37	Co^{2+}	−67.3	−51.4	−155.1	−2023.4
38	Co^{3+}		123.8		
39	Cr^{2+}	−138.8	−164.7		−1818.8
40	Cr^{3+}	5481.0	−204.9		
41	$Cr(H_2O)_6^{3+}$	−1970.6			—
42	CrO_4^{2-}	−863.1	−706.2	38.5	—
43	$HCrO_4^-$	−890.3	−742.6	69.0	—
44	$Cr_2O_7^{2-}$	−1460.5	−1257.2	213.8	—
45	Cs^+	−247.6	−281.9	133.1	−247.7
46	Cu^+	51.9	50.4	−26.3	
47	Cu^{2+}	64.4	65.0	−98.6	−2069.4
48	F^-	−332.5	−278.7	−13.7	−457.3
49	Fe^{2+}	−87.8	−84.9	−113.3	−1889.1
50	Fe^{3+}	−47.6	−9.7	−305.8	−4330.4
51	$Fe(CN)_6^{3-}$	640.2	719.6		—
52	$Fe(CN)_6^{4-}$	530.1	686.2		—

[A] methanoic (formic) ion [B] ethanoic (acetic) ion

	Ion	$\Delta H_f^\ominus$ kJ mol⁻¹	$\Delta G_f^\ominus$ kJ mol⁻¹	$S^\ominus$ J mol⁻¹ K⁻¹	$\Delta H_h^\ominus$ kJ mol⁻¹
53	H		**−215.4**$^{H^-}$		**−1075.3**$^{H^+}$
54	Hg_2^{2+}		153.9		
55	Hg_2^{3+}		164.8		
56	I^-	−13.2	−51.5	111.3	−306.7
57	I_3^-	−51.4	−51.4	239.3	
58	IO^-	−107.4	−38.4	−5.3	—
59	IO_3^-	−221.2	−127.9	118.4	
60	IO_4^-	−147.2			—
61	ICl^-		−161.0		—
62	I_2Cl^-		−132.5		—
63	IBr_2^-		−122.9		—
64	I_2Br^-	−127.9	−109.9	197.5	—
65	K^+	−252.3	−283.2	102.5	−305.4
66	Li^+	−278.3	−293.7	14.2	−499.1
67	Mg^{2+}	−461.8	−455.9	−117.9	−1891.2
68	Mn^{2+}	−218.7	−223.3	−83.6	−1814.2
69	MnO_4^-	−518.3	−425.0	190.0	—
70	NH_4^+	−132.4	−79.3	113.4	−280.7
71	$N_2H_5^+$	−7.4	82.4	150.6	—
72	NO_2^-	−104.5	−37.1	140.2	—
73	NO_3^-	−207.3	−111.2	146.4	—
74	Na^+	−240.0	−261.8	59.0	−389.9
75	Ni^{2+}	−63.9	−46.3	−159.3	−2074.8
76	OH^-	−229.9	−157.2	−10.7	−460.2
77	HO_2^-	−160.2	−67.3	23.8	—
78	PO_3^-	−976.9			—
79	PO_4^{3-}	−1279.8	−1020.8	−221.7	—
80	$P_2O_7^{4-}$	179.1	−1923.7	−104.5	—
81	HPO_4^{2-}	−1294.3	−1091.5	−33.4	—
82	$H_2PO_4^-$	−1298.5	−1132.6	90.4	—
83	HPO_3^{2-}	−968.9			—
84	$H_2PO_3^{2-}$	−969.3			—
85	$H_2PO_2^-$	−613.7			—

References: R7. $\Delta H_h^\ominus$; R62.

	Ion	$\Delta H_f^\ominus$ kJ mol⁻¹	$\Delta G_f^\ominus$ kJ mol⁻¹	$S^\ominus$ J mol⁻¹ K⁻¹	$\Delta H_h^\ominus$ kJ mol⁻¹
86	PH_4^+		67.8		—
87	Pb^{2+}	1.6	−24.2	21.3	−1448.9
88	Pb^{3+}		302.1		
89	Pt^{2+}		230.1		
90	$PtCl_4^{2-}$	−516.2	−384.4	384.9	
91	$PtCl_6^{2-}$	−700.3	−515.0	220.1	—
92	Rb^+	−250.1	−282.1	124.3	−280.7
93	S^{2-}	33.1	85.8	−14.5	
94	S_2^{2-}	30.1	79.5	28.5	
95	S_3^{2-}	25.9	73.6	66.1	
96	S_4^{2-}	23.0	69.0	103.3	
97	S_5^{2-}	21.3	65.7	140.6	
98	HS^-	−17.5	−11.9	62.8	—
99	SO_3^{2-}	−635.4	−486.5	−29.2	—
100	HSO_3^-	−626.1	−527.7	139.7	—
101	SO_4^{2-}	−909.2	−744.5	20.1	—
102	HSO_4^-	−887.2	−755.9	131.8	—
103	$S_2O_3^{2-}$	−652.2	−518.7	121.3	—
104	$S_4O_6^{2-}$	−1224.1	−1030.4	259.4	—
105	SeO_4^{2-}	−599.0	−441.3	54.0	—
106	$HSeO_4^-$	−581.5	−452.2	149.4	—
107	Sn^{2+}	−8.7	−26.2		
108	Sn^{4+}	30.5	15.3		
109	Sr^{2+}	−545.5	−557.2	−39.2	−1413.8
110	TeO_3^{2-}	−596.5			—
111	$Te(OH)_3^+$	−608.3	−496.1	111.7	—
112	Ti^{2+}		−337.5		
113	Ti^{3+}		−302.0		
114	U^{2+}		−292.8		
115	U^{3+}		−312.0		
116	Zn^{2+}	−152.3	−147.1	−106.4	−2013.3
117	$Zn(OH)_4^{2-}$		−863.5		—
118	$Zn(NH_3)_4^{2+}$		−304.1		—

Standard electrode potentials

$E^{\ominus}$ standard electrode potential $dE^{\ominus}/dT$ temperature coefficient of $E^{\ominus}$ p partial pressure

In each case the voltage given is the e.m.f. of a cell in which the system $Pt[H_2(g)]\|2H^+(aq)$ forms the **left-hand electrode**.

Electrode system	$E^{\ominus}$(298 K)/V	($dE^{\ominus}/dT$)/mV K^{-1}
$[\frac{3}{2}N_2(g)+H^+(aq)], [HN_3(g)]\|Pt$	−3.40	−1.193
$Li^+(aq)\|Li(s)$	−3.03	−0.534
$Rb^+(aq)\|Rb(s)$	−2.93	−1.245
$K^+(aq)\|K(s)$	−2.92	−1.080
$Ca^{2+}(aq)\|Ca(s)$	−2.87	−0.175
$Na^+(aq)\|Na(s)$	−2.71	−0.772
$Mg^{2+}(aq)\|Mg(s)$	−2.37	+0.103
$Ce^{3+}(aq)\|Ce(s)$	−2.33	+0.101
$Th^{4+}(aq)\|Th(s)$	−1.90	+0.280
$Be^{2+}(aq)\|Be(s)$	−1.85	+0.565
$U^{3+}(aq)\|U(s)$	−1.80	−0.070
$Al^{3+}(aq)\|Al(s)$	−1.66	+0.504
$Mn^{2+}(aq)\|Mn(s)$	−1.19	−0.080
$[SO_4^{2-}(aq)+H_2O(l)], [SO_3^{2-}(aq)+2OH^-(aq)]\|Pt$	−0.93	−1.389
$Zn^{2+}(aq)\|Zn(s)$	−0.76	+0.091
$Cr^{3+}(aq)\|Cr(s)$	−0.74	+0.468
$[As(s)+3H^+(aq)], AsH_3(g)\|Pt$	−0.60	−0.050
$E^{\ominus} = -0.60-0.0591\,pH-0.0197\lg p(AsH_3)$		
$[2SO_3^{2-}(aq)+3H_2O(l)], [S_2O_3^{2-}(aq)+6OH^-(aq)]\|Pt$	−0.58	−1.146
$Fe(OH)_3(s), [Fe(OH)_2(s)+OH^-(aq)]\|Pt$	−0.56	−0.96
$[H_3PO_3(aq)+2H^+(aq)], [H_3PO_2(aq)+H_2O(l)]\|Pt$	−0.499	−0.36
$E^{\ominus} = -0.499-0.0591\,pH+0.0295\lg([H_3PO_3]/[H_3PO_2])$		
$S(s), S^{2-}(aq)\|Pt$	−0.48	−0.93
$Fe^{2+}(aq)\|Fe(s)$	−0.44	+0.052
$Cr^{3+}(aq), Cr^{2+}(aq)\|Pt$	−0.41	
$Cd^{2+}(aq)\|Cd(s)$	−0.40	−0.093
$[Se(s)+2H^+(aq)], H_2Se(g)\|Pt$	−0.40	−0.28
$E^{\ominus} = -0.399-0.0591\,pH-0.0295\lg[H_2Se]$		
$Ti^{3+}(aq), Ti^{2+}(aq)\|Pt$	−0.37	
$PbSO_4(s), [Pb(s)+SO_4^{2-}(aq)]\|Pt$	−0.36	−1.015
$Co^{2+}(aq)\|Co(s)$	−0.28	+0.06
$E^{\ominus} = -0.277+0.0295\lg[Co^{2+}]$		
$[H_3PO_4(aq)+2H^+(aq)], [H_3PO_3(aq)+H_2O(l)]\|Pt$	−0.276	−0.36
$E^{\ominus} = -0.276-0.0591\,pH+0.0295\lg([H_3PO_4]/[H_3PO_3])$		
$Ni^{2+}(aq)\|Ni(s)$	−0.250	+0.06
$[2SO_4^{2-}(aq)+4H^+(aq)],[S_2O_6^{2-}(aq)+2H_2O(l)]\|Pt$	−0.22	+0.52
$Sn^{2+}(aq)\|Sn(white,s)$	−0.14	−0.282
$Pb^{2+}(aq)\|Pb(s)$	−0.13	−0.451
$[CrO_4^{2-}(aq)+4H_2O(l)],[Cr(OH)_3(s)+5OH^-(aq)]\|Pt$	−0.13	−1.675
$[CO_2(g)+2H^+(aq)],[CO(g)+H_2O(l)]\|Pt$	−0.10	
$E^{\ominus} = -0.103-0.0591\,pH+0.0295\lg(p_{CO_2}/p_{CO})$		

Electrode system	**$E^{\ominus}$(298 K)/V**	**($dE^{\ominus}/dT$)/mV K^{-1}**
$2H^{+}(aq)\vert[H_2(g)]Pt$	± 0.00	± 0.000
$[HCO_2H(aq)+H^{+}(aq)],[H_2O(l)+HCHO(aq)]\vert Pt$	$+0.06$	
$E^{\ominus} = +0.056-0.0591\ pH + 0.0295\ lg([HCO_2H]/[HCHO])$		
$[2H^{+}(aq)+S(s)],H_2S(aq)\vert Pt$	$+0.14$	-0.209
$E^{\ominus} = +0.142-0.0591\ pH - 0.0295\ lg[H_2S]$		
$[Sn^{4+}(aq)1.0M\ HCl],[Sn^{2+}(aq)(1.0M\ HCl)]\vert Pt$	$+0.15$	
$Cu^{2+}(aq),Cu^{+}(aq)\vert Pt$	$+0.15$	$+0.073$
$[4H^{+}(aq)+SO_4^{2-}(aq)],[H_2SO_3(aq)+H_2O(l)]\vert Pt$	$+0.17$	$+0.81$
$AgCl(s),[Ag(s)+Cl^{-}(aq)]\vert Pt$	$+0.22$	-0.658
$[PbO_2(s)+2H_2O(l)],[Pb(OH)_2(s)+2OH^{-}(aq)]\vert Pt$	$+0.25$	-1.194
$[HAsO_2(aq)+3H^{+}(aq)],[As(s)+2H_2O(l)]\vert Pt$	$+0.25$	-0.510
$E^{\ominus} = 0.248-0.0591\ pH + 0.0197\ lg[HAsO_2]$		
$Hg_2Cl_2(s),[2Hg(s)+2Cl^{-}(aq)]\vert Pt$	$+0.27$	-0.317
$[PbO_2(s)+H_2O(l)],[PbO(s)+2OH^{-}(aq)]\vert Pt$	$+0.28$	
$Cu^{2+}(aq)\vert Cu(s)$	$+0.34$	$+0.008$
$Fe(CN)_6^{3-}(aq),Fe(CN)_6^{4-}(aq)\vert Pt$	$+0.36$	
$[O_2(g)+2H_2O(l)],4OH^{-}(aq)\vert Pt$	$+0.40$	-1.680
$[2H_2SO_3(aq)+2H^{+}(aq)],[S_2O_3^{2-}(aq)+3H_2O(l)]\vert Pt$	$+0.40$	-1.26
$[S_2O_3^{2-}(aq)+6H^{+}(aq)],[2S(s)+3H_2O(l)]\vert Pt$	$+0.47$	
$E^{\ominus} = +0.465-0887\ pH + 0.0148\ lg[S_2O_3^{2-}]$		
$[IO^{-}(aq)+H_2O(l)],[I^{-}(aq)+2OH^{-}(aq)]\vert Pt$	$+0.49$	
$[4H_2SO_3(aq)+4H^{+}(aq)],[S_4O_6^{2-}(aq)+6H_2O(l)]\vert Pt$	$+0.51$	-1.31
$E^{\ominus} = +0.509-0.0394\ pH + 0.0098\ lg([H_2SO_3]^4/[S_4O_6^{2-}])$		
$Cu^{+}(aq)\vert Cu(s)$	$+0.52$	-0.058
$[TeO_2(s)+4H^{+}(aq)],[Te(s)+2H_2O(l)]\vert Pt$	$+0.53$	-0.370
$I_2(aq),\ 2I^{-}(aq)\vert Pt$	$+0.54$	-0.148
$[H_3AsO_4(aq)+2H^{+}(aq)],\ [HAsO_2(aq)+2H_2O(l)]\vert Pt$	$+0.56$	-0.364
$E^{\ominus} = +0.560-0.0591\ pH + 0.0295\ lg([H_3AsO_4]/[HAsO_2])$		
$[S_2O_6^{2-}(aq)+4H^{+}(aq)],\ 2H_2SO_3(aq)\vert Pt$	$+0.57$	$+1.10$
$E^{\ominus} = +0.57-0.1182\ pH + 0.0295\ lg([S_2O_6^{2-}]/[H_2SO_3]^2)$		
$[Sb_2O_5(s)+6H^{+}(aq)],\ [2SbO^{+}(aq)+3H_2O(l)]\vert Pt$	$+0.58$	
$E^{\ominus} = +0.581-0.0886\ pH - 0.0295\ lg[SbO^{+}]$		
$[MnO_4^{2-}(aq)+2H_2O(l)],\ [MnO_2(s)+4OH^{-}(aq)]\vert Pt$	$+0.59$	-1.778
$[2H^{+}(aq)+O_2(g)],\ H_2O_2(aq)\vert Pt$	$+0.68$	-1.033
$E^{\ominus} = 0.682-0.0591\ pH + 0.0295\ lg(p_{O_2}/[H_2O_2])$		
$[C_6H_4O_2(aq)+2H^{+}(aq)],\ C_6H_4(OH)_2(aq)\vert Pt$	$+0.70$	-0.731
$Fe^{3+}(aq),Fe^{2+}(aq)\vert Pt$	$+0.77$	$+1.188$
$Hg_2^{2+}(aq)\vert Hg(s)$	$+0.79$	
$Ag^{+}(aq)\vert Ag(s)$	$+0.80$	-1.000
$[2NO_3^{-}(aq)+4H^{+}(aq)],[N_2O_4(g)+2H_2O(l)]\vert Pt$	$+0.80$	$+0.107$
$[ClO^{-}(aq)+H_2O(l)],[Cl^{-}(aq)+2OH^{-}(aq)]\vert Pt$	$+0.89$	-1.079
$2Hg^{2+}(aq),Hg_2^{2+}(aq)\vert Pt$	$+0.92$	
$[NO_3^{-}(aq)+3H^{+}(aq)],[HNO_2(aq)+H_2O(l)]\vert Pt$	$+0.94$	-0.80
$[HNO_2(aq)+H^{+}(aq)],[NO(g)+H_2O(l)]\vert Pt$	$+0.99$	

Electrode system	$E^{\ominus}$(298 K)/V	$(dE^{\ominus}/dT)$/mV K^{-1}
$[HIO(aq)+H^+(aq)],[I^-(aq)+H_2O(l)]\mid Pt$	+0.99	
$E^{\ominus} = +0.987-0.0295\,pH+0.0295\,lg([HIO]/[I^-])$		
$[VO^{2+}(aq)+2H^+(aq)],[VO^{2+}(aq)+H_2O(l)]\mid Pt$	+1.00	
$[H_6TeO_6(s)+2H^+(aq)],[TeO_2+4H_2O(l)]\mid Pt$	+1.02	+0.13
$[N_2O_4(g)+4H^+(aq)],[2NO(g)+2H_2O(l)]\mid Pt$	+1.03	−0.011
$Br_2(l),2Br^-(aq)\mid Pt$	+1.07	−0.629
$Br_2(aq),2Br^-(aq)\mid Pt$	+1.09	−0.478
$[2IO_3^-(aq)+12H^+(aq)],[I_2(aq)+6H_2O(l)]\mid Pt$	+1.19	−0.364
$E^{\ominus} = +1.19-0.0709\,pH+0.0059\,lg([IO_3^-]^2/[I_2])$		
$[MnO_2(s)+4H^+(aq)],[Mn^{2+}(aq)+2H_2O(l)]\mid Pt$	+1.23	−0.661
$Tl^{3+}(aq),Tl^+(aq)\mid Pt$	+1.25	+0.89
$[Cr_2O_7^{2-}(aq)+14H^+(aq)],[2Cr^{3+}(aq)+7H_2O(l)]\mid Pt$	+1.33	−1.263
$E^{\ominus} = 1.333-0.1379\,pH+0.0098\,lg([Cr_2O_7^{2-}]/[Cr^{3+}]^2)$		
$Cl_2(aq),2Cl^-(aq)\mid Pt$	+1.36	−1.260
$[PbO_2(s)+4H^+(aq)],[Mn^{2+}(aq)+4H_2O(l)]\mid Pt$	+1.46	−0.238
$Mn^{3+}(aq),Mn^{2+}(aq)\mid Pt$	+1.51	+1.23
$[MnO_4^-(aq)+8H^+(aq)],[Mn^{2+}(aq)+4H_2O(l)]\mid Pt$	+1.51	−0.66
$2BrO_3^-(aq),[Br_2(aq)+6H_2O(l)]\mid Pt$	+1.52	−0.418
$E^{\ominus} = +1.52-0.0709\,pH+0.0059\,lg([BrO_3^-]^2/[Br_2])$		
$[2HBrO(aq)+2H^+(aq)],[Br_2(aq)+2H_2O(l)]\mid Pt$	+1.57	
$E^{\ominus} = +1.574-0.0591\,pH+0.0295\,lg([HBrO]^2/[Br_2])$		
$[2HClO(aq)+2H^+(aq)],[Cl_2(aq)+2H_2O(l)]\mid Pt$	+1.59	
$[2HBrO(aq)+2H^+(aq)],[Br_2(l)+2H_2O(l)]\mid Pt$	+1.60	
$E^{\ominus} = +1.596-0.0591\,pH+0.0591\,lg([HBrO])$		
$[H_5IO_6(aq)+H^+(aq)],[IO_3^-(aq)+3H_2O(l)]\mid Pt$	+1.60	
$[2HClO(aq)+2H^+(aq)],[Cl_2(g)+2H_2O(l)]\mid Pt$	+1.63	
$E^{\ominus} = +1.630-0.0591\,pH+0.0295\,lg([HClO]^2/p_{Cl_2})$		
$[2HCl(aq)+6H^+(aq)],[Cl_2(g)+4H_2O(l)]\mid Pt$	+1.64	
$[2ClO_2^-(aq)+8H^+(aq)],[Cl_2(g)+4H_2O(l)]\mid Pt$	+1.68	
$[Cl_2O(g)+2H^+(aq)],[Cl_2(g)+H_2O(l)]\mid Pt$	+1.68	
$[PbO_2(s)+SO_4^{2-}(aq)+4H^+(aq)],[PbSO_4(s)+2H_2O(l)]\mid Pt$	+1.69	+0.326
$[MnO_4^-(aq)+4H^+(aq)],[MnO_2(s)+2H_2O(l)]\mid Pt$	+1.70	−0.666
$E^{\ominus} = +1.695-0.0788\,pH+0.0197\,lg[MnO_4^-]$		
$Ce^{4+}(aq),Ce^{3+}(aq)\mid Pt$	+1.70(in M $HClO_4$)	
$[H_2O_2(aq)+2H^+(aq)],2H_2O(l)\mid Pt$	+1.77	−0.658
$E^{\ominus} = 1.776-0.0591\,pH+0.0295\,lg[H_2O_2]$		
$Co^{3+}(aq),Co^{2+}(aq)\mid Pt$	+1.81(in M HNO_3)	
$Ag^{2+}(aq),Ag^+(aq)\mid Pt$	+1.98	
$S_2O_8^{2-}(aq),2SO_4^{2-}(aq)\mid Pt$	+2.01	−1.26
$E^{\ominus} = +2.010+0.0295\,lg([S_2O_8^{2-}]/[SO_4^{2-}]^2)$		
$[O_3(g)+2H^+(aq)],[O_2(g)+H_2O(l)]\mid Pt$	+2.08	−0.483
$E^{\ominus} = +2.076-0.0591\,pH+0.0295\,lg(p_{O_3}/p_{O_2})$		
$[F_2O(g)+2H^+(aq)],[2F^-(aq)+H_2O(l)]\mid Pt$	+2.15	−1.184
$[FeO_4^{2-}(aq)+8H^+(aq)],[Fe^{3+}(aq)+4H_2O(l)]\mid Pt$	+2.20	−0.85
$F_2(g), 2F^-(aq)\mid Pt$	+2.87	−1.830
$[H_4XeO_6(aq)+2H^+(aq)],[XeO_3(g)+3H_2O(l)]\mid Pt$	+3.0	
$[F_2(g)+2H^+(aq)],2HF(aq)\mid Pt$	+3.06	−0.60

References: R68, R74, R75.

Standard enthalpy changes on formation of some aqueous solutions

Z mole ratio of solution = $n(H_2O)/n$(solute), where n stands for amount of substance
$\Delta H_f^\ominus(298\ K)$ molar enthalpy change on formation of solution from elements of solute and pure water

All values of $\Delta H_f^\ominus$ are negative. Superscripts give non-standard values of Z.

$-\Delta H_f^\ominus(298\ K)/kJ\ mol^{-1}$

	Z	1	2	5	10	20	50	100	200	500	1000	2000	∞
1	H_2O_2	189.81	190.46	190.95	191.08	191.15	191.15						191.17
2	HF		317.11	318.67	318.97	319.21^{25}	319.31	319.41	319.48	319.75	320.21	321.33	332.63
3	HCl	121.55	140.96	155.77	161.32	163.85	165.36	165.92	166.27	166.57	166.73	166.85	167.16
4	$HClO_4$		106.27	126.23	129.79	130.04	129.54	129.24	129.08	129.03	129.03	129.08^{A}	129.33
5	HBr	72.72	93.72	111.74	116.96	119.08	120.16	120.56	120.81	121.03	121.16	121.26	121.55
6	HI		35.82^{3}	46.40	51.61	53.53	54.21	54.56	54.60	54.74	54.84	54.92	55.19
7	HIO_3							216.31	216.73	217.57^{400}	218.41^{800}		
8	SO_2							326.58	327.84	329.75	331.38	333.22	337.15^{10^4}
9	H_2SO_3							612.41	613.67	615.58	617.21	619.01	622.99^{10^4}
10	H_2SO_4	841.79	855.44	872.48	880.13	884.92	886.77	887.64	888.63	890.49	892.34	894.29	909.27
11	NH_3	75.36	77.66	79.27	79.81	80.02	80.15	80.19		80.22	80.21	80.14^{5000}	79.69
12	NH_4OH	363.49	364.33	365.29	365.66	365.86	365.99	366.03	366.04	366.05	366.04	366.02	362.50
13	HNO_3	187.63	194.56	202.77	205.82	206.82^{25}	206.85	206.86		206.97	207.04	207.11	207.36
14	NH_4NO_3		349.30^{3}	347.48	345.05	342.53^{25}	341.15	340.23	339.87	339.67	339.64	339.67	339.87
15	NH_4Cl			299.53^{8}	299.44	299.21	299.09	299.10	299.17	299.27	299.35	299.42	299.66
16	H_3PO_4	$1271.77^{0.75}$	1278.63	1283.94	1286.50	1287.96	1288.95	1289.41	1289.83	1290.36	1290.90	1291.58	1296.71
17	$ZnCl_2$		444.76^{4}	448.57	455.97	464.43^{25}	470.91	476.98	480.57	482.12^{400}	482.96^{800}		487.35
18	$ZnSO_4$	1052.61			1052.61^{18}	1053.15	1054.61	1054.95	1055.34	1055.83	1056.30		1059.93
19	$Zn(NO_3)_2$	$505.85^{1.5}$	513.80	542.37	560.15	564.97	565.17	564.80	564.97	565.59^{400}			
20	$CuCl_2$				232.13	240.50	247.61	250.96	253.22	254.97^{400}	256.23	256.90	
21	$CuSO_4$						836.79	837.26	837.64	838.23	838.85	839.48	843.12
22	$Cu(NO_3)_2$				347.73	351.67	351.50	350.95	350.79	350.62^{400}	350.62^{800}		
23	$MnSO_4$					1115.12	1117.46	1119.09	1120.31	1121.31^{400}	1122.48	1123.03	1126.75
24	$MgCl_2$				776.76	786.80	791.36	792.83	793.79	794.67	795.17	795.59	796.88
25	$CaCl_2$					872.41^{25}	873.87	874.69	875.29	875.79	876.17		877.89
26	LiCl		429.36	436.94	441.64	443.45	444.43	444.97	445.09	445.30^{400}	445.46^{800}		445.92
27	NaCl			409.11^{8}	409.06	408.24	407.27	406.89	406.75	406.74^{400}	406.80	406.86	407.11
28	$NaNO_3$			453.84^{6}	452.29	449.57^{25}	447.77	446.98	446.43	446.09	446.03	446.03	446.22
29	NaOH		455.61^{3}	464.49	469.23	469.59	469.25	469.06	469.03	469.10	469.19	469.29	469.60
30	KOH		467.65^{3}	474.09	478.49	479.81	480.19	480.31	480.42	480.59	480.72	480.84	481.16
31	KCl							418.46	418.29	418.29^{400}	418.33^{800}	418.43^{3200}	418.65

^{A} also 129.16^{10^4}. *Reference*: R7.

Solubility products for ions in aqueous solution

$A_pB_q(s) \rightleftharpoons pA^+(aq) + qB^-(aq)$ $\qquad K_{sp} = [A^+(aq)]^p[B^-(aq)]^q$

	Equilibrium			K_{sp} (298 K) $mol^{(p+q)}\,dm^{-3(p+q)}$	$p+q$
1	$Al(OH)_3(s)$	⇌	$Al^{3+}(aq) + 3OH^-(aq)$	1.0×10^{-32}	4
2	$Au(OH)_3(s)$	⇌	$Au^{3+}(aq) + 3OH^-(aq)$	5.5×10^{-46}	4
3	$As(OH)_3(s)$	⇌	$As^{3+}(aq) + 3OH^-(aq)$	2.0×10^{-1}	4
4	$BaSO_4(s)$	⇌	$Ba^{2+}(aq) + SO_4^{2-}(aq)$	1.0×10^{-10}	2
5	$BaC_2O_4(s)$	⇌	$Ba^{2+}(aq) + C_2O_4^{2-}(aq)$	1.7×10^{-7}	2
6	$BaCO_3(s)$	⇌	$Ba^{2+}(aq) + CO_3^{2-}(aq)$	5.5×10^{-10}	2
7	$BaCrO_4(s)$	⇌	$Ba^{2+}(aq) + CrO_4^{2-}(aq)$	1.17×10^{-10}	2
8	$Be(OH)_2(s)$	⇌	$Be^{2+}(aq) + 2OH^-(aq)$	2.0×10^{-18} 291 K	2
9	$Bi(OH)_3(s)$	⇌	$Bi^{3+}(aq) + 3OH^-(aq)$	4.0×10^{-31}	4
10	$CaCO_3(s)$	⇌	$Ca^{2+}(aq) + CO_3^{2-}(aq)$	5.0×10^{-9}	2
11	$CaC_2O_4(s)$	⇌	$Ca^{2+}(aq) + C_2O_4^{2-}(aq)$	2.3×10^{-9}	2
12	$Ca_3(PO_4)_2(s)$	⇌	$3Ca^{2+}(aq) + 2PO_4^{3-}(aq)$	1.0×10^{-26}	5
13	$CaC_4H_4O_6(s)$	⇌	$Ca^{2+}(aq) + C_4H_4O_6^{2+}(aq)$	7.7×10^{-7}	2
14	$CaSO_4(s)$	⇌	$Ca^{2+}(aq) + SO_4^{2-}(aq)$	2.0×10^{-5}	2
15	$CdCO_3(s)$	⇌	$Cd^{2+}(aq) + CO_3^{2-}(aq)$	2.5×10^{-14}	2
16	$CdS(s)$	⇌	$Cd^{2+}(aq) + S^{2-}(aq)$	8.0×10^{-27}	2
17	$CaF_2(s)$	⇌	$Ca^{2+}(aq) + 2F^-(aq)$	4.0×10^{-11}	3
18	$Ce(OH)_3(s)$	⇌	$Ce^{3+}(aq) + 3OH^-(aq)$	1.6×10^{-20}	4
19	$Cr(OH)_2(s)$	⇌	$Cr^{2+}(aq) + 2OH^-(aq)$	1.0×10^{-17}	3
20	$Cr(OH)_3(s)$	⇌	$Cr^{3+}(aq) + 3OH^-(aq)$	1.0×10^{-30}	4
21	$Co(OH)_2(s)$	⇌	$Co^{2+}(aq) + 2OH^-(aq)$	6.3×10^{-16}	3
22	$Co(OH)_3(s)$	⇌	$Co^{3+}(aq) + 3OH^-(aq)$	4.0×10^{-45}	4
23	$Cu(OH)_2(s)$	⇌	$Cu^{2+}(aq) + 2OH^-(aq)$	2.0×10^{-19}	3
24	$Cu^{II}CrO_4(s)$	⇌	$Cu^{2+}(aq) + CrO_4^{2-}(aq)$	3.6×10^{-6}	2
25	$Cu(IO_3)_2(s)$	⇌	$Cu^{2+}(aq) + 2IO_3^-(aq)$	7.6×10^{-8}	3
26	$CuS(s)$	⇌	$Cu^{2+}(aq) + S^{2-}(aq)$	6.3×10^{-36} 1.0×10^{-41} 291 K	2
27	$CuBr(s)$	⇌	$Cu^+(aq) + Br^-(aq)$	3.2×10^{-8}	2
28	$Cu_2S(s)$	⇌	$2Cu^+(aq) + S^{2-}(aq)$	2.5×10^{-48} 1.0×10^{-51} 291 K	3

	Equilibrium			K_{sp} (298 K) $mol^{(p+q)}\,dm^{-3(p+q)}$	$p+q$
46	$MgCO_3(s)$	⇌	$Mg^{2+}(aq) + CO_3^{2-}(aq)$	1.0×10^{-5}	2
47	$MgF_2(s)$	⇌	$Mg^{2+}(aq) + 2F^-(aq)$	6.6×10^{-9}	3
48	$MgNH_4PO_4(s)$	⇌	$Mg^{2+}(aq) + NH_4^+(aq) + PO_4^{3-}(aq)$	2.5×10^{-13}	3
49	$Hg(OH)_2(s)$	⇌	$Hg^{2+}(aq) + 2OH^-(aq)$	6.3×10^{-24}	3
50	$HgSe(s)$	⇌	$Hg^{2+}(aq) + Se^{2-}(aq)$	1.0×10^{-59}	2
51	HgS (black)(s)	⇌	$Hg^{2+}(aq) + S^{2-}(aq)$	1.6×10^{-52}	2
52	HgS (red)(s)	⇌	$Hg^{2+}(aq) + S^{2-}(aq)$	4.0×10^{-53}	2
53	$Hg_2Br_2(s)$	⇌	$Hg_2^{2+}(aq) + 2Br^-(aq)$	5.75×10^{-23}	3
54	$Hg_2Cl_2(s)$	⇌	$Hg_2^{2+}(aq) + 2Cl^-(aq)$	1.6×10^{-18}	3
55	$Hg_2(CN)_2(s)$	⇌	$Hg_2^{2+}(aq) + 2CN^-(aq)$	5.0×10^{-40}	3
56	$Hg_2I_2(s)$	⇌	$Hg_2^{2+}(aq) + 2I^-(aq)$	4.5×10^{-29}	3
57	$Hg_2C_2O_4(s)$	⇌	$Hg_2^{2+}(aq) + C_2O_4^{2-}(aq)$	1.0×10^{-13}	2
58	$Hg_2SO_4(s)$	⇌	$Hg_2^{2+}(aq) + SO_4^{2-}(aq)$	6.55×10^{-7}	2
59	$NiCO_3(s)$	⇌	$Ni^{2+}(aq) + CO_3^{2-}(aq)$	6.6×10^{-9}	2
60	$Ni(OH)_2(s)$	⇌	$Ni^{2+}(aq) + 2OH^-(aq)$	6.3×10^{-18}	3
61	γ-NiS(s)	⇌	$Ni^{2+}(aq) + S^{2-}(aq)$	2.0×10^{-26} 1.1×10^{-27} 291 K	3
62	$K_2[PtCl_6](s)$	⇌	$2K^+(aq) + [PtCl_6]^{2-}(aq)$	1.1×10^{-5}	3
63	$KClO_4(s)$	⇌	$K^+(aq) + ClO_4^-(aq)$	1.07×10^{-2}	2
64	$AgCl(s)$	⇌	$Ag^+(aq) + Cl^-(aq)$	2.0×10^{-10}	2
65	$AgBr(s)$	⇌	$Ag^+(aq) + Br^-(aq)$	5.0×10^{-13}	2
66	$AgI(s)$	⇌	$Ag^+(aq) + I^-(aq)$	8.0×10^{-17}	2
67	$AgBrO_3(s)$	⇌	$Ag^+(aq) + BrO_3^-(aq)$	6.0×10^{-5}	2
68	$AgIO_3(s)$	⇌	$Ag^+(aq) + IO_3^-(aq)$	2.0×10^{-8}	2
69	$Ag_2CrO_4(s)$	⇌	$2Ag^+(aq) + CrO_4^{2-}(aq)$	3.0×10^{-12}	3
70	$AgCNS(s)$	⇌	$Ag^+(aq) + CNS^-(aq)$	2.0×10^{-12}	2
71	$Ag_2CO_3(s)$	⇌	$2Ag^+(aq) + CO_3^{2-}(aq)$	6.3×10^{-12}	3
72	$Ag_2Cr_2O_7(s)$	⇌	$2Ag^+(aq) + Cr_2O_7^{2-}(aq)$	1.02×10^{-11}	3
73	$AgCN(s)$	⇌	$Ag^+(aq) + CN^-(aq)$	2.3×10^{-16}	2
74	$Ag_3PO_4(s)$	⇌	$3Ag^+(aq) + PO_4^{3-}(aq)$	1.25×10^{-20} 293 K	4

	Equilibrium			K_{sp} (298 K) / $mol^{(p+q)}\ dm^{-3(p+q)}$	$p+q$
29	$Fe^{III}_4[Fe^{II}(CN)_6]_3(s)$	⇌	$4Fe^{3+}(aq) + 3[Fe^{II}(CN)_6]^{4-}(aq)$	3.0×10^{-41}	7
30	$FeCO_3(s)$	⇌	$Fe^{2+}(aq) + CO_3^{2-}(aq)$	3.5×10^{-11}	2
31	$FeC_2O_4(s)$	⇌	$Fe^{2+}(aq) + C_2O_4^{2-}(aq)$	2.1×10^{-7}	2
32	$FeS(s)$	⇌	$Fe^{2+}(aq) + S^{2-}(aq)$	6.3×10^{-18}	2
33	$Fe(OH)_2(s)$	⇌	$Fe^{2+}(aq) + 2OH^-(aq)$	6.0×10^{-15}	3
34	$Fe(OH)_3(s)$	⇌	$Fe^{3+}(aq) + 3OH^-(aq)$	8.0×10^{-40}	4
35	$PbCl_2(s)$	⇌	$Pb^{2+}(aq) + 2Cl^-(aq)$	2.0×10^{-5}	3
36	$Pb_3(AsO_4)_2(s)$	⇌	$3Pb^{2+}(aq) + 2AsO_4^{3-}(aq)$	4.1×10^{-36}	5
37	$Pb(N_3)_2(s)$	⇌	$Pb^{2+}(aq) + 2N_3^-(aq)$	2.6×10^{-9}	3
38	$PbBr_2(s)$	⇌	$Pb^{2+}(aq) + 2Br^-(aq)$	3.9×10^{-5}	3
39	$PbCO_3(s)$	⇌	$Pb^{2+}(aq) + CO_3^{2-}(aq)$	6.3×10^{-14}	2
40	$PbF_2(s)$	⇌	$Pb^{2+}(aq) + 2F^-(aq)$	2.7×10^{-8}	3
41	$PbI_2(s)$	⇌	$Pb^{2+}(aq) + 2I^-(aq)$	7.1×10^{-9}	3
42	$PbC_2O_4(s)$	⇌	$Pb^{2+}(aq) + C_2O_4^{2-}(aq)$	3.4×10^{-11}	2
43	$PbSO_4(s)$	⇌	$Pb^{2+}(aq) + SO_4^{2-}(aq)$	1.6×10^{-8}	2
44	$PbS(s)$	⇌	$Pb^{2+}(aq) + S^{2-}(aq)$	1.25×10^{-28}	2
45	$Mg(OH)_2(s)$	⇌	$Mg^{2+}(aq) + 2OH^-(aq)$	2.0×10^{-11}	3

	Equilibrium			K_{sp} (298 K) / $mol^{(p+q)}\ dm^{-3(p+q)}$	$p+q$
75	$Ag_2SO_4(s)$	⇌	$2Ag^+(aq) + SO_4^{2-}(aq)$	1.6×10^{-5}	3
76	$Ag_2S(s)$	⇌	$2Ag^+(aq) + S^{2-}(aq)$	6.3×10^{-50}	3
77	$SrCO_3(s)$	⇌	$Sr^{2+}(aq) + CO_3^{2-}(aq)$	1.1×10^{-10}	2
78	$SrF_2(s)$	⇌	$Sr^{2+}(aq) + 2F^-(aq)$	2.45×10^{-9}	3
79	$SrC_2O_4(s)$	⇌	$Sr^{2+}(aq) + C_2O_4^{2-}(aq)$	5.0×10^{-8}	2
80	$Sn(OH)_2(s)$	⇌	$Sn^{2+}(aq) + 2OH^-(aq)$	1.4×10^{-28}	3
81	$Zn(OH)_2(s)$	⇌	$Zn^{2+}(aq) + 2OH^-(aq)$	2.0×10^{-17}	3
82	$ZnCO_3(s)$	⇌	$Zn^{2+}(aq) + CO_3^{2-}(aq)$	1.4×10^{-11}	2
83	$Zn(CN)_2(s)$	⇌	$Zn^{2+}(aq) + 2CN^-(aq)$	2.6×10^{-13} 291 K	3
84	$ZnC_2O_4(s)$	⇌	$Zn^{2+}(aq) + C_2O_4^{2-}(aq)$	7.5×10^{-9}	2
85	α-ZnS(s)	⇌	$Zn^{2+}(aq) + S^{2-}(aq)$	1.6×10^{-24}	
				5.0×10^{-26} 291 K	2
86	β-ZnS(s)	⇌	$Zn^{2+}(aq) + S^{2-}(aq)$	2.5×10^{-22}	
				1.1×10^{-24} 291 K	2
87	$Th(OH)_4(s)$	⇌	$Th^{4+}(aq) + 4OH^-(aq)$	1.25×10^{-45}	5
88	$TlCl(s)$	⇌	$Tl^+(aq) + Cl^-(aq)$	1.75×10^{-4}	2

Molar conductivity of ions in aqueous solution

λ molar conductivity of ions at infinite dilution. See page 111 **CHM** for conductivity of water.

	Cation	$\lambda/\Omega^{-1}\ cm^2\ mol^{-1}$		Cation	$\lambda/\Omega^{-1}\ cm^2\ mol^{-1}$
1	Li^+	39	11	Fe^{2+}	108
2	Na^+	50	12	Co^{2+}	110
3	Ag^+	62	13	Sr^{2+}	119
4	K^+	74	14	Pb^{2+}	119
5	NH_4^+	74	15	Ca^{2+}	119
6	Zn^{2+}	106	16	Ba^{2+}	127
7	Ni^{2+}	106	17	Hg^{2+}	127
8	Mg^{2+}	106	18	Al^{3+}	189
9	Mn^{2+}	107	19	Fe^{3+}	205
10	Cu^{2+}	107	20	H^+	350

	Anion	$\lambda/\Omega^{-1}\ cm^2\ mol^{-1}$		Anion	$\lambda/\Omega^{-1}\ cm^2\ mol^{-1}$
21	IO_3^-	41	31	NO_3^-	71
22	$CH_3CO_2^-$	41 (ethanoic)	32	Cl^-	76
23	HCO_3^-	45	33	I^-	77
24	HSO_4^-	52	34	Br^-	78
25	HCO_2^-	55 (methanoic)	35	CN^-	82
26	F^-	55	36	CO_3^{2-}	119
27	BrO_3^-	56	37	$C_2O_4^{2-}$	148 (ethandioic)
28	MnO_4^-	61	38	SO_4^{2-}	160
29	ClO_3^-	65	39	OH^-	197
30	ClO_4^-	67	40	PO_4^{3-}	240

References: R1, R2, R69 (for both tables).

Equilibrium constants for acids and bases in aqueous solution

$K_a = [H^+][B^-]/[A]$, where $A \rightleftharpoons H^+ + B^-$, and K_a is the equilibrium constant.
$pK_a = -lg(K_a/mol\ dm^{-3})$ pH = pKa − log [acid]/[base]
Similarly for bases, K_b is the equilibrium constant.
Values relate to concentrations between 0.01 and 0.1 mol dm^{-3}.

Acid or ion	Equilibrium (all in aqueous solution)	K_a(298 K)/mol dm^{-3}	pK_a
Sulphuric	$H_2SO_4 \rightleftharpoons H^+ + HSO_4^-$	very large.	
Nitric	$HNO_3 \rightleftharpoons H^+ + NO_3^-$	40	−1.4
Chromic	$H_2CrO_4 \rightleftharpoons H^+ + HCrO_4^-$	10	-1.0^{U}
Trichloroethanoic	$CCl_3CO_2H \rightleftharpoons H^+ + CCl_3CO_2^-$	2.3×10^{-1}	0.7^{X}
Iodic	$HIO_3 \rightleftharpoons H^+ + IO_3^-$	1.7×10^{-1}	0.8
Dichloroethanoic	$CHCl_2CO_2H \rightleftharpoons H^+ + CHCl_2CO_2^-$	5.0×10^{-2}	1.3^{X}
Sulphurous	$H_2SO_3 \rightleftharpoons H^+ + HSO_3^-$	$1.6 \times 10^{-2\dagger}$	1.8^{V}
Phosphorous	$H_3PO_3 \rightleftharpoons H^+ + H_2PO_3^-$	1.6×10^{-2}	1.8^{Y}
Chlorous	$HClO_2 \rightleftharpoons H^+ + ClO_2^-$	1.0×10^{-2}	2.0
Hydrogen sulphate[I]	$HSO_4^- \rightleftharpoons H^+ + SO_4^{2-}$	1.0×10^{-2}	2.0
Phosphoric	$H_3PO_4 \rightleftharpoons H^+ + H_2PO_4^-$	7.9×10^{-3}	2.1^{Z}
Iron(III)[I]	$Fe(H_2O)_6^{3+} \rightleftharpoons H^+ + Fe(H_2O)_5(OH)^{2+}$	6.0×10^{-3}	2.2
Chloroethanoic	$CH_2ClCO_2H \rightleftharpoons H^+ + CH_2ClCO_2^-$	1.3×10^{-3}	2.9^{X}
Hydrofluoric	$HF \rightleftharpoons H^+ + F^-$	5.6×10^{-4}	$3.3^{\dagger}$
Nitrous	$HNO_2 \rightleftharpoons H^+ + NO_2^-$	4.7×10^{-4}	3.3
Methanoic (formic)	$HCO_2H \rightleftharpoons H^+ + HCO_2^-$	1.6×10^{-4}	3.8
Benzoic	$C_6H_5CO_2H \rightleftharpoons H^+ + C_6H_5CO_2^-$	6.3×10^{-5}	4.2
Anilinium[I]	$C_6H_5NH_3^+ \rightleftharpoons H^+ + C_6H_5NH_2$	2.0×10^{-5}	4.6
Ethanoic (acetic)[D]	$CH_3CO_2H \rightleftharpoons H^+ + CH_3CO_2^-$	1.7×10^{-5}	4.8^{X}
Butanoic	$CH_3(CH_2)_2CO_2H \rightleftharpoons H^+ + CH_3(CH_2)_2CO_2^-$	1.5×10^{-5}	4.8
Propanoic (propionic)	$CH_3CH_2CO_2H \rightleftharpoons H^+ + CH_3CH_2CO_2^-$	1.3×10^{-5}	4.9
Aluminium[I]	$Al(H_2O)_6^{3+} \rightleftharpoons H^+ + Al(H_2O)_5(OH)^{2+}$	1.0×10^{-5}	5.0
Dihydrogen phosphite[I]	$H_2PO_3^- \rightleftharpoons H^+ + HPO_3^-$	6.3×10^{-7}	6.2^{Y}
Carbonic	$H_2O + CO_2^{A} \rightleftharpoons H^+ + HCO_3^-$	4.5×10^{-7}	6.4^{T}
Hydrogen chromate[I]	$HCrO_4^- \rightleftharpoons H^+ + CrO_4^{2-}$	3.2×10^{-7}	6.5^{U}
Hydrogen sulphide	$H_2S \rightleftharpoons H^+ + HS^-$	8.9×10^{-8}	7.1^{S}
Hydrogen sulphite[I]	$HSO_3^- \rightleftharpoons H^+ + SO_3^{2-}$	6.2×10^{-8}	7.2^{V}
Dihydrogen phosphate[I]	$H_2PO_4^- \rightleftharpoons H^+ + HPO_4^{2-}$	6.2×10^{-8}	7.2^{Z}
Hypochlorous	$HClO \rightleftharpoons H^+ + ClO^-$	3.7×10^{-8}	7.4
Hypobromous	$HBrO \rightleftharpoons H^+ + BrO^-$	2.1×10^{-9}	8.7
Boric	$H_3BO_3 \rightleftharpoons H^+ + H_2BO_3^-$	5.8×10^{-10}	9.2
Ammonium[I]	$NH_4^+ \rightleftharpoons H^+ + NH_3$	5.6×10^{-10}	9.3
Hydrocyanic	$HCN \rightleftharpoons H^+ + CN^-$	4.9×10^{-10}	9.3
Silicic	$H_2SiO_3 \rightleftharpoons H^+ + HSiO_3^-$	1.3×10^{-10}	9.9
Hydrogen carbonate[I]	$HCO_3^- \rightleftharpoons H^+ + CO_3^{2-}$	4.8×10^{-11}	10.3^{T}
Hydrogen peroxide	$H_2O_2 \rightleftharpoons H^+ + HO_2^-$	2.4×10^{-12}	11.6
Hydrogen silicate[I]	$HSiO_3^- \rightleftharpoons H^+ + SiO_3^{2-}$	$1.3 \times 10^{-12\dagger}$	11.9
Hydrogen phosphate[I]	$HPO_4^{2-} \rightleftharpoons H^+ + PO_4^{3-}$	4.4×10^{-13}	12.4^{Z}
Hydrogen sulphide[I]	$HS^- \rightleftharpoons H^+ + S^{2-}$	$1.2 \times 10^{-13\dagger}$	12.9^{S}
Water	$H_2O \rightleftharpoons H^+ + OH^-$	1.0×10^{-14B}	14.0

Notes
† Discrepancy between sources.
[A] Some dissolved CO_2 forms the unionized molecule H_2CO_3 for which $K_a \approx 2 \times 10^{-4}$ mol dm^{-3} and $pK_a \approx 3.7$
[B] This is $K_w/mol^2\ dm^{-6} = [H^+][OH^-]/mol^2\ dm^{-6}$. Value is exact at 297 K. See page 111 **CHM**.
[D] See also page 111 **CHM**. [STUVWXYZ] Compare values with the same letter.
[I] **ION**

Base	Equilibrium (all in aqueous solution)	K_b(298 K)/mol dm^{-3}	pK_b
Lead hydroxide	$Pb(OH)_2 \rightleftharpoons PbOH^+ + OH^-$	9.6×10^{-4}	3.0
Zinc hydroxide	$Zn(OH)_2 \rightleftharpoons ZnOH^+ + OH^-$	9.6×10^{-4}	3.0
Silver hydroxide	$AgOH \rightleftharpoons Ag^+ + OH^-$	1.1×10^{-4}	4.0
Ammonium hydroxide	$NH_3(aq) + H_2O(l) \rightleftharpoons NH_4^+(aq) + OH^-(aq)$	1.8×10^{-5}	4.8
Hydrazine	$N_2H_4 + H_2O \rightleftharpoons N_2H_5^+ + OH^-$	$1.2 \times 10^{-7\dagger}$	6.1
Hydroxylamine	$NH_2OH + H_2O \rightleftharpoons NH_3OH^+ + OH^-$	$6.6 \times 10^{-9\dagger}$	8.2
Beryllium hydroxide	$Be(OH)_2 \rightleftharpoons Be^{2+} + 2OH^-$	5.0×10^{-11}	10.3

Indicators: Buffer solutions

		$pK_{indicator}$	pH range		
			acid		*alkaline*
1	Methyl violet	0.8	yellow	0.0–1.6	blue
2	Malachite green	1.0	yellow	0.2–1.8	blue/green
3	Thymol blue (acid)	1.7	red	1.2–2.8	yellow
4	Methyl yellow (in ethanol)	3.5	red	2.9–4.0	yellow
5	Methyl orange–xylene cyanole soln.	3.7	purple	3.2–4.2	green
6	Bromophenol blue	4.0	yellow	2.8–4.6	blue
7	Congo red	4.0	violet	3.0–5.0	red
8	Bromocresol green	4.7	yellow	3.8–5.4	blue
9	Methyl red	5.1	red	4.2–6.3	yellow
10	Azolitmin (litmus)		red	5.0–8.0	blue
11	Bromocresol purple	6.3	yellow	5.2–6.8	purple
12	Bromothymol blue	7.0	yellow	6.0–7.6	blue
13	Phenol red	7.9	yellow	6.8–8.4	red
14	Thymol blue (base)	8.9	yellow	8.0–9.6	blue
15	Phenolphthalein (in ethanol)	9.3†	colourless	8.2–10.0	red
16	Thymolphthalein	9.7	colourless	8.3–10.6	blue
17	Alizarin yellow R	12.5	yellow	10.1–13.0†	orange/red

Note
Most indicators are 0.1 % solutions in H_2O unless stated otherwise.
Warning
Certain indicators are poisonous and should be handled carefully, particularly when concentrated.

Buffer solutions

The following mixtures give the indicated pH at 298 K.

pH	*x*	Composition of solutions
1.0	67.0	25 cm^3 of 0.2 mol dm^{-3} KCl + *x* cm^3 of 0.2 mol dm^{-3} HCl
1.5	20.7	
2.0	6.5	
2.5	38.8	50 cm^3 of 0.1 mol dm^{-3} potassium hydrogen phthalate + *x* cm^3 of 0.1 mol dm^{-3} HCl
3.0	22.3	
3.5	8.2	
4.0	0.1	
4.5	8.7	50 cm^3 of 0.1 mol dm^{-3} potassium hydrogen phthalate + *x* cm^3 of 0.1 mol dm^{-3} NaOH
5.0	22.6	
5.5	36.6	
6.0	5.6	50 cm^3 of 0.1 mol dm^{-3} potassium dihydrogen phosphate + *x* cm^3 of 0.1 mol dm^{-3} NaOH
6.5	13.9	
7.0	29.1	
7.5	40.9	
8.0	46.1	
8.5	15.2	50 cm of 0.025 mol dm^{-3} borax + *x* cm^3 of 0.1 mol dm^{-3} HCl
9.0	4.6	
9.5	8.8	50 cm^3 of 0.025 mol dm^{-3} borax + *x* cm^3 of 0.1 mol dm^{-3} NaOH
10.0	18.3	
10.5	22.7	
11.0	4.1	50 cm^3 of 0.05 mol dm^{-3} disodium hydrogen phosphate + *x* cm^3 of 0.1 mol dm^{-3} NaOH
11.5	11.1	
12.0	26.9	
12.5	20.4	25 cm^3 of 0.2 mol dm^{-3} KCl + *x* cm^3 of 0.2 mol dm^{-3} NaOH
13.0	66.0	

References: R2 (for both pages).

Equilibrium constants for some gaseous reactions

T temperature
ΔH molar enthalpy change (for reaction)
ΔG Gibbs free energy change (for reaction)
K_p equilibrium constant (from partial pressures)
$K^{\ominus}$ see reaction (it may be non-dimensional)

T/K	10^3 K/T	$K_p/K^{\ominus}$	lg $K_p/K^{\ominus}$	ΔH/kJ mol^{-1}	ΔG/kJ mol^{-1}
Reaction $N_2O_4(g) \rightleftharpoons 2NO_2(g)$ $K^{\ominus}$ = atm					
298	3.36	1.15×10^{-1}	−0.94	58.0	5.4
350	2.86	3.89	+0.59	57.9	−3.9
400	2.50	4.79×10^{1}	+1.68	57.7	−12.9
450	2.22	3.47×10^{2}	+2.54	57.6	−21.9
500	2.00	1.70×10^{3}	+3.23	57.4	−30.9
550	1.82	6.03×10^{3}	+3.78	57.2	−39.9
600	1.67	1.78×10^{4}	+4.25	57.1	−48.8
Reaction $N_2(g) + 3H_2(g) \rightleftharpoons 2NH_3(g)$ $K^{\ominus}$ = atm^{-2}					
298	3.36	6.76×10^{5}	+5.83	−92.4	−33.3
400	2.50	4.07×10^{1}	+1.61	−96.9	−12.3
500	2.00	3.55×10^{-2}	−1.45	−101.3	13.9
600	1.67	1.66×10^{-3}	−2.78	−105.8	31.9
700	1.43	7.76×10^{-5}	−4.11	−110.2	55.1
800	1.25	6.92×10^{-6}	−5.16	−114.6	79.1
900	1.11	1.00×10^{-6}	−6.00	−119.0	103.3
1100	0.91	5.0×10^{-8}	−7.70		
Reaction $H_2(g) + CO_2(g) \rightleftharpoons H_2O(g) + CO(g)$ $K^{\ominus}$ = 1					
298	3.36	1.00×10^{-5}	−5.00	41.2	28.5
500	2.00	7.76×10^{-3}	−2.11	40.5	20.2
700	1.43	1.23×10^{-1}	−0.91	39.9	12.2
800	1.25	2.88×10^{-1}	−0.54	39.5	8.2
900	1.11	6.03×10^{-1}	−0.22	39.1	4.2
1000	1.00	9.55×10^{-1}	−0.02	38.8	0.3
1100	0.91	1.45	+0.16	38.5	−3.47
1200	0.83	2.10	+0.32	38.1	−7.36
1300	0.77	2.82	+0.45	37.8	−11.1
Reaction $2SO_2(g) + O_2(g) \rightleftharpoons 2SO_3(g)$ $K^{\ominus}$ = atm^{-1}					
298	3.36	4.0×10^{24}	+24.60	−19.7	
500	2.00	2.5×10^{10}	+10.40		
700	1.43	3.0×10^{4}	+4.48		
1100	0.91	1.3×10^{-1}	−0.89		
Reaction $H_2(g) + I_2(g) \rightleftharpoons 2HI(g)$ $K^{\ominus}$ = 1					
298	3.36	794	+2.9	−9.6	
500	2.00	160	+2.2		
700	1.43	54	+1.7		
764	1.31	46 (experimental value)			
1100	0.91	25	+1.4		

T/K	10^3 K/T	$K_p/K^\ominus$	lg $K_p/K^\ominus$	ΔH/kJ mol^{-1}	ΔG/kJ mol^{-1}
Reaction $H_2O(g) + C(s) \rightleftharpoons H_2(g) + CO(g)$ $K^\ominus$ = atm					
298	3.36	1.00×10^{-16}	−16.0	131.3	91.3
500	2.00	2.52×10^{-7}	−6.60	134.4	63.3
700	1.43	2.82×10^{-3}	−2.55	137.6	34.2
800	1.25	5.37×10^{-2}	−1.27	139.1	19.5
900	1.11	5.75×10^{-1}	−0.24	140.7	4.18
1000	1.00	3.72	+0.57	142.3	−11.0
1100	0.91	1.70×10^{1}	+1.23	143.8	−26.0
1200	0.83	6.60×10^{1}	+1.82	145.4	−41.8
1300	0.77	2.04×10^{2}	+2.31	146.9	−57.6
Reaction $Ag_2CO_3(s) \rightleftharpoons Ag_2O(s) + CO_2(g)$ $K^\ominus$ = atm					
298	3.36	3.16×10^{-6}	−5.5	81.6	31.4
350	2.86	3.98×10^{-4}	−3.4	81.2	23.0
400	2.50	1.41×10^{-2}	−1.85	80.3	14.2
450	2.22	1.86×10^{-1}	−0.73	79.9	6.3
500	2.00	1.48	+0.17	79.5	−1.7
550	1.82	8.91	+0.95	78.7	−10.0
600	1.67	63.1	+1.8	78.2	−20.5
Reaction $CaCO_3(s) \rightleftharpoons CaO(s) + CO_2(g)$ $K^\ominus$ = atm					
298	3.36	1.6×10^{-23}	−22.8	177.8	130.1
500	2.00	6.3×10^{-11}	−10.2	177.4	97.5
700	1.43	1.3×10^{-5}	−4.9	177.0	65.3
800	1.25	5.0×10^{-4}	−3.3	177.0	49.8
900	1.11	1.0×10^{-2}	−2.0	177.0	33.9
1000	1.00	1.3×10^{-1}	−0.9	176.6	18.0
1100	0.91	7.9×10^{-1}	−0.1	176.6	2.1
1200	0.83	4.0	+0.6	176.1	−13.8
1300	0.77	15.9	+1.2	176.1	−29.7
Reaction $N_2(g) + O_2(g) \rightleftharpoons 2NO(g)$ $K^\ominus$ = 1					
293	3.36	4×10^{-31}	−30.4	180	
700	1.43	5×10^{-13}	−12.3		
1100	0.91	4×10^{-8}	−7.4		
1500	0.67	1×10^{-5}	−5.0		

Vapour pressures of selected liquids and gases

This table gives values of T/K where T is the temperature at which the vapour pressure of the liquid, p, reaches the indicated value.

p/mmHg	**1**	**10**	**40**	**100**	**400**	**760**						
p/atm						**1**	**2**	**5**	**10**	**20**	**40**	**60**
Ammonia	164.1[s]	181.3[s]	194.0[s]	204.8	227.8	239.6	254.5	277.9	298.9	323.3	352.1	371.5
Hydrogen	9.9[s]	11.9[s]	13.6[s]	15.3	18.7	20.7	23.0	27.2	31.4			
Oxygen	54.1[s]	62.6	69.1	74.4	84.4	90.3	97.2	108.7	120.0	133.2	149.1	
CCl_2F_2	154.7	175.4	191.6	204.6	229.3	243.4	261.0	289.3	315.6	347.2	273.2	
$CHCl_2F$	181.9	205.7	224.4	239.3	267.0	282.1	301.6	332.2	360.2	394.4	435.8	
CCl_4	223.2[s]	253.6	277.5	296.2	331.0	349.9	375.2	414.9	451.2	495.2	549.2	
CO_2	138.9[s]	153.7[s]	164.6[s]	173.0[s]	187.5[s]	195.0[s]	204.1[s]	216.5	233.7	254.3	279.1	295.6
CS_2	199.4	228.5	250.7	268.1	301.2	319.7	342.3	378.0	409.5	448.7	496.0	529.2
Ethanol	241.9	270.9	292.2	308.1	336.7	351.6	370.7	399.2	425.0	456.2	491.2	515.2
Methanol	229.2	257.0	278.2	294.4	323.1	337.9	357.2	385.7	411.2	441.0	476.7	497.2
Benzene	236.5[s]	261.7[s]	280.8	299.3	333.8	353.3	377.0	415.7	452.0	494.7	545.5	
Methane	67.3[s]	77.7[s]	85.5[s]	91.8	104.4	111.7	120.9	134.9	148.4	164.7	186.9	
Ethane	113.7	130.3	143.4	153.9	173.5	184.6	198.2	220.4	241.2	266.8	296.8	
Propane	144.3	164.7	180.8	193.6	217.6	231.1	247.6	274.6	300.1	331.3	368.0	
Butane	171.7	195.4	214.1	229.0	256.9	272.7	292.0	323.2	352.7	389.2		
Pentane	196.6	223.1	244.0	260.6	291.7	309.3	331.2	365.6	397.9	437.5		
Hexane	219.3	248.2	270.9	431.2	322.8	341.9	366.2	404.9	439.8	482.6		
Heptane	239.2	271.1	295.5	315.0	351.2	371.6	398.0	438.9	476.0	520.7		
Octane	259.2	292.4	318.3	338.9	377.2	398.8	425.9	469.4	509.0	454.6		
Nonane	274.6	311.2	339.2	361.3	401.4	424.0						
Decane	289.7	328.9	358.7	381.8	423.8	447.3						
Hendecane	305.9	347.1	377.6	401.3	445.1	469.0						
Dodecane	321.0	363.2	394.9	419.4	464.2	489.4	522.4	573.2	619.0			
Ethoxyethane	198.9	225.1	245.5	261.7	291.1	307.8	329.2	363.2	395.2	432.2		

[s] solid.

References: R2, R4 (4–217).

Vapour pressure of ice, water, and mercury as a function of temperature

t temperature *p* saturation vapour pressure

Note changes of multiplying factor.

Ice

t/°C	p/Pa	t/°C	p/Pa	t/°C	p/Pa	t/°C	p/Pa	t/°C	p/Pa
−90	0.01	−70	0.26	−50	3.94	−30	38.10	−10	260
−80	0.05	−60	1.08	−40	12.90	−20	103	0	610

Water

t/°C	$p/10^2$ Pa	t/°C	$p/10^4$ Pa	t/°C	$p/10^5$ Pa	t/°C	$p/10^6$ Pa	t/°C	$p/10^6$ Pa
−15	1.91	75	3.85	115	1.69	205	1.72	295	8.00
−10	2.87	80	4.73	120	1.99	210	1.91	300	8.59
−5	4.22	85	5.78	125	2.32	215	2.11	305	9.21
0	6.10	90	7.01	130	2.70	220	2.32	310	9.87
5	8.72	91	7.28	135	3.13	225	2.55	315	10.56
10	12.3	92	7.56	140	3.61	230	2.80	320	11.29
15	17.0	93	7.85	145	4.16	235	3.06	325	12.06
20	23.4	94	8.14	150	4.76	240	3.35	330	12.87
25	31.7	95	8.45	155	5.43	245	3.65	335	13.72
30	42.4	96	8.77	160	6.18	250	3.98	340	14.61
35	56.2	97	9.09	165	7.00	255	4.32	345	15.55
40	73.8	98	9.43	170	7.92	260	4.69	350	16.53
45	95.8	99	9.79	175	8.92	265	5.08	355	17.56
50	123	100	10.13	180	10.03	270	5.50	360	18.65
55	157	101	10.50	185	11.23	275	5.94	365	19.80
60	199	102	10.88	190	12.55	280	6.41	370	21.02
65	250	105	12.08	195	13.98	285	6.91	374	22.06
70	312	110	14.33	200	15.54	290	7.44	374.15[c]	22.12

Mercury

t/°C	$p/10^{-2}$ Pa	t/°C	p/Pa	t/°C	p/100 Pa	t/°C	$p/10^3$ Pa	t/°C	$p/10^5$ Pa
−300	0.06	70	6.44	170	8.17	270	16.47	370	1.28
−200	0.24	80	11.84	180	11.73	280	20.92	380	1.52
−100	0.81	90	21.09	190	16.56	290	26.34	390	1.79
0	2.47	100	36.38	200	23.05	300	32.90	400	2.10
10	6.53	110	60.95	210	31.62	310	40.78	461	5.00
20	16.01	120	99.42	220	42.84	320	50.17	518	10.00
30	37.02	130	138.12	230	57.31	330	61.30	585	20.00
40	81.05	140	246.0	240	75.81	340	74.39	630	30.00
50	168.9	150	374.3	250	99.17	350	89.69	680	45.00
70	336.5	160	538.5	260	128.40	360	107.50	753	75.00

[c] critical temperature. $V_c(H_2O) = 5.7 \times 10^{-5}\ m^3\ mol^{-1}$.

Note

Order of magnitude critical conditions for Hg may be calculated from van der Waals coefficients, giving $T_c = 1550$°C, $p_c = 1.05 \times 10^8$ Pa, $V_c = 1.7 \times 10^{-5}\ m^3\ mol^{-1}$.

References: R4 (4–274).

Stability constants for complexes of metal ions in aqueous solution

The equilibrium $ML_{n-1} + L \rightleftharpoons ML_n$, where M denotes a metal ion and L a ligand, has stepwise stability constants:

$$K_n = [ML_n]/[ML_{n-1}][L]$$

For example, $Cu(H_2O)_3Cl^+(aq) + Cl^-(aq) \rightleftharpoons Cu(H_2O)_2Cl_2(aq) + H_2O$ has the stability constant:

$$K_2 = [Cu(H_2O)_2Cl_2]/[Cu(H_2O)_3Cl^+][Cl^-], \text{ where } \lg K_2 = 1.6.$$

If a total of p ligand ions (or molecules) can form a complex, the overall stability constant is:

$$K_{(p)} = K_1 K_2 \ldots K_p = [ML_p]/[M][L]^p$$

Values of K_n and $K_{(p)}$ are very sensitive to temperature and to the concentration of other ions present. Values given here are for infinite dilution in pure water and may have been calculated from a formula rather than measured.

Ion	Ligand	lg K_1	lg K_2	lg K_3	lg K_4	lg K_5	lg $K_{(p)}(T)$	p	T/K
$Cu(H_2O)_4^{2+}$	Cl^-	2.80	1.60	0.49	0.73	—	5.62	4	291
	$NH_3(aq)$	4.25	3.61	2.98	2.24	−0.52	13.08	4	291
	$C_7H_5O_3^-$ A	10.6	6.3	—	—	—	16.9	2	
	$C_6H_6O_2$ B	17.0	8.0	—	—	—	25.0	2	
Fe^{3+}	SCN^-	2.95	1.94	1.4	0.8	0.02	7.1	5	298
	F^-	5.30	4.46	3.22	2.00	0.36	15.34	5	
Co^{2+}	$NH_3(aq)$	1.99	1.51	0.93	0.64	0.06	4.39	6	303
Ni^{2+}	$NH_3(aq)$	2.67	2.12	1.61	1.07	0.63	8.01	6	303
Ag^+	$NH_3(aq)$	3.32	3.92	—	—	—	7.23	2	298
Zn^{2+}	$NH_3(aq)$	2.18	2.25	2.31	1.96	—	8.70	4	303
Cd^{2+}	$NH_3(aq)$	2.51	1.96	1.30	0.79	—	6.65	4	303
	CN^-	5.18	4.42	4.32	3.19	—	17.11	4	298
Hg^{2+}	$NH_3(aq)$ C	8.8	8.7	1.0	0.8	—	19.3	4	295
	CN^- D	18.00	16.70	3.83	2.98	—	41.52	4	293

Overall stability constants for metal ion EDTA[E] complexes at 293 K

Ion	lg K	Ion	lg K	Ion	lg K
Ag^+	7.3	Co^{3+}	36 in 0.1 KCl	Mn^{2+}	14.0
Al^{3+}	16.1	Cu^{2+}	18.8	Na^{2+}	1.7 in 0.1 KCl
Ba^{2+}	7.7	Fe^{2+}	14.3	Ni^{2+}	18.6
Ca^{2+}	10.6	Fe^{3+}	25.1	Pb^{2+}	18.0
Cd^{2+}	16.5	Hg^{2+}	21.8	Sr^{2+}	8.6
Co^{2+}	16.3	Mg^{2+}	8.7	Zn^{2+}	16.5

A 2-hydroxybenzoate
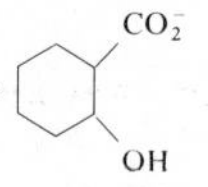

B 1,2-dihydroxybenzene
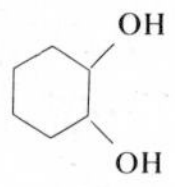

C in 2 mol dm^{-3} NH_4NO_3 solution.

D in 0.1 mol dm^{-3} $NaNO_3$ solution.

E ethylenediamine tetra-acetic acid.
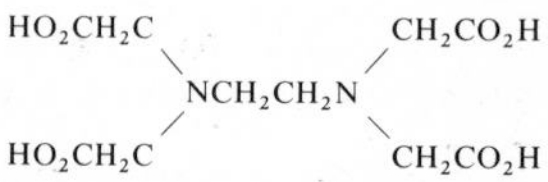

Reference: R69.

Lattice energies of ionic crystals

ΔH_1 experimental lattice energy of crystal, that is, enthalpy change when crystal is formed from gaseous ions in the standard state. Values of $-\Delta H_1(298\ K)/kJ\ mol^{-1}$ are given for the pairs of ions indicated. **All values of ΔH_1 are negative.**

	F^-	Cl^-	Br^-	I^-	O^{2-}	S^{2-}
Li^+	1029	849	804	753		
Na^+	915	781	743	699		
K^+	813	710	679	643		
Rb^+	779	685	656	624		
Ag^+	943	890	877	867		
Be^{2+}	3456	2983	2895	2803	4519	
Mg^{2+}	2883	2489	2414	2314	3933	3255
Ca^{2+}	2582	2197	2125	2038	3523	3021
Sr^{2+}	2427	2109	2046	1954	3310	2874
Ba^{2+}	2289	1958	1937	1841	3125	2745
Zn^{2+}		2686	2648	2594	4058	3565
Cd^{2+}	2770	2502	2481	2356	3812	3356
Hg^{2+}		2611	2611	2636	3933	3523
Pb^{2+}	2469	2234	2209	2079	3556	3063
Mn^{2+}		2464			3849	3519
Cu^{2+}		2761			4142	3724
Cs^+	735	641	626	594		
NH_4^+	733	676	644	607		

Some enthalpy changes on neutralization

ΔH_r enthalpy change on reaction

Reaction	$\Delta H_r(298\ K)/kJ\ mol^{-1}$
$HCl(aq) + NaOH(aq) \rightarrow NaCl(aq) + H_2O$	−57.9
$HBr(aq) + NaOH(aq) \rightarrow NaBr(aq) + H_2O$	−57.6
$HNO_3(aq) + NaOH(aq) \rightarrow NaNO_3(aq) + H_2O$	−57.6
$CH_3CO_2H(aq) + NaOH(aq) \rightarrow CH_3CO_2Na(aq) + H_2O$	−56.1
$HCl(aq) + NH_3(aq) \rightarrow NH_3Cl(aq) + H_2O$	−53.4
$H^+(aq) + NH_4OH \rightarrow NH_4^+(aq) + H_2O$	−51.5
$CH_3CO_2H(aq) + NH_3(aq) \rightarrow CH_3CO_2NH_3(aq) + H_2O$	−50.4
$H_2S(aq) + OH^- \rightarrow HS^-(aq) + H_2O$	−32.2
$\frac{1}{2}Cu^{2+}(aq) + OH^- \rightarrow \frac{1}{2}Cu(OH)_2(aq)$	−30.1
$\frac{1}{2}Mg^{2+}(aq) + OH^- \rightarrow \frac{1}{2}Mg(OH)_2(aq)$	−4.4

Variation of ionization constants and conductivity with temperature

κ electrolytic conductivity
K_a ionization constant for ethanoic acid
K_w ionization constant for water

T/K	273	283	293	298	303	313	233	373
$\kappa(water)/10^{-8}\ \Omega^{-1}\ cm^{-1}$	1.2	2.3	4.2	5.5	7.0	11.3	17	
$K_w/10^{-14}\ mol^2\ dm^{-2}$	0.11	0.29	0.68	1.01	1.47	2.92	5.6	51.3
$K_a(CH_3CO_2H)/10^{-5}\ mol\ dm^{-1}$	1.66	1.73	1.75	1.75	1.75	1.70	1.63	

Reference: R72 (for all three tables).

General introduction to properties of solid materials

Data on the properties of various materials follow. Two points should be noted.

1 The values given should be regarded as typical, rather than exact, because in most cases they depend on the composition of the sample, on its previous history, and possibly on humidity or other external factors. For some of the more variable properties, it is only possible to give a range of values.

2 It is not safe to draw conclusions from the figures given without making sure one understands the definition of the quantity measured. The figures given here may suggest why materials are useful for certain applications, but are too brief for serious design work. Only a very small sample of the more important materials is included.

Metals (See pages 113–117.) Very few metals are used in a pure form; see the footnotes on pages 114–115. Some properties vary appreciably over the useful working range of temperature: typical variations are given on page 116.

Strength and hardness may be improved by *alloying*, by *cold working* (that is, rolling, drawing, or otherwise deforming at room temperature) and by *tempering* (that is, suddenly cooling from a high temperature). Certain alloys may be hardened by sudden quenching from a high temperature, followed by reheating to a lower temperature to allow *precipitation* (or *age*) *hardening* to take place by the formation of precipitates within the metal. These processes also reduce ductility and may cause brittleness, so that usually a compromise must be achieved between strength and brittleness. The table on page 117 gives examples of the effects of these processes, which do not normally affect elastic properties or density appreciably.

When two values of σ and ε are given, the first relates to the softest annealed condition obtainable and the second to the hardest fine-grain or cold-worked condition.

Structural materials (See page 118.) Many of these are of natural origin and/or of composite nature, so the variability is particularly noticeable. The theoretical strength must be divided by quite a substantial safety factor to allow for the effects of variability, shape, and joint holes. Strength may vary considerably with the orientation of the stress. The effects of moisture and fire are of great concern to the engineer.

Plastic materials (See page 119). The properties of commerical samples of these depend very markedly on the fillers which are used. These may be introduced to achieve a desired property or simply to save expensive material. Properties may also depend on the method of manufacture. In some cases the property of the material is far more characteristic of the filler than of the plastic, for example, fibre-glass and carbon fibre materials. In these, the function of the plastic is to stick the fibres together and transmit the stresses uniformly among them.

Glasses (See page 120.) Most glasses consist predominantly of silica, SiO_2, with admixtures of other oxides which reduce the temperature required for working and impart other desirable properties, at the expense of increasing the thermal expansivity and hence the liability to crack under thermal shock.

The compositions given are typical percentages by mass and the exact values vary from batch to batch.

Ceramics (See page 120.) A very large number of ceramic materials are available, some based on metal oxides rather than on clays. The four examples given are representative of the main classes of these materials. All ceramic materials are brittle and most ceramics are more or less porous.

Properties of ferromagnetic materials

μ_{ri} initial relative permeability
μ_{rm} maximum relative permeability
B_s $= B - \mu_0 H$, saturation magnetic flux density
H_c coercivity
B_r remanence
W hysteresis loss per cycle per unit volume for $B_{max} = 1$ T (or 0.5 T)
T_C Curie temperature
ρ electrical resistivity
$(BH)_{max}$ maximum energy product on hysteresis curve, figure of merit for the material
H value of magnetic field strength at which $(BH)_{max}$ occurrs

Soft magnetic materials

Material	μ_{ri} / 1000	μ_{rm} / 1000	B_s / T	H_c / A m^{-1}	B_r / T	W / J m^{-3}	T_C / K	ρ / 10^{-8} Ω m
Fe (single crystal)		1500	2.16	12		**30**$^{0.5\,T}$	1043	10
Fe (99% pure)	0.25	7	2.16	80	1.3	500	1043	11
Fe (1% C steel)			2.00	600				
Fe (cast annealed)			1.70	400		1000		
Fe (2% Si dynamo)	1.0	6	2.10	60		250	1003	35
Fe (3% Si grain oriented)	5.0	40	1.98	8		30	993	48
Ni (99% pure)	0.25	2	0.61	120	0.3		631	7
Co			1.76	950			1388	9
NiFeMo(79:16:5)[A]	100	1000	0.79	0.16	0.55	**0.8**$^{0.5\,T}$	673	60
NiFeMo(79:17:4)[B]	20	100	0.87	0.16	0.5	20	733	55
NiFe(45:55)[C]	2.5	2.5	1.60	24		120	673	45
NiFeCo(45:30:25)[D]	0.4	2.0	1.55	96		250	988	19
NiFeCu(30:59:11)[E]	0.06	0.065		240			573	70
CuMnAl(61:26:13)[F]	0.8		0.48	550			603	7
$MnZn(Fe_2O_4)_2$[G]	1.5	2.5	0.34	16	0.1	10	423	2×10^7
$NiZn(Fe_2O_4)_2$[G]	0.8	2.5	0.37	80	0.2	14	523	10^{11}

[A] supermalloy. [B] 4-79 permalloy. [C] 45 permalloy. [D] Perminvar (constant permeability alloy).
[E] 36 Isoperm (constant permeability alloy). [F] Heusler alloy. [G] Ferroxcube type ferrites.

Permanent magnetic materials

Material	Composition	B_r / T	H_c / kA m^{-1}	$(BH)_{max}$ / kJ m^{-3}	at H / kA m^{-1}
Carbon steel	Fe(1% C, ? Mn)	0.9	4.4	1.6	2.7
Cobalt steel	Fe(2% Co, 4% Cr, 0.9% C)	1.0	6.0	2.9	4.2
Alnico 1	FeNiAlCo(62:21:12:5)	0.65	43	11.0	25
Magnadur	$BaF_{12}O_{19}$ anisotropic	0.36	110	20	86
Ticonal C Hycomax II	FeCoNiAlTiCu(41.5:29:14:7:4.5:4)	0.85	95	32	59.5
Columax Ticonal GX	FeCoNiAlCu(51:24:14:8:3) (columnar grain orientation)	1.35	58	59.5	51
Cobalt platinum	PtCo(77:23)	0.65	360	72	206

Note
The properties of magnetic materials are greatly affected by impurities, heat treatment, and previous history of the specimen.
See page 15 CON for a definition of *H*.
References: R1, R4.

Physical and mechanical properties of pure metals

Values relate to commercially pure metals at room temperature and may vary between specimens. Different values will be found in other tables.

cs	crystal system (see page 58 **TCE**)	T_m	normal melting temperature
n	number of solid phases	Δh_S^L	specific enthalpy change (latent heat) on fusion
r	nearest neighbour distance		
ρ_m	density	c_p	specific heat capacity. $c_p^{\ominus} = 0.1\ J\ g^{-1}\ K^{-1}$
α	thermal expansivity	λ	thermal conductivity

	Metal	cs	n	r / nm	ρ_m / $g\ cm^{-3}$	α / $10^{-6}\ K^{-1}$	T_m / K	Δh_S^L / $J\ g^{-1}$	c_p / $c_p^{\ominus}$	λ[A] / $W\ cm^{-1}\ K^{-1}$
1	Aluminium[B]	FCC	1	0.29	2.70	23.0	932	412	8.78	2.38
2	Antimony	RBL	3	0.29	6.68	11.0	903	163	2.13	0.18
3	Bismuth	TRG	1	0.31	9.75	13.5	545	54	1.27	0.09
4	Cadmium	HCP	1	0.30	8.65	31.5	594	54	2.29	1.00
5	Chromium	BCC	2	0.25	7.19	7.0	2176	280	4.64	0.87
6	Cobalt	FCC	3	0.25	8.90	13.7	1768	280	4.31	1.00
7	Copper[C]	FCC	1	0.26	8.94	16.7	1356	205	3.81	3.85
8	Gold	FCC	1	0.29	19.32	14.0	1336	628	1.27	3.10
9	Iridium	FCC	1	0.27	22.42	6.5	2727	138	1.35	1.48
10	Iron	BCC	4	0.25	7.86	11.7	1812	269	4.38	0.80
11	Lanthanum	HCP	4	0.38	6.19	5.0	1193	113	2.00	
12	Lead[D]	FCC	1	0.35	11.35	28.9	601	25	1.26	0.38
13	Magnesium	HCP	1	0.32	1.74	25.0	923	377	9.80	1.50
14	Manganese	CUB	4	0.89[I]	7.42	22.8	1517	262	5.11	
15	Molybdenum	BCC	1	0.27	10.22	5.0	2890		3.01	1.43
16	Nickel	FCC	2	0.25	8.90	12.8	1728	305	0.44	0.91
17	Niobium	BCC	1	0.29	8.55	7.1	2770	288	2.65	0.52
18	Platinum[E]	FCC	1	0.28	21.45	8.9	2043	113	1.36	0.73
19	Rhodium	FCC	2	0.27	12.41	8.4	2239	212	2.43	1.52
20	Silver[F]	FCC	1	0.29	10.50	19.2	1234	105	1.05	4.18
21	Sodium	BCC	1	0.37	0.97	69.6	371	113	1.22	1.35
22	Tantalum	BCC	1	0.29	16.60	6.5	3270	173	1.51	0.58
23	Tin	TET	3	0.32	7.31	21.2	505	57	2.24	0.64
24	Titanium	HCP	2	0.30	4.54	8.5	1950	322	4.73	0.20
25	Tungsten[G]	BCC	1	0.27	19.35	4.5	3650	184	1.42	1.91
26	Uranium	BCC	3	0.28	18.95	13.5	1406	650	1.17	0.28
27	Zinc[H]	HCP	1	0.27	7.13	29.7	693	100	3.84	1.13
28	Zirconium	HCP	2	0.32	6.53	5.4	2125	183	2.76	0.22

[A] these quantities vary with alloying additions and with previous treatment.
[B] used pure for electrical conductors, air conditioning plant, and garden furniture.
[C] used pure for electrical conductors, water pipes, and cylinders.
[D] used pure for electrical storage batteries and cable sheaths.
[E] used pure for electrical contacts and thermometry.
[F] used pure for electrical contacts and decorative plating.
[G] used pure for electric lamp filaments.
[H] used pure for dry cells and anti-corrosion plating.
[I] lattice constant.

ρ_e electrical resistivity
ρ_e' $= d\rho/\rho\, dT$. Temperature coefficient of ρ_e
E Young modulus
K bulk modulus
G shear modulus
ν Poisson ratio
σ_u ultimate tensile strength
ε elongation at fracture
BHN Brinel hardness number

		ρ_e[A] / $10^{-8}\,\Omega\,m$	ρ_e'[A] / $10^{-3}\,K^{-1}$	E / 10^{10} Pa	K / 10^{10} Pa	G / 10^{10} Pa	ν	σ_u[AD] / 10^7 Pa	ε[AE] / %	BHN[A]
1	Al	2.45	4.5	7.0[B]	7.6	2.6[C]	0.34	5 to 11.4	60 to 5	20 to 27
2	Sb	39.0	5.1	7.8			0.33	1		30
3	Bi	107.0	4.6	3.2	3.2	1.2	0.30			7
4	Cd	6.8	4.2	5.0	4.2	1.9	0.21	7	50	21
5	Cr	12.7	3.0	27.9	16.0	11.5		8		70
6	Co	5.6	6.6	20.6			0.34	23 to 91		120
7	Cu	1.56	4.3	13.0[B]	13.8	4.8[C]	0.44	22 to 43	50 to 5	45 to 100
8	Au	2.04	4.0	7.8[B]	21.7	2.7[C]	0.42	12 to 22	30 to 4	33 to 58
9	Ir	4.7	4.5	51.5			0.44	22	7	170
10	Fe	8.9	6.5	21.1[B]	17.0	8.2[C]	0.29	21	50	
11	La	62.4	2.18	3.9		1.5	0.29	13	8	40
12	Pb	19.0	4.2	1.6	4.6	0.6		1.5	6	
13	Mg	3.9	4.3	4.5	3.6	1.7	0.31	9 to 22		30 to 47
14	Mn	136.0		15.7			0.39			
15	Mo	5.2	4.4	34.3				16.5		
16	Ni	6.1	6.8	20.0	17.7	7.6	0.37	34 to 99	50 to 8	90 to 210
17	Nb	15.2	2.6	10.5	17.0	3.8	0.38	26 to 69	49 to 1	80 to 160
18	Pt	9.8	3.9	16.6[B]	22.8	6.1	0.34	12		38
19	Rh	4.3	4.4	29.4			0.32	95 to 21		100
20	Ag	1.5	4.1	8.3[B]	10.4	3.0[C]		14 to 35	25 to 50	25
21	Na	4.8								
22	Ta	12.6	3.5	18.6	19.6	6.9	0.39	34 to 124	40 to 1	80 to 180
23	Sn	11.5	4.6	5.0	5.8	1.8[C]	0.33	1	60	5
24	Ti	43.1	3.8	11.6	10.8	4.4		23	54	
25	W	4.9	4.8	41.1	31.1	16.1		12	1	225
26	U	29.0		16.6		8.3	0.21	38.6	4	
27	Zn	5.5	4.2	10.8	7.2	4.3		13.9	50	
28	Zr	42.4	4.4	7.4				34 to 56	35 to 10	64 to 200

[A] these quantities vary with alloying additions and with previous treatment.
[B] temperature coefficients $\alpha_E/10^{-4}\,K^{-1}$: Al −4.8, Cu −3.7, Au −4.8, Fe −2.3, Pt −1.0, Ag −7.5.
[C] temperature coefficients $\alpha_G/10^{-4}\,K^{-1}$: Al −5.2, Cu −3.1, Au −3.3, Fe −2.8, Ag −4.5, Sn −5.9.
[D] σ_u is the maximum force before fracture divided by original cross-sectional area and is a measure of strength.
[E] ε is the permanent fractional extension occurring before fracture and is a measure of ductility.
References: R17, R53, R54, R55, R56.

Dependence on temperature of some properties of selected metals

Electrical resistivity $\sigma/10^{-8}\ \Omega$ m

Electrical resistivity, particularly at low temperatures, is sensitive to impurity concentration and cold working.

T/K	**20**	**40**	**80**	**160**	**273**	**373**	**573**	**973**	**1473**
Aluminium			0.3		2.45	3.55	5.9	24.7^{Liq}	32.1^{Liq}
Copper	0.0008	0.058	0.29	0.77	1.55	2.38	3.61	6.7	22.3
Iron	0.007	0.37	0.64	3.55	8.70	16.61[A]	31.5[A]	85.5[A]	122.0[A]
Lead	0.59		4.7		19.8	27.8	50	107.6^{Liq}	**126.3**[B]
Tungsten	0.005	0.066	0.60	2.33	4.82	7.3	12.4	24	39

[A] these figures relate to a different specimen from those at low temperatures. [B] liq 1273 K.

Thermal conductivity λ/kW m^{-1} K^{-1}

T/K	**4.2**	**20**	**76**	**194**	**273**	**373**	**573**	**973**
Aluminium	3200	5700	420	239	238	230	226	
Copper	12000	10500	660	410	400	380	380	350
Iron	77	300	180	89	82	69	55	34
Lead	2500	59	40	36	35	34	32	
Tungsten	2600	5400	260	178	170	160	150	120

Linear expansivity $\alpha/10^{-6}$ K^{-1}

T/K	**25**	**50**	**100**	**200**	**300**	**400**	**500**	**600**	**800**	**1200**
Aluminium	0.5	3.8	12.2	20.0	23.2	24.9	26.4	28.3	33.8	
Copper	0.6	3.8	10.5	15.1	16.8	17.7	18.3	18.9	20.0	23.4
Iron		1.6	5.6	10.0	11.7	12.9	14.3	15.5	16.6	21.4$^{\gamma\ \text{phase}}$
Lead	14.5	21.6	25.0	27.5	28.9	29.8	32.1			
Tungsten			2.7	4.1	4.5	4.6	4.6	4.7	4.8	5.1

Molar heat capacity C_p/J mol^{-1} K^{-1}

'Classical' value is $3R = 25$ J mol^{-1} K^{-1} at all temperatures, where R is the gas constant.

T/K	**10**	**20**	**30**	**50**	**100**	**200**	**400**	**800**	**1200**
Aluminium	0.04	0.21	0.84	3.80	13.1	21.5	25.7	30.6	29.3^{Liq}
Copper	0.054	0.46	1.71	6.22	16.1	22.7	25.1	27.6	30.1^{Liq}
Iron	0.084	0.25	0.75	3.05	12.0	21.5	27.4	38.6	34.2$^{\gamma\ \text{phase}}$
Lead	2.80	11.0	16.4	21.4	24.5	25.8	27.4	30.0	28.7^{Liq}
Tungsten	0.046	0.326	1.42	5.93	16.0	15.0	25.0	26.5	27.8

C_p (liq Fe, 2000 K) = 44 J mol^{-1} K^{-1}.

Ultimate tensile strength $\sigma_u/10^6$ Pa

T/K	**70**	**205**	**277**	**373**	**477**	**589**	**673**	**773**
Aluminium	220	100	90	75	42	17		
Copper	330	260	210	190	160		130	90

These values should be taken to indicate the order of magnitude of changes in σ_u only. Exact values are very sensitive to impurity (alloy constituents) and heat treatment or cold working.

References: R17, R53, R54, R55, R56.

Typical effects of cold working, heat treatment, and alloying on the mechanical properties of metals

R reduction in thickness by cold working
σ_y yield stress
σ_p 0.1% proof stress (this is a measure of σ_y)
σ_u ultimate tensile stress
ε elongation on fracture
T temperature of tempering
W mass fraction of alloying component

See page 112 for explanations and definitions.

Cold working of rolled copper strip annealed initially

$R/\%$	$\sigma_p/10^8$ Pa	$\sigma_u/10^8$ Pa	$\varepsilon/\%$
0	0.6	2.1	58
10	1.8	2.4	38
20	2.4	2.7	23
30	2.7	3.2	15
40	3.0	3.3	10
50	3.2	3.5	8
60	3.3	3.8	7
70	3.5	3.9	6
80	3.6	4.1	5

Tempering of plain carbon steel

This contains 0.45 per cent C and small additions of Si, Mn, S, and P. It is initially hardened by quenching. Tempering is carried out by maintaining at temperature T until no further change in properties is observed.

T/K	$\sigma_p/10^8$ Pa	$\sigma_u/10^8$ Pa	$\varepsilon/\%$
Initial condition	7.1	9.8	12
573	6.6	9.8	15
673	6.9	9.6	17
773	6.3	9.0	21
873	5.4	7.8	25
973	4.7	6.8	28

Iron–carbon alloy

Plain carbon steel containing small proportions of Si, Mn, S, and P.

W(C)/%	$\sigma_y/10^8$ Pa	$\sigma_u/10^8$ Pa	$\varepsilon/\%$
0.10	2.6	3.7	45
0.22	3.3	4.8	36
0.39	3.2	5.4	34
0.54	3.6	6.9	25
0.81	3.7	7.9	19
1.04	4.1	8.4	15

Copper–zinc alloy (brasses)

W(Cu)/%	W(Zn)/%	$\sigma_p/10^8$ Pa	$\sigma_u/10^8$ Pa	$\varepsilon/\%$
100	0	0.45	2.3	50
90	10	0.75	2.6	63
80	20	0.90	3.0	67
70	30	1.05	3.3	70
60	40	1.35	3.6	85

References: R17, R53, R54, R55, R56.

Properties of structural and building materials

ρ	density	f	safety factor for σ_{max} [A]
E	Young modulus	p_{max}	compressive strength
σ_{max}	tensile strength	T_{max}	shear strength
α	thermal expansivity	λ	thermal conductivity
ε	moisture expansivity (relative humidity 40% to 90%)	C	combustibility
		M.R.	moisture resistance; VG = very good, G = good, F = fair, P = poor

	Material	ρ / kg m^{-3}	E / GN m^{-2}	σ_{max} / MN m^{-2}	f	p_{max} / MN m^{-2}	T_{max} / MN m^{-2}	α / 10^{-6} K	ε / 10^{-3}	λ / W m^{-1} K^{-1}	C / °C	M.R.	
	Metals												
1	Mild steel	7700	200	250[Y]	1.5	250[Y]	250[Y]	12	—	60	400	G[H]	1
2	High tensile steel	7700	200	340[Y]	1.3	340[Y]	330[Y]	12	—	60	400		2
3	Unalloyed aluminium	2700	70	60 to 120[Y]	varies	60 to 120[Y]	60 to 70[Y]	24	—	200	200	VG[pure]	3
4	High strength Al alloy	2800	70	240 to 400[Y]	varies	240 to 400[Y]	160 to 280[Y]	24	—	100	200	G	4
	Timber (dry, 18% moisture)												
5	Douglas fir (imported)	600	16‖ 1⊥	18‖	1.3 to 2.5	15‖ 2.5⊥	1.9⊥	3‖[E] 35⊥	0.5‖ 4.0⊥	0.4‖ 0.11⊥	burns	F[H]	5
6	Oak	720	9[av] 5[min]	21‖	1.3 to 2.5	15‖ 4.4⊥	3.1⊥	3‖[E]	0.5‖ 4.0⊥	0.16⊥	burns	F[H]	6
7	Western red cedar	380	7[av] 4[min]	11‖	1.3 to 2.5	9‖ 1.5⊥	1.4⊥	3‖[E]	0.5‖ 4.0⊥	0.09⊥	burns	F[H]	7
8	Balsa	200	6‖ 0.2⊥	25‖	—	1.5‖	1.5⊥	0.2‖[E] 20⊥	15⊥[K]	0.2‖ 0.07⊥	burns		8
	Boards												
9	Douglas fir plywood	450 to 600	7 to 11	9[C] to 15[B]	[F]	6[C] to 10[B]	(2)	5 to 10[E]	0.7 to 3.4‖	0.12 to 0.19⊥	burns	F[H]	9
10	Birch plywood	600 to 700	4 to 10	8[C] to 16[B]	[F]	5[C] to 8[B]	(2)	5 to 10[E]	0.7 to 3.4‖	0.17 to 0.20⊥	burns	F[H]	10
11	Standard hardboard[D]	800 to 1000	4 to 6	25 to 55	6	10 to 15		[E]	1.0 to 3.5	0.07 to 0.10	burns	P	11
12	Chipboard[D]	450 to 1300	2 to 4	2 to 10		5 to 10		[E]	0.7 to 8.3	0.10 to 0.25	burns	P	12
13	Plasterboard	700 to 1300	—	2 to 5		—		[E]	0.1 to 0.7	0.15 to 0.20	weakens	P	13
14	Asbestos cement sheet[D]	1700 to 2000	18 to 20	20 to 35		20 to 30		[E]	0.2 to 0.8	0.25 to 0.35	shatters	G	14
15	Woodwool–cement[D]	400 to 800	—	0.3 to 2		—		[E]	—	0.05 to 0.10	weakens	G	15
	Bricks and blocks												
16	Engineering brick	1800 to 2000	20	depends	15 to 30[G]	50 to 100		6	0.05	1.00 to 1.50	does	VG	16
17	Common brick	1500 to 1800	7	on	12[G]	7 to 70		6	0.1	0.80 to 1.20	not	VG	17
18	Breeze block	1300 to 1500	20 to 40	joints	12[G]	4 to 6		12	0.3 to 0.7	0.35 to 0.45	burn	G	18
19	Aerated concrete block[D]	600 to 1200	15 to 30			4 to 8		12	0.3 to 0.7	0.08 to 0.40		G	19
	Concrete												
20	1:2:4 mix	2200 to 2400	40	cracks	3	20 to 35		12	0.2 to 0.6	1.40 to 1.50	stable	VG	20
21	High strength mix	2200 to 2400	40	unless	3	50 to 70		12	0.2 to 0.6	1.40 to 1.50	stable	VG	21
22	Lightweight concrete[D]	800 to 1200	15 to 40	reinforced	4	6 to 15		12	0.2 to 0.7	0.10 to 0.60	stable	G	22
	Plastics												
23	Glass reinforced polyester[J]	1500 to 2000	5 to 7	70 to 500	4 to 10	100 to 400		20 to 30	—		stable[I]	FG	23
24	Rigid	1250 to 2500	2 to 4	40 to 60		40 to 60		50 to 70	—		200	FG	24
25	Epoxide resin	1200 to 2500	1 to 5	30 to 80		100 to 200		40 to 60	—		250	G	25

‖ parallel to grain or to plies. ⊥ perpendicular to grain or to plies. [A] maximum safe stress is σ_{max}/f. [B] parallel to face grain. [C] perpendicular to face grain. [D] E, σ_{max}, λ, $1/\varepsilon$ increase with ρ (and binder content). [E] α is masked by ε. [F] depends on condition of timber. [G] includes strength of mortar. Depends on ratio of height to thickness (r). Figures given for $r = 1$. $f(12) = 2f(1)$, $f(21) = 4f(1)$.

[H] if suitably coated. [I] if special fire-resisting grade. [J] lower figures for randomly directed fibres. Larger figures for stress parallel to unidirectional fibres. [K] 10% to 20% moisture. [Y] yield strength.

References: supplied by C.I.R.I.A. from manufacturers' leaflets.

Properties of plastic materials

ρ	density	E	Young modulus	α	thermal expansivity	E_b	electrical breakdown field
n	refractive index	τ_f	flexural strength	λ	thermal conductivity	ε_r	relative permittivity
σ_u	ultimate tensile strength	p_{max}	compressive strength	t_{max}	maximum operating temperature	p	specific price (1969)
e	elongation at fracture	c_V	specific heat capacity	ρ_e	electrical resistivity		

		ρ / g cm^{-3}	n	σ_u / MPa m^{-2}	e / %	E / MPa m^{-2}	
1	Acrylic (e.g. Perspex)	1.17 to 1.20	1.49	55 to 70	2 to 10	2500 to 3500	**1**
2	Polychloroethane (PVC)	1.25[F] 1.39[R]	1.52	20[F] 60[R]	300[F] 2[R]	2400 to 2500	**2**
3	Polyethylene (polythene) low density	0.92	1.51	15	600	150	**3**
4	Polyethylene (polythene) high density	0.96		29	350	1000	**4**
5	Polyethenylbenzene (polystyrene)	1.05	1.6	40	2.5	35 000	**5**
6	Polyester (unsaturated) cast window filler	1.2	(clear)	35			**6**
7	Polyester laminate, 70% woven glass fibre	1.65	(opaque)	350			**7**
8	Polypropylene	0.9	1.49	35	100	900 to 1300	**8**
9	Polymethylpentene (TPX)	0.83	(clear)	28	15	1100	**9**
10	Polyphenylethanal fabric laminate (e.g. Tufnul)	1.27 to 1.55	(brown)	190		6700	**10**
11	Phenolic resin (Bakelite) woodflour filler	1.35 to 1.45	(brown)	50	0.6	6000 to 8000	**11**
12	Phenolic resin (Bakelite) asbestos filler	1.7 to 2.0	(black)	55	0.34	1000 to 14 000	**12**
13	Rubber (natural) soft vulcanized	0.93 to 1.17	(opaque)	32	850	1 (e = 25%)	**13**
14	Rubber (natural) carbon filler	2.5	(opaque)	35	650	10 (e = 500%)	**14**

	τ_f / MPa m^{-2}	p_{max} / MPa m^{-2}	c_V / J g^{-1} K^{-1}	α / 10^{-6} K^{-1}	λ / W m^{-1} K^{-1}	t_{max} / °C	ρ_e / Ω m	E_b / kV mm^{-1}	ε_r	p(1969) / £ kg^{-1}	
1	83 to 20	75130	1.5	90		340 to 380	10^{13}	14 to 16	3.3	0.4	**1**
2	93[R]	9[F] 55[R]	1 to 2[F] 0.9[R]	240[F] 50[R]		293[F] 255[R]	10^{14}	12 to 52	2.2	0.13	**2**
3			2.3			363	10^{14}	28	2.2	0.16	**3**
4						394	10^{14}	20	2.35	0.21	**4**
5	60	95	1.3	70		359	10^{11}	16	2.45	0.16	**5**
6	120	110	2.1	80	23	343	10^{14}	8	4.0	0.24	**6**
7	400	350		12	0.17	453	10^{13}	60	5.0	0.54	**7**
8					12					0.25	**8**
9			2.2	117	17	453	10^{14}	2.8		0.84[A]	**9**
10		480		$80^{\perp}$ $20^{\parallel}$		393				0.16	**10**
11	70	200	1.5	50	34	408	10^{14}	275	5		**11**
12	75	240	1.3	30	60	413	10^{14}	325	5 to 20		**12**
13		2000	2.1	220	15	250	10^{12}	0.25	2.5	0.24[B]	**13**
14			1.6	160	17		10^{11}		7.0		**14**

[A] likely to fall. [B] for unvulcanized rubber. Vulcanization is part of the fabrication process, so no typical price can be given for vulcanized material. [F] flexible PVC. [R] rigid PVC.

References: manufacturers' leaflets.

Properties of typical commercial glasses and ceramics

ρ	density	T_a	annealing temperature	v	apparent porosity		
n	refractive index	T_s	softening temperature	σ	modulus of rupture (bending test)		
V	constringence (reciprocal dispersive power)[N]	ρ_e	electrical resistivity	t_f	firing temperature		
α	thermal linear expansivity	ε_r	relative permittivity (293 K, 1 MHz)	λ	thermal conductivity		
E	Young modulus						

	Glass	Applications	ρ / g cm^{-3}	n (589 nm)	V	α / 10^{-6} K^{-1}	T_a / K	T_s / K	ρ_e / Ω m	ε_r	E / GPa	Composition
1	Vitreous silica	Tableware, immersion heaters	2.20	1.458		0.54	1413	1940	10^{12}	3.8	70	99.5 % SiO_2
2	Vycor	Tableware	2.18	1.458		0.8	1183	1773	5×10^9	3.8	68	96 % SiO_2, 3 % B_2O_3
3	Container	Jars and bottles	2.49	1.520		8.5	821	1003	10^7	7.6	70	73 % SiO_2, 15 % Na_2O[D]
4	Sheet	Windows, electric lamps	2.46	1.510		8.5	821	1003	3×10^6	7.0	70	73 % SiO_2, 13 % Na_2O[E]
5	Borosilicate	Laboratory and ovenware	2.23	1.474		3.2	838	1093	10^8	4.6	69	80 % SiO_2, 12 % B_2O_3
6	Alumino-silicate	Combustion tubes[A]	2.53	1.534		4.2	988	1188	3×10^{11}	6.3	89	57 % SiO_2, 21 % Al_2O_3[F]
7	High lead	Electrical components	4.28	1.693		9.1	703	853	6×10^{11}	9.5	53	35 % SiO_2, 58 % PbO[G]
8	Solder glass					8.9	613	718				16 % B_2O_3, 84 % PbO
9	Light Ba crown	Optical	2.90	1.541	59.4	8.2	843			6.90	73	57 % SiO_2, 27 % BaO[H]
10	Dense Ba crown	Optical	3.56	1.612	59.0	6.4	878			8.21	79	36 % SiO_2, 45 % BaO[I]
11	Light flint	Optical	3.26	1.578	40.8	8.0	758			6.57	60	53 % SiO_2, 38 % PbO[J]
12	Dense flint	Optical	3.55	1.613	36.9	8.6	733			7.42	56	48 % SiO_2, 45 % PbO[K]
13	Glass fibre[B]	Textiles	2.46	1.512		8.7	801	983	5×10^6	7.9	73	72 % SiO_2, 13 % Na_2O[L]
14	Glass fibre[C]	'fibreglass'	2.53	1.548		5.0	848	1103	$>10^{15}$	6.4	77	55 % SiO_2, 18 % CaO[M]

	Ceramic	ρ / g cm^{-3}	v / %	E / GPa	σ / MPa	α / 10^{-6} K^{-1}	λ / W m^{-1} K^{-1}	ρ_e / Ω m	t_f / °C
1	Earthenware	2.5	15 to 20	50	56	7	1.6		1400
2	Bone china	2.8	0 to 2	90	112	8	1.6		1500
3	Electrical porcelain	2.5	0	70	105	7	1.6	10^{10} to 10^{12}	1500
4	High alumina (90 % Al_2O_3)	3.7	0	250 to 380	280 to 380	7.5	12 to 26	10^9 to 10^{12}	1950

[A] also boiler sight glasses. [B] soda-lime. [C] E glass, weather resistant. [D] also 10 % CaO.
[E] also 9 % CaO, 3 % Mg. [F] also 6 % CaO. [G] also 7 % K_2O. [H] also 14 % K_2O.
[I] also 8 % B_2O_3. [J] also 10 % K_2O. [K] also 5 % Na_2O. [L] also 9 % CaO. [M] also 15 % Al_2O_3.

[N] $V = (n_d - 1)/(n_F - n_c)$, where d is He d-line (588 nm); F, H F-line (486 nm) and C, H C-line (656 nm). (These are standard optical wavelengths.)

References: Glass Research Institute and British Ceramics R.A., manufacturers' leaflets.

Electrical conductors and resistors

Copper wire

D_b diameter of bare conductor. Preferred sizes in bold.
D_i diameter of conductor plus grade I (350 V breakdown) enamel insulation (II denotes grade II insulation)
R resistance per unit length
ε minimum elongation on fracture
s.w.g. near equivalent standard wire gauge (now obsolete)
D_s diameter of quoted s.w.g. (given to illustrate the basis of s.w.g.)

D_b / mm	D_i / mm	R (293 K)[1] / $\Omega\ m^{-1}$	ε / %	s.w.g.	D_s / in
0.016	0.020	85.75	—	—	—
0.020	0.025	54.88	—	50	0.0010
0.025	0.031	35.12	—	49	0.0012
0.032	0.040	21.44	—	—	
0.040	0.050	13.72	—	48	0.0016
0.050	0.062	8.781	10	47	0.0020
0.063	0.078	5.531	12	46	0.0024
0.080	0.098	3.430	14	44	0.0032
0.100	0.129^{II}	2.195	16	42	0.0040
0.125	0.149	1.405	17	38	0.0048
0.160	0.187	0.8575	19	37	0.0068
0.200	0.230	0.5488	21	36	0.0076
0.250	0.284	0.3512	22	33	0.0100

D_b / mm	D_i / mm	R (293 K)[1,2] / $10^{-2}\ \Omega\ m^{-1}$	ε / %	s.w.g.	D_s / in
0.315	0.352	22.12	23	30[3]	0.0124
0.400	0.442	13.72	24	27	0.0164
0.500	0.548	8.781	25	25	0.020
0.630	0.684	5.531	27	23	0.024
0.800	0.861	3.430	28	21	0.032
1.000	1.068	2.195	30	19	0.040
1.250	1.325	1.405	31	18	0.048
1.600	1.683	0.858	32	16	0.064
2.000	2.092	0.549	33	14	0.080
2.500	2.631^{II}	0.351	33	12	0.140
3.150	3.294^{II}	0.221	34	10	0.128
4.00	4.160^{II}	0.137	35	8	0.160
5.00	5.177^{II}	0.088	36	6	0.192

[1] tolerance ±10% on fine wires to ±3% on thick wires. [2] note change of scale. [3] exact equivalence of metric and s.w.g. sizes.

International colour code for 3-core flex

brown: **live** blue: **neutral** yellow/green: **earth**

(Old British standard red: live black: neutral green (sometimes brown): earth)

International code for resistors

1st letter (shows position of decimal point): R ohms K kilohms M megohms
2nd letter (shows tolerance): F ±1% G ±2% J ±5% K ±10% M ±20%

Thus: 1ROM denotes 1.0 Ω ± 20% 100K0K denotes 100 kΩ ± 10% 6K8G denotes 6.8 kΩ ± 2%
4R7J denotes 4.7 Ω ± 5% 4M7F 4.7 MΩ ± 1%

Preferred values for resistors

Bold type: available in ±5%, ±10% and ±20% tolerance ranges
Normal type: available in ±5%, and ±10% tolerance ranges only
Italic type: available in ±5% tolerance range only

Figures are repeated over each decade from 0.22 Ω to 22 MΩ. Values outside this range are not always available.

10 *11* 12 *13* **15** *16* 18 *20* **22** *24* 27 *30* **33** *36* 39 *43* **47** *51* 56 *62* **68** *75* 82 *91* **100**

Old colour code for resistors

Colour	Black	Brown	Red	Orange	Yellow	Green	Blue	Purple	Grey	White	Silver	Gold
Band A 1st sig. fig.	0	1	2	3	4	5	6	7	8	9	—	—
Band B 2nd sig. fig.	0	1	2	3	4	5	6	7	8	9	—	—
Band C Multiplier	1	10	100	1000	10^4	10^5	10^6	—	—	—	0.01	0.1
Band D Tolerance	—	—	—	—	—	—	—	—	—	—	±10%	±5%

Composition resistors: all bands equal width. Wire wound resistors: band A double width. No band D implies ±20%.

References: R63, R70.

Physical properties of liquids

M	molar mass	p_{sat}	saturation vapour pressure (298 K)
ρ	density (273 K)	Δh_m	specific enthalpy change (latent heat) on fusion (at T_m). $h^\ominus = 10^5\ J\ kg^{-1}$
α	cubic expansivity (293 K)		
T_m	normal melting temperature (1 atm)	Δh_b	specific enthalpy change (latent heat) on evaporation (at T_b). $h^\ominus = 10^4\ J\ kg^{-1}$
T_b	normal boiling temperature (1 atm)		

	Liquid	$\frac{M}{g\ mol^{-1}}$	$\frac{\rho}{g\ m^{-3}}$	$\frac{\alpha^\dagger}{10^{-3}\ K^{-1}}$	$\frac{T_m}{K}$	$\frac{T_b}{K}$	$\frac{p_{sat}}{Pa}$	$\frac{\Delta h_m}{h^\ominus}$	$\frac{\Delta h_b}{h^\ominus}$
1	Water	18.0	1.00	0.21	273.2	373.2	2261	33.44	226.1
2	Heavy water	20.0	1.10		277.0	374.6		31.70	
3	Mercury	200.6	13.55	0.18	234.3	630.1		1.15	29.5
4	Pentane	72.2	0.62	1.61	143.5	309.2	56392		35.9
5	Hexane	86.2	0.66		177.8	341.9	16093		33.2
6	Heptane	100.2	0.68		182.5	371.6	4655		32.5
7	Octane	114.2	0.70		216.4	398.8	1330		29.2
8	Dichloromethane	84.9	1.32	1.37	178.0	382.9	44954	5.42	33.0
9	Trichloromethane	119.4	1.48	1.27	209.7	334.9	20615	7.79	24.9
10	Tetrachloromethane	153.8	1.58	1.24	250.2	349.7	11571	1.69	19.5
11	Dibromomethane	173.9	2.48		220.6	370.1	4522		
12	Carbon disulphide	76.1	1.26	1.22	162.2	319.5	39235	5.77	35.2
13	Methanol	32.0	0.79	1.20	175.5	337.9	12502	6.91	110.3
14	Ethanol	46.1	0.79	1.12	159.1	351.4	5586	10.89	83.9
15	Propan-1-ol	60.1	0.80	0.96	147.0	370.4	1862		68.7
16	Propane-1,2,3-triol (glycerol)	92.1	1.26	0.51	291.3	563.2	133	19.87	
17	Benzene	78.1	0.87	1.24	278.7	353.3	9975	12.70	39.4
18	Cyclohexane	84.2	0.77		279.7	353.9	10241	3.18	35.7
19	Phenylamine (aniline)	93.1	1.02	0.86	267.0	457.6	133	8.81	43.4
20	Methylbenzene (toluene)	92.1	0.86	1.07	178.2	383.8	2926		35.9
21	1,2-dimethylbenzene[A]	106.2	0.88	0.97	248.0	417.6	665	12.81	34.7
22	1,3-dimethylbenzene[A]	106.2	0.86	1.01	225.3	412.3	798	10.89	34.3
23	1,4-dimethylbenzene[A]	106.2	0.86	1.01	286.4	411.5	931	16.48	33.9
24	Ethanoic (acetic) acid	60.1	1.04	1.07	289.8	391.1	1596	19.47	39.4
25	Propanone (acetone)	58.1	0.78	1.49	178.5	329.4	23541	9·79	52.2
26	Ethoxyethane (ether)	74.1	0.71	1.66	156.9	307.7	57855		37.2
27	Turpentine	136.2	0.86	0.97	263.2	429.2			28.7
28	Silicone oil[B]	163.3	0.76	1.60	205.2	372.7			

† many discrepancies between sources.
[A] *o*, *m*, and *p*-xylene respectively.
[B] dimethyl silicone, low viscosity oil.

References: R1, R2, R4, R45, R46, R47.

κ	isothermal compressibility (293 K). $\kappa^\ominus = 10^{11}\ \mathrm{Pa}^{-1}$
c_p	specific heat capacity. $c_p^\ominus = 100\ \mathrm{J\ g^{-1}\ K^{-1}}$
λ	thermal conductivity. $\lambda^\ominus = 0.1\ \mathrm{W\ m^{-1}\ K^{-1}}$
c	speed of sound (293 K)
η	viscosity (298 K). $\eta^\ominus = 10^{-4}\ \mathrm{kg\ m^{-1}\ s^{-1}}$
γ	surface tension (293 K)
ε	relative permittivity (dielectric constant) (293 K, 0 Hz)
n	refractive index

	Formula	$\kappa^{\dagger}/\kappa^\ominus$	$c_p/c_p^\ominus$	$\lambda^{\dagger}/\lambda^\ominus$	c/m s^{-1}	$\eta^{\dagger A}/\eta^\ominus$	γ^{B}/N m^{-1}	ε	n(589 nm)
1	H_2O	0.46	4.17	6.0	1483	8.91	7.28	80.10	1.3320
2	D_2O	0.47	4.10	5.8	1384			79.80	1.3280
3	Hg		0.14	80.3	1451	15.50	40.70	—	—
4	$CH_3(CH_2)_3CH_3$	0.32		1.4	1044	2.24	1.60	1.84	1.3547
5	$CH_3(CH_2)_4CH_3$	1.54	2.26	1.3	1085	2.98	1.84	1.89	1.3723
6	$CH_3(CH_2)_5CH_3$	1.44	2.05	1.4	1161	3.96	2.03	1.92	1.3851
7	$CH_3(CH_2)_6CH_3$	1.16	2.22	1.5	1192	6.14	2.48	1.95	1.3951
8	CH_2Cl_2	0.97	1.22		1064	4.25	2.80	9.08	1.4212
9	$CHCl_3$	1.01	0.98	1.2	995	5.42	**2.71**[S]	4.81	1.4429
10	CCl_4	1.05	0.84	1.1	938	8.80	2.69	2.24	1.4570
11	CH_2Br_2	0.65			971			7.73	1.5389
12	CS_2	0.93	0.99	1.6	1166	3.63	3.23	2.64	
13	CH_3OH	1.23	2.53	2.0	1122	5.53	2.26	33.00	1.3265
14	CH_3CH_2OH	1.11	2.41	1.7	1177	10.60	2.23	25.70	1.3594
15	$CH_3CH_2CH_2OH$	1.00	2.41	1.6	1223	22.70	2.30	20.10	1.3836
16	$CH_2OHCHOHCH_2OH$	0.21	2.42	2.9	1930	942.00	6.30	42.50	
17	C_6H_6	0.96	1.70	1.5	1321	6.01	**2.888**[S]	**2.28**[S]	1.4979
18	C_6H_{12}	1.10	1.83		1278	8.95	2.50	**2.02**[S]	1.4235
19	$C_6H_5NH_2$	0.56	2.05	1.7	1659	3.71	4.29	6.89	
20	$C_6H_5CH_3$	0.89	1.68	1.8	1322	5.50	2.84	2.39	1.4941
21	$C_6H_4(CH_3)_2$		1.73	1.4	1352	7.54	3.01	2.57	1.5029
22	$C_6H_4(CH_3)_2$	0.85	1.68	1.6		5.79	2.89	2.38	1.4946
23	$C_6H_4(CH_3)_2$		1.67			6.03	2.84	2.27	1.4933
24	CH_3CO_2H	0.91	2.03	1.7	1585	11.55	2.76	6.15	1.3698
25	CH_3COCH_3	1.27	2.17	1.9	1197	3.16	2.37	21.30	1.3563
26	$C_2H_5OC_2H_5$	1.87	2.28	1.4		2.22	**1.696**[S]	4.34	1.3495
27	$C_{10}H_{16}$	1.28	1.75		1225		2.70		1.4700
28	$CH_3Si(CH_3)_2OSi(CH_3)_3$		1.37	1.0	795	4.95	1.60	2.18	1.3750

† many discrepancies between sources.
[A] decreases rapidly with temperature, increases with pressure (doubles at about 10^8 Pa).
[B] γ decreases rapidly with temperature. For many liquids, the empirical Eötvos relation holds: $\mathrm{d}\{\gamma(M/\rho)^{2/3}\}/\mathrm{d}T = -2.12\times10^{-7}$ N m mol$^{-2/3}$ K^{-1}, which has been used to estimate M.
[S] standard value for calibrating instruments.

Physical properties of gases

M molar mass
T_b normal boiling temperature
c_p specific heat capacity at constant pressure
γ ratio c_p/c_V
η viscosity
α_V volume expansivity
α_p temperature coefficient of pressure
z compressibility factor pV/RT
T_c critical temperature
p_c critical pressure
ρ_c critical density
l mean free path
d molecular diameter (derived from viscosity measurements)

	Gas		M / g mol^{-1}	T_b / K	c_p(273 K) / 0.1 J g^{-1} K^{-1}	γ(273 K)	η(273 K) / 10^{-5} N s m^{-2}	α_V(273 K) / 10^{-3} K^{-1}	α_p(273 K) / 10^{-3} K^{-1}	z(273 K, 1 atm)	T_c / K	p_c / 10^5 Pa	ρ_c / 10^2 kg m^{-3}	l(1 atm) / 10^{-8} m	d / 10^{-10} m
1	Ideal monatomic gas				$207.8/M$	1.67	0	3.66	3.66	1.00000	—	—	—	∞	0
2	Air					1.40	1.71	3.67	3.67	0.99956	132	37.7		5.98	3.74
3	Oxygen	O_2	32	90	9.09	1.40	1.92	4.86	3.67	0.99922	155	50.6	4.10	6.33	3.54
4	Nitrogen	N_2	28	77	10.36	1.40	1.66	3.67	3.67	0.99968	126	33.9	3.11	5.88	3.75
5	Hydrogen	H_2	2	20	141.50	1.41	0.84	3.66	3.66	1.0006	33	12.9	0.31	11.1	2.97
6	Helium	He	4	4	$52.25^{-180\,°C}$	$1.63^{-180\,°C}$	1.86	3.66	3.66		5	2.3	0.69	17.4	2.58
7	Neon	Ne	20	27	10.30	1.64	2.97	3.66	3.66		44	27.2	4.84	12.4	2.79
8	Argon	Ar	40	87	5.24	1.67	2.10	3.68	3.67	0.99921	151	48.5	5.31	6.26	3.42
9	Chlorine	Cl_2	71	239	4.81	1.36	1.23	3.83	3.80		417	76.9	5.73	2.74	4.40
10	Carbon monoxide	CO	28	82	10.36	1.40	1.66	3.67	3.67		133	34.8	3.01	5.86	3.71
11	Carbon dioxide	CO_2	44	273	8.32	1.30	1.38	3.74	3.73	0.99479	304	73.6	4.68	3.90	3.90
12	Sulphur dioxide	SO_2	64	263	6.33	$1.26^{\dagger}$	1.17	3.90	3.84		431	78.6	5.24	2.74	4.29
13	Methane	CH_4	16	112	22.06	1.31	1.03	3.68	3.68	$0.9984^{300\,K}$	191	46.2	1.62	4.81	3.80
14	Ethane	C_2H_6	30	185	16.15	1.22	0.85			$0.9926^{300\,K}$	305	48.8	2.03		4.42
15	Propane	C_3H_8	44	229	$2.23^{-43\,°C}$	1.13	0.80			$0.9848^{300\,K}$	370	42.4	2.20		5.08
16	Butane	C_4H_{10}	58	273	$2.27^{-5\,°C}$		$0.83^{16\,°C}$			$0.9712^{300\,K}$	425	37.8	2.28		5.00
17	2-methyl propane (iso-butane)	C_4H_{10}	58	261	$2.20^{-16\,°C}$	$1.11^{15\,°C}$	$0.76^{23\,°C}$			$0.9731^{300\,K}$	408	36.4	2.21		5.34
18	Ammonia	NH_3	17	240	21.88	$1.34^{\dagger}$	0.92	3.77	3.79		405	112	2.35	5.83	2.97
19	Hydrogen sulphide	H_2S	34	213	10.00	1.32	1.17	3.77	3.76		374	89.8	3.49		
20	Ethene (ethylene)	C_2H_4	28	169	15.02	1.26	0.91	3.72	3.74		283	51.0	2.27	3.43	4.23
21	Ethyne (acetylene)	C_2H_2	26	189	$16.04^{15\,°C}$	1.26	0.94	3.74	3.73		309	$62.2^{\dagger}$	2.31		4.22
22	Dinitrogen oxide	N_2O	44	185	8.25	1.30	1.35	$3.73^{\dagger}$	$3.72^{\dagger}$		310	72.4	$4.59^{\dagger}$	3.87	3.88
23	Nitrogen oxide	NO	30	121	9.70	1.39	1.78	3.67	3.67		180	65.6	5.20		3.47
24	Nitrogen dioxide	NO_2	46	294	6.80	1.31					431	101	5.60		
25	Refrigerant 12 (Freon 12)	CCl_2F_2	121	243	$0.61^{30\,°C}$	1.14	$1.27^{30\,°C}$				385	41.0	5.55		
26	Refrigerant 11 (Freon 11)	CCl_3F	137	297	0.67	1.14	$1.14^{30\,°C}$				471	43.6	5.54		

Note
Specific enthalpies of evaporation, $\Delta h_L^G(T_b)$/J g^{-1}: H_2 450, O_2 213, He 21, CO_2 607, NH_3 1376, CCl_2F_2 165, CCl_3F 182. †discrepancy between sources.
References: R1, R2, R4, R45, R46, R47.

Compressibility of selected gases

z compressibility factor, $= pV_m/RT$
B_V, C_V, D_V virial coefficients in $pV_m/RT = 1 + B_V(T)/V_m + C_V(T)/V_m^2 + D_V(T)/V_m^3$ U cm^3 mol^{-1}

Hydrogen

T/K	1 atm	4 atm	7 atm	10 atm	40 atm	70 atm	100 atm	B_V/U	C_V/U^2	D_V/U^3
				z						
40	0.9845	0.9362	0.8853	0.8317				−51.52	1400	−10400
100	0.9998	0.9992	0.9987	0.9983	1.0029	1.0222	1.0560	− 1.90	412	13000
200	1.0007	1.0028	1.0048	1.0068	1.0283	1.0513	1.0760	11.93	254	8850
300	1.0006	1.0024	1.0042	1.0059	1.0238	1.0420	1.0607	15.01	250	6000
400	1.0005	1.0020	1.0034	1.0048	1.0193	1.0339	1.0486			
500	1.0004	1.0016	1.0028	1.0040	1.0160	1.0280	1.0400			
600	1.0003	1.0012	1.0023	1.0034	1.0136	1.0237	1.0337			

Critical constants: $T_c = 32.99$ K, $p_c = 1.294$ MPa, $\rho_c = 0.031$ g cm^{-3}, $z_c = 0.30$.
Van der Waals constants: $a = 0.0247$ Pa m^6 mol^{-2}, $b = 26.7$ m^3 mol^{-1}.

Air

T/K	1 atm	4 atm	7 atm	10 atm	40 atm	70 atm	100 atm	B_V/U	C_V/U^2	D_V/U^3
				z						
100	0.9809							−153.15	−3253.5	9.40
200	0.9977	0.9907	0.9837	0.9767	0.9080	0.8481	0.8105	−38.24	1323.5	5.46
300	0.9997	0.9988	0.9980	0.9972	0.9914	0.9900	0.9933	−7.480	1288.5	3.46
400	1.0002	1.0008	1.0014	1.0021	1.0095	1.0188	1.0299	6.367	1194.2	2.16
500	1.0003	1.0014	1.0024	1.0035	1.0145	1.0265	1.0393	14.048	1119.2	1.40
1000	1.0003	1.0013	1.0023	1.0033	1.0133	1.0233	1.0333	27.129	904.3	
2000	1.0004	1.0009	1.0014	1.0020	1.0076	1.0132	1.0188			
3000	1.0252	1.0133	1.0107	1.0095	1.0092	1.0119	1.0151			

Critical constants: $T_c = 132.45$ K, $p_c = 30.5$ MPa, $\rho_c = 0.311$ g cm^{-3}, $z_c = 0.29$.
Van der Waals constants: $a = 0.14$ Pa m^6 mol^{-2}, $b = 39.1$ m^3 mol^{-1} (for N_2).

Carbon dioxide

T/K	1 atm	4 atm	7 atm	10 atm	40 atm	70 atm	100 atm
				z			
300	0.9950	0.9798	0.9644	0.9486	0.7611		
400	0.9982	0.9927	0.9871	0.9815	0.9252	0.8697	0.8155
500	0.9993	0.9971	0.9950	0.9928	0.9721	0.9531	0.9365
600	0.9998	0.9990	0.9983	0.9976	0.9916	0.9874	0.9850
700	1.0000	0.9999	0.9999	1.0000	1.0008	1.0031	1.0068
800	1.0001	1.0004	1.0008	1.0011	1.0054	1.0108	1.0172
900	1.0001	1.0007	1.0012	1.0018	1.0079	1.0147	1.0224
1000	1.0002	1.0008	1.0015	1.0022	1.0092	1.0167	1.0248
1500	1.0002	1.0010	1.0017	1.0025	1.0100	1.0176	1.0253

Critical constants:
$T_c = 304.2$ K
$p_c = 7.38$ MPa
$\rho_c = 0.468$ g cm^{-3}
$z_c = 0.274$
Van der Waals constants:
$a = 0.3636$ Pa m^6 mol^{-2}
$b = 42.67$ m^3 mol^{-1}

Butane

T/K	1 atm	4 atm	7 atm	10 atm	40 atm	70 atm	100 atm	B_V/U
				z				
300	0.9712	0.8606[H]						
350	0.9840	0.9274	0.8346	0.7119[H]				
400	0.9888	0.9553	0.9063	0.8541				
450	0.9920	0.9680	0.9350	0.9908	0.5949	0.3358	0.4095	0.9816
500	0.9944	0.9773	0.9543	0.9313	0.7644	0.5693	0.5214	0.9745
600	0.9972	0.9887	0.9775	0.9664	0.8913	0.8193	0.7780	1.0051
700	0.9985	0.9940	0.9882	0.9825	0.9464	0.9164	0.9026	1.0674
800	0.9992	0.9968	0.9938	0.9909	0.9743	0.9643	0.9637	1.1199
900	0.9997	0.9985	0.9971	0.9958	0.9902	0.9909	0.9975	1.1545
1000	0.9999	0.9996	0.9992	0.9989	0.9998	1.0066	1.0173	1.1751
1500	1.0003	1.0013	1.0026	1.0040	1.0151	1.0304	1.0458	1.1888

Critical constants:
$T_c = 425.16$ K
$p_c = 3.784$ MPa
$\rho_c = 0.228$ g cm^{-3}
$z_c = 0.274$
Van der Waals constants:
$a = 1.466$ Pa m^6 mol^{-2}
$b = 122.6$ m^3 mol^{-1}

[H] liquid. *References*: R1, R2, R4, R45, R46, R47.

Temperatures and the 1968 International Practical Temperature Scale: Ranges of standard thermometers

Reference pressure for boiling and freezing temperatures is 101.325 kPa. Defining points for the 1968 International Practical Temperature Scale (IPTS) are named in bold type.

	T_{68}/K	t_{68}/°C
Absolute zero (unattainable)	0	−273.15
Helium boils	4.215	−268.935
Triple point of hydrogen[A]	**13.81**	**−259.34**
Hydrogen[A] **vapour pressure = 33 330.6 Pa**	**17.042**	**−256.108**
Hydrogen[A] **boils**	**20.28**	**−252.87**
Neon boils	**27.102**	**−246.048**
Triple point of oxygen	**54.361**	**−218.789**
Oxygen boils	**90.188**	**−182.962**
Ethanol melts	161	−112
Carbon dioxide sublimes[S]	194.67	−78.48
Lowest recorded land surface temperature	205	−68
($CaCl_2 + 6H_2O$): ice (1 : 0.7) freezing mixture	218.3	−54.9
Mercury melts[S]	234.29	−38.86
Ethylene glycol: water 50:50 (antifreeze) freezes	236.7	−36.5
Triple point of water (definition of K)	**273.16**	**0.01**
Room temperature	288 to 293	15 to 20
Standard for thermochemistry	298.15	25.0
Hot weather	303	30
Highest recorded land temperature	330	57
Ethanol boils	351.6	78.4
Water boils } alternative defining points	**373.15**	**100.00**
Tin melts } alternative defining points	**505.1181**	**231.9681**
Mercury boils[S]	629.81	356.66

	T_{68}/K	t_{68}/°C
Zinc melts	**692.73**	**419.58**
Dull red (black body)	800	530
Bright red (black body)	1180	900
Silver melts	**1235.08**	**961.93**
Gold melts	**1337.58**	**1064.43**
White heat	1500 and above	1300 and above
Iron melts	1808	1535
Bunsen burner flame (town gas)	2033	1760
Oxy-hydrogen flame	3073	2800
Tungsten filament	3100 to 3300	2800 to 3000
Tungsten melts[S]	3660	3387
Electric arc	3700	3427
Oxy-acetylene flame	3773	3500
Carbon sublimes	5100	4827
Tungsten vaporizes	5570	5297
Surface of Sun (varies with method of measurement)	6000	5700
Nitroglycerine explosion (calculated)	7000	6700
Hottest star (surface)	25000	
Solar corona	10^6	
Stellar interior, nuclear bomb	10^8	

[A] hydrogen must achieve equilibrium between para and ortho molecules. [S] secondary standard.

Ranges of standard thermometers

1 Below 5 K, helium vapour pressure. Scales of 1958 (^{4}He) and 1962 (^{3}He). p_{sat} saturated vapour pressure of helium.

p_{sat}/Pa	10^{-2}	10^{-1}	1.0	10	10^2	10^3	10^4	10^5	1.01×10^5
$T_{58}(^4He)$/K	0.549	0.643	0.771	0.953	1.23	1.67	2.48	4.20	4.125
$T_{62}(^3He)$/K	0.228	0.276	0.345	0.452	0.632	0.966	1.66	3.18	3.190

2 13.81 K to 903.89 K, platinum resistance thermometer. 4 different formulae used over different ranges.

3 903.89 K to 1337.58 K, Pt/$Pt_{90}Rh_{10}$ thermocouple. E.M.F. of thermocouple $E(T_{68}) = a + bT_{68} + cT_{68}^2$. a, b, and c are constants.

4 Above 1337.58 K, disappearing filament optical pyrometer.

References: R1, R2, R4.

Temperature scales and temperature measurement

T, θ temperature R gas constant k Boltzmann constant
$\rho(T)$ electrical resistivity, for Pt, Cu, and W respectively, at temperature T
U thermocouple e.m.f. for $Pt/Pt_{90}Rh_{10}$, copper/constantan, and chromel/alumel respectively. Cold junction is at 273.15 K.

The figures given may be interpolated to obtain approximate thermometer calibrations.
For more accurate work, see R4 (page 4.13) for ρ_{Pt} and ρ_{Cu}, R1 (page 92) for ρ_W, R2 (page E47) for U.

$\frac{T}{K}$	$\frac{\theta_C}{°C}$	$\frac{\theta_F}{°F}$	$\frac{RT}{kJ\ mol^{-1}}$	$\frac{kT}{eV}$	$\frac{\rho_{Pt}(T)}{\rho_{Pt}(°C)}$	$\frac{\rho_{Cu}(T)}{\rho_{Cu}(°C)}$	$\frac{\rho_W(T)}{\rho_W(°C)}$	$\frac{U_{Pt/PtRh}}{mV}$	$\frac{U_{Cu/con}}{mV}$	$\frac{U_{ch/al}}{mV}$
73.2	−200	−328	0.61	0.006	0.177	0.117	0.122			
123.2	−150	−238	1.02	0.011					−4.60	−4.81
173.2	−100	−148	1.44	0.015	0.599	0.557			−3.35	−3.49
223.2	−50	−58	1.86	0.019					−1.81	−1.86
273.2	0	32	2.27	0.024	1.000	1.000	1.000			
323.2	50	122	2.69	0.028				0.30	2.03	2.02
373.2	100	212	3.10	0.032	1.392	1.431	1.490	0.64	4.28	4.10
423.2	150	302	3.52	0.036				1.03	6.70	6.13
473.2	200	392	3.93	0.041	1.773	1.862		1.44	9.29	8.13
523.2	250	482	4.35	0.045				1.87	12.01	10.16
573.2	300	572	4.77	0.049	2.142	2.299	2.531	2.32	14.86	12.21
623.2	350	662	5.18	0.054				2.78	17.82	14.29
673.2	400	752	5.60	0.058	2.499	2.747		3.25	20.87	16.40
723.2	450	842	6.01	0.062				3.73		18.51
773.2	500	932	6.43	0.067	2.844	3.210	3.673	4.22		20.65
823.2	550	1022	6.84	0.071				4.72		22.78
873.2	600	1112	7.26	0.075	3.178	3.695		5.22		24.91
923.2	650	1202	7.68	0.080				5.74		27.03
973.2	700	1292	8.09	0.084	3.499	4.207	4.898	6.26		29.17
1023.2	750	1382	8.51	0.088				6.79		31.23
1073.2	800	1472	8.92	0.093	3.809	4.750		7.33		33.30
1123.2	850	1562	9.34	0.097				7.88		35.34
1173.2	900	1652	9.75	0.101	4.108	5.332		8.43		37.36
1223.2	950	1742	10.17	0.105				9.00		39.35
1273.2	1000	1832	10.58	0.110	4.395	5.959	6.735	9.57		41.31
1323.2	1050	1922	11.00	0.114				10.15		43.25
1373.2	1100	2012	11.42	0.118	4.672			10.74		45.16
1423.2	1150	2102	11.83	0.123				11.34		47.04
1473.2	1200	2192	12.25	0.127	4.937		7.959	11.94		48.89
1523.2	1250	2282	12.66	0.131				12.54		50.69
1573.2	1300	2372	13.08	0.136	5.190			13.14		52.46
1623.2	1350	2462	13.49	0.140				13.74		54.20
1673.2	1400	2552	13.91	0.144	5.431			14.34		
1723.2	1450	2642	14.33	0.149				14.94		
1773.2	1500	2732	14.74	0.153	5.660			15.53		
1823.2	1550	2822	15.16	0.157				16.12		
1873.2	1600	2912	15.57	0.161				16.72		
1923.2	1650	3002	15.99	0.166				17.31		
1973.2	1700	3092	16.40	0.170				17.89		
2023.2	1750	3182								

References: R1, R2, R4.

Equations and formulae: physics, chemistry, and mathematics

Recommended symbols given on page 6 to 11 **UCS** are used, with a minimum of explanation. The list is intended only to refresh the memory. It is necessary to consult a textbook to find out the meaning of the formulae and the assumptions made in deriving them.

Kinematics		
Linear motion	$\boldsymbol{a} = \mathrm{d}\boldsymbol{v}/\mathrm{d}t = \mathrm{d}^2\boldsymbol{s}/\mathrm{d}t^2$	
	$v = u + at$	constant a only
	$v^2 = u^2 + 2as$	constant a only
Circular motion	$v = r\omega$	
	$a = v^2/r$	
Dynamics		
Linear motion	$\boldsymbol{F} = m\boldsymbol{a} = \mathrm{d}(m\boldsymbol{v})/\mathrm{d}t$	
impulse	$\boldsymbol{F}t = \Delta p = \Delta(m\boldsymbol{v}) = m\boldsymbol{v} - m\boldsymbol{v}_0$	
work	$W = F\Delta s = \Delta E_k = \Delta(mv^2/2)$	$\boldsymbol{F} \parallel \boldsymbol{s}$
	$= mv^2/2 - mv_0^2/2 = -\Delta E_p$	
conservation of mechanical energy	$E_k + E_p = E_T(\text{constant})$	ideal case
Gravitation	$F = -GM_1M_2/r^2$	
	$E_p = -GM_1M_2/r$	
	$\approx mgh$	near surface of Earth
Kepler's laws	$r^2\omega = \text{constant}$	
	$\omega^2 r^3 = GM$	
Rotational motion		
moment of inertia	$I = \sum mr^2 = Mk^2$	in general
	$I = mr^2/2$	for disk about perpendicular axis through centre
	$I = mr^2/4$	for disk about diameter
	$I = ml^2/12$	for bar about perpendicular axis through centre
	$I = 2mr^2/3$	for hollow sphere about diameter
	$I = 2mr^2/5$	for solid sphere about diameter
perpendicular axes theorem	$I_z = I_x + I_y$	for plane lamina
parallel axes theorem	$I_a = I_c + Mh^2$	I_c relates to $\parallel$ axis through centre of mass
kinetic energy	$E_k = I\omega^2/2$	
torque	$T = Fr = \mathrm{d}(I\omega)/\mathrm{d}t$	$\boldsymbol{r} \perp \boldsymbol{F}$
Simple harmonic motion		
displacement	$x = x_0 \begin{matrix}\sin\\ \cos\end{matrix} (\omega t + \phi)$	
acceleration	$a = \mathrm{d}^2x/\mathrm{d}t^2 = -\omega^2 x$	
period (frequency $= 1/T$)	$T = 2\pi/\omega = 2\pi\sqrt{i/f}$	i inertia, f force per unit displacement
	$= 2\pi\sqrt{l/g}$	for simple pendulum
	$= 2\pi\sqrt{I/\tau}$	for torsional oscillations
Vectors		
resolution	$A_\theta = \lvert A \rvert \cos\theta$ = component at angle θ to $\boldsymbol{A}$	
	$A^2 = A_x^2 + A_y^2 + A_z^2$	A_x, A_y, and A_z are perpendicular components

Pressure	$p = \rho g h$	
work done on expansion	$W = p\Delta V$	
Elasticity		
Stress	$\sigma = F/A$	
Strain	$\varepsilon = \Delta l/l_0$	
Young modulus	$E = \sigma/\varepsilon$	
Stored energy density	$E_p = \sigma\varepsilon/2 = E(\Delta l)^2/2l_0^2$	
Poisson ratio	$\mu = -\varepsilon(\text{lateral})/\varepsilon(\text{longitudinal})$	
Shear stress	$\tau = F/A$	F acts parallel to 'surface'
Shear strain	$\gamma = \dfrac{\Delta l(\parallel F)}{l(\perp F)} = \Delta\theta$	θ is angle of shear
Shear modulus	$G = \tau/\gamma$	
Bulk modulus	$K = -p/(\nabla V/V_0)$	
Optics		
Spherical mirror	$1/u + 1/v = 1/f = 2/r$ $m = v/u = (v/f) - 1$	new Cartesian sign convention
Refractive index	$n_{1,2} = \sin i/\sin r = n_1/n_2 = c_2/c_1$	
Prism	$n = \sin\dfrac{A + D_{\min}}{2} \Big/ \sin\dfrac{A}{2}$	
Dispersive power	$\omega = (n_b - n_r)/(n_y - 1)$	n for blue and red hydrogen and yellow sodium (or helium) lines
Lens	$1/v - 1/u = 1/f = (n-1)(1/r_1 - 1/r_2)$ $m = v/u$ $1/F = 1/f_1 - 1/f_2$ $l_1 l_2 = f^2$	new Cartesian sign convention thin lenses in contact distances from principal foci
Telescope	$M = f_o/f_e$	
Resolving power	$\phi = 1.22\lambda/d_0 \approx \lambda/d_0$	d_0 diameter of objective
Newton's rings	$r^2 = pR\lambda$	for pth dark ring, R radius of curvature of lens
Thin film	$2nt\cos r = p\lambda$	for dark fringe in reflection, p = integer
Diffraction grating	$d(\sin i + \sin\theta) = p\lambda$	for maximum, p = integer. d grating constant
dispersive power	$\omega = p/(d\cos\theta)$	
resolving power	$\lambda/\mathrm{d}\lambda = nN$	N total number of slits n order of diffraction
Waves	$c = \nu\lambda$	
Doppler effect	$\nu_1/\nu_2 = c/(c - v_s)$ $= (c - v_o)/c$	moving source moving observer
Lambert's law of absorption	$I = I_0 \exp(-\alpha l)$	
Sound		
Speed	$c = (K/\rho)^{\frac{1}{2}}$ $c = (\gamma p/\rho)^{\frac{1}{2}}$ $c = (F/m)^{\frac{1}{2}}$	solids, liquids, and gases gas string, m mass per unit length, F tension

Equations and formulae: physics, chemistry, and mathematics

Electrostatics		
Coulomb's law	$F = -Q_1Q_2/4\pi\varepsilon_r\varepsilon_0 r^2$	F positive in direction of r increasing
Potential energy	$E_p = Q_1Q_2/4\pi\varepsilon_0 r$	
Potential	$V = Q/4\pi\varepsilon_r\varepsilon_0 r$	
Field strength	$E = \lim_{Q\to 0} F/Q = -\mathrm{d}V/\mathrm{d}x$	
Work done moving charge	$W = Q\Delta V = QEl$	$l \parallel E$
Capacitance	$C = Q/V$	
	$= A\varepsilon_r\varepsilon_0/d$	for parallel plates. V p.d.
series connection	$1/C = 1/C_1 + 1/C_2 + \cdots$	
parallel connection	$C = C_1 + C_2 + \cdots$	
stored energy	$E_p = QV/2 = CV^2/2 = Q^2/2C$	
Current electricity	$I = \mathrm{d}Q/\mathrm{d}t$	in general
	$I = nQv$	n charges moving with speed v
Ohm's law	$I = V/R$	V p.d. across R
Uniform conductor	$R = \rho l/A = l/\sigma A$	ρ resistivity, σ conductivity
Power	$P = VI\ (= I^2R = V^2/R)$	(if Ohm's law is obeyed)
Series connection	$R = R_1 + R_2 + \cdots$	
Parallel connection	$1/R = 1/R_1 + 1/R_2 + \cdots$	
Kirchoff's laws	**1** Total current flowing into junction is zero. $\sum I_i = 0$	
	2 Sum of p.d.s. round any closed circuit equals total e.m.f. $\sum I_iR_i = \sum E_i$	
Electromagnetism		
Biot Savart law	$\mathrm{d}B = \mu_0 I\,\mathrm{d}s\sin\theta/4\pi r^2$	$\perp I\mathrm{d}s$ and r, in sense of R.H. screw along $I\mathrm{d}s$
Ampère's law	$\oint B\,\mathrm{d}s\cos\theta = \mu_0 I$	I total current within path of integration
Long straight conductor	$B = \mu_0 I/2\pi r$	B circumferential in sense of R.H. screw rotated along I
Circular coil (on axis)	$B = \mu_0 NIr^2/2(r^2+x^2)^{3/2}$	B along axis, in direction of R.H. screw rotated in sense of I
	$= \mu_0 NI\sin^3\alpha/2r$	2α is angle subtended by coil at field point
Solenoid (on axis)	$B = \mu_0 nI(\cos\phi_1 - \cos\phi_2)/2$ $\rightarrow \mu_0 nI$ for infinite solenoid	Direction as above. $2\phi_1, 2\phi_2$ angles subtended by ends of solenoid at field point
Force on moving charge	$F = BQv\sin\theta$	
Force on current	$F = IlB\cos\theta$	$\perp B$ and l in sense of L.H. rule
Torque on dipole	$T = mB\sin\theta$	m dipole moment
Torque on coil	$T = ANIB\sin\theta$	θ angle between normal to coil (R.H. screw +ve) and field

Electromagnetic induction

E.m.f. round closed-loop	$E = -\mathrm{d}\phi/\mathrm{d}t = -\mathrm{d}(BA)/\mathrm{d}t$	A area enclosed
Self inductance	$\phi = LI$	
Mutual inductance	$\phi_2 = M_{12}I_1 = M_{21}I_1$	ϕ_2 flux linking circuit 2
Stored energy	$E_p = LI^2/2$	

Varying currents and a.c.

LRC circuit	$V_{\text{inst}} = L(\mathrm{d}I/\mathrm{d}t)_{\text{inst}} + RI_{\text{inst}} + Q_{\text{inst}}/C$	
RC circuit	$Q = CV_0(1 - \mathrm{e}^{-t/RC})$	growth of charge, constant V_0
	$Q = CV_0\,\mathrm{e}^{-t/RC} = \mathrm{e}^{-t/\tau}$	decay of charge, initial V_0
RL circuit	$I = (V_0/R)(1 - \mathrm{e}^{-Rt/L})$	growth of current, constant V_0
	$I = I_0\,\mathrm{e}^{-Rt/L} = I_0\,\mathrm{e}^{-t/\tau}$	decay of current, initial I_0
a.c. series circuit	$E = E_0 \cos \omega t$	
	$I = (E_0/Z)\cos(\omega t - \phi)$	$Z = (R^2 + (\omega L - 1/\omega C)^2)^{\frac{1}{2}}$ $\tan\phi = (\omega L - 1/\omega C)/R$
	$I_{\text{r.m.s.}} = E_{\text{r.m.s.}}/Z$	E and I are often used to denote r.m.s. values without subscript
	$E_{\text{r.m.s.}} = E_0/\sqrt{2} = 0.707\,E_0$	E_0 peak value e.m.f.
Resonant frequency	$\nu_0 = 1/2\pi\sqrt{LC}$	
	$Z(\nu_0) = R$	

Temperature

Definition of temperature	$\theta/100\,°\text{C} = \dfrac{X(\theta) - X(0\,°\text{C})}{X(100\,°\text{C}) - X(0\,°\text{C})}$	empirical scale, X may be any temperature dependent property
Thermocouple	$E = A + B\theta + C\theta^2$	A, B, C constants
	$E_{\text{a,c}} = E_{\text{a,b}} + E_{\text{b,c}}$	a, b, c materials
Resistance thermometer	$R(\theta) = R(0\,°\text{C})\{1 + \alpha\theta + \beta\theta^2 + \cdots\}$	α, β constants
Newton's law of cooling	$\mathrm{d}\theta/\mathrm{d}t = -k(\theta - \theta_{\text{ambient}})$	k constant
Linear expansion	$l(\theta) = l(0\,°\text{C})(1 + \alpha\theta + \beta\theta^2 + \cdots)$	α is linear expansivity if β may be ignored. Varies with temperature range
Cubic expansion	$V(\theta) = V(0\,°\text{C})(1 + \gamma\theta + \cdots)$	where $\gamma \approx 3\alpha$

Properties of ideal gases

Ideal gas law	$pV = nRT = nm\overline{c^2}/3$	n amount of substance
Average kinetic energy of gas molecule	$E_k = 3kT/2$	$k = R/L$ = Boltzmann constant
Molar heat capacity	$C_V = (3 + f)R/2$	f number of degrees of freedom for rotational and vibrational motion
Adiabatic gas law	$pV^\gamma = c$	c constant, γ c_p/c_V
Work done in expansion	$W = \int_{V_1}^{V_2} p\,\mathrm{d}V = nRT\ln(V_2/V_1)$	isothermal
	$= (p_1V_1 - p_2V_2)/(\gamma - 1)$	adiabatic
Relation between molar heat capacities	$C_p - C_V = R$	

Equations and formulae: physics, chemistry, and mathematics

Properties of imperfect gases

Van der Waals equation	$(p+a/V^2)(V-b) = nRT$	a, b constants; $a \sim n^2$, $b \sim n$
Critical conditions	$T_c = 8a/27Rb,\ p_c = a/27b^2,\ V_c = 3b$	in terms of Van der Waals constants a and b
Boyle temperature	$T_B = a/Rb$	
Inversion temperature	$T_i = 2T_B$	

Radiation

Wien's law for black body	$\lambda_{max}T = 2.9 \times 10^{-3}$ m K	
Kirchoff's law	$\varepsilon(\lambda)/a(\lambda) = dQ/d\lambda = c$	c constant
Stefan's law	$P = \sigma\varepsilon AT^4$	where $\sigma = 3.74 \times 10^{-16}$ W m^{-2} K^{-4}
Planck's law	$E_\lambda\, d\lambda = c_1\lambda^{-5}\, d\lambda(e^{c_2/\lambda T} - 1)^{-1}$	$c_1 = 2\pi hc^2 = 3.74 \times 10^{-16}$ W m^2; $c_2 = hc/k = 1.44 \times 10^{-2}$ m K

Thermodynamics

First Law of Thermodynamics	$dQ = dU + dW$	
Thermal conduction	$P = dQ/dt = \lambda A\, d\theta/dz$	λ thermal conductivity
through cylindrical shell	$P = 2\pi\lambda l(\theta_1 - \theta_2)/\ln(r_2/r_1)$	
Carnot engine	$\eta = (Q_1 - Q_2)/Q_1 = (T_1 - T_2)/T_1$	
Entropy	$dS = \Delta Q/T = k\,\Delta \ln \omega$	
Enthalpy	$H = U + pV$	
Heat capacity	$C_V = (dU/dT)_V$	
	$C_p = (dH/dT)_p$	
Gibbs function	$G = H - TS = U + pV - TS$	
	$dG = V\,dp - S\,dT$	

Physical chemistry

Cell e.m.f.	$E = -\Delta G/nF$	n number of electrons transferred per molecule
Clausius–Clapeyron equation	$dp/dT = \Delta H_b/T(V_{vap} - V_{liq})$	
Trouton's rule	$\Delta H_b/T_b(1\text{ atm}) \approx 88$ J mol^{-1} K^{-1}	for normal non-associated liquids
Vapour pressure over curved surface	$\delta p = 2\gamma\rho_{vap}\{r(\rho_{liq} - \rho_{vap})\}$	γ surface tension, r radius of curvature
Osmotic pressure	$\Pi = cRT/M$	c concentration of solute, M molar mass of solute
Phase rule	$f = c - p + 2$	degrees of freedom, components, phases
Equilibrium constant	$K = [C]^p[D]^q/[A]^m[B]^n$	A, B reactants; C, D products; m, n, p, q coefficients
Reaction rates	$d[A]/dt = -k$	zero order
	$= -kN$	first order
	$= -kN^2$	second order
	$= kN_AN_B$	bimolecular

Atomic physics

Radioactivity	$A = \mathrm{d}N/\mathrm{d}t = -\lambda N$	
	$N = N_0\,\mathrm{e}^{-\lambda t}$	
	$T_{\frac{1}{2}} = (\ln 2)/\lambda = 0.693/\lambda$	
α emission	$Z \to Z-2,\ A \to A-4$	
β^- emission	$Z \to Z+1,\ A \to A$	
β^+ emission	$Z \to Z-1,\ A \to A$	
γ absorption	$I = I_0\,\mathrm{e}^{-\mu x}$	
Particle in magnetic field	$r = mv/Be$	r radius of curvature of path, $B \perp v$
Rutherford scattering	$N \sim Z^2 t \operatorname{cosec}^4(\phi/2)/(M_\alpha v^2)^2$	t thickness
Bragg diffraction	$2d \sin\theta = n\lambda$	n integer
Photoelectric effect	$h\nu = \phi + mv^2/2$	ϕ work function
De Broglie wave	$\lambda = h/p = h/mv$	
Bohr atom	$E_n = -mZ^2e^4/8h^2\varepsilon_0^2 n^2$	n integer
	$h\nu = \Delta E$	
	$\bar{\nu} = 1/\lambda = R_\infty(1/n_1^2 - 1/n_2^2)$	L angular momentum (about z axis)
	$L(= mvr) = nh/2\pi$	
	$a_n = n^2h^2\varepsilon_0/\pi e^2$	a radius of maximum probability
Mass energy equation	$E = mc^2$	
Uncertainty relation	$\Delta x\,\Delta p \geq h/2\pi$	

Mathematics formulae

Differentials and integrals

Functions in column A are the differentials of those in column B. Functions in column B are the indefinite integrals of those in column A.

A differential	**B integral**
anx^{n-1}	ax^n
ax^n	$ax^{n+1}/(n+1)$
x^{-1}	$\ln x$
$a\,\mathrm{e}^{ax}$	e^{ax}
$-\cos x$	$\sin x$
$\sin x$	$-\cos x$
$\sec^2 x$	$\tan x$
$(1-x^2)^{-\frac{1}{2}}$	$\sin^{-1} x$ or $-\cos^{-1} x$
$(1+x^2)^{-1}$	$\tan^{-1} x$
$u(\mathrm{d}v/\mathrm{d}x) + v(\mathrm{d}u/\mathrm{d}x)$	uv
$\{v(\mathrm{d}u/\mathrm{d}x) - u(\mathrm{d}u/\mathrm{d}x)\}/v^2$	u/v
$\sin^2 x$	$x/2 - (\sin 2x)/4$
$\cos^2 x$	$x/2 + (\sin 2x)/4$

Equations and formulae: physics, chemistry, and mathematics

Trigonometric functions

$\sin\theta = y/r = 1/\mathrm{cosec}\,\theta$ $\quad\cos\theta = x/r = 1/\sec\theta$ $\quad\tan\theta = y/x = \sin\theta/\cos\theta = 1/\cot\theta$

$\cos^2\theta + \sin^2\theta = 1$ $\quad 1+\tan^2\theta = \sec^2\theta$ $\quad 1+\cot^2\theta = \mathrm{cosec}^2\theta$

$\sin(\theta\pm\phi) = \sin\theta\cos\phi \pm \cos\theta\sin\phi$

$\cos(\theta\pm\phi) = \cos\theta\cos\phi \mp \sin\theta\sin\phi$

$\tan(\theta\pm\phi) = (\tan\theta\pm\tan\phi)/(1\mp\tan\theta\tan\phi)$

$$\sin\theta\pm\sin\phi = 2\,{}^{\sin}_{\cos}\left(\frac{\theta+\phi}{2}\right){}^{\cos}_{\sin}\left(\frac{\theta-\phi}{2}\right)$$

$\sin 2\theta = 2\sin\theta\cos\theta$

$\cos 2\theta = \cos^2\theta - \sin^2\theta = 2\cos^2\theta - 1 = 1 - 2\sin^2\theta$

$\tan 2\theta = 2\tan\theta/(1-\tan^2\theta)$

$$\cos\theta\pm\cos\phi = \pm 2\,{}^{\cos}_{\sin}\left(\frac{\theta+\phi}{2}\right){}^{\cos}_{\sin}\left(\frac{\theta-\phi}{2}\right)$$

Cosine rule	$a^2 = b^2 + c^2 - 2bc\cos A$	for any triangle
Sine rule	$a/\sin A = b/\sin B = c/\sin C$	for any triangle

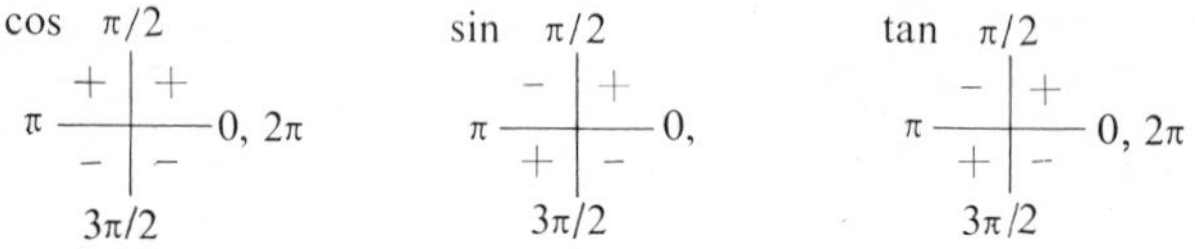

Series

$e^x = 1 + x + x^2/2! + x^3/3! + \cdots$

$\sin x = x - x^3/3! + x^5/5! - \cdots$

$\cos x = 1 - x^2/2! + x^4/4! - \cdots$

$\ln(1+x) = x - x^2/2 + x^3/3 - \cdots$ $\qquad |x| < 1$

$(1+x)^n = 1 + nx + n(n-1)x^2/2! + n(n-1)(n-2)x^3/3! + \cdots$ $\qquad |x| < 1$. Series terminates for any x if n is a positive integer

Coordinate geometry

Straight line	$y = mx + c$	
	$y - y_0 = m(x - x_0)$	through (x_0, y_0)
Circle	$(y-a)^2 + (y-b)^2 = R^2$	centre at a, b

Algebra

$ax^2 + by + c = 0 \Rightarrow x = \{-b \pm \sqrt{b^2 - 4ac}\}/2a$

$a^2 - b^2 = (a+b)(a-b)$ $\quad (a\pm b)^2 = a^2 \pm 2ab + b^2$ $\quad a^3 \mp b^3 = (a\mp b)(a^2 \pm ab + b^2)$

Geometry

Perimeter of circle	$L = 2\pi r$	
Area of triangle	$S = \frac{1}{2}bh = \frac{1}{2}bc\sin A$	
Area of circle	$S = \pi r^2$	
Surface area of sphere	$S = 4\pi r^2$	
Surface area of cone	$S = \pi r(r+l)$	l = slant height
Volume of sphere	$V = 4\pi r^3/3$	
Volume of cone	$V = \pi r^2 h/3$	

AX.XB = CX.XD for any chords including tangents

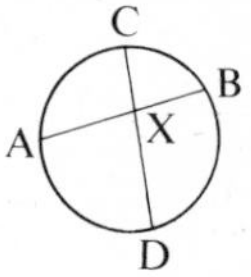

Centres of gravity

Circular arc	$CG = (r\sin\theta)/\theta$	along radius of symmetry. θ is angle subtended at C
Circular sector lamina	$CG = (2r\sin\theta)/3\theta$	along radius of symmetry. θ is angle subtended at C
Triangular lamina (ABC)	$AG = 2AM/3$	M is midpoint of BC
Semicircular lamina	$CG = 4r/3\pi$	along radius of symmetry
Hollow cone (without base)	$VG = 2h/3$	on axis. V is vertex
Solid cone	$VG = 3h/4$	on axis. V is vertex
Hemisphere	$CG = 3r/8$	along radius of symmetry

The exponential function and natural logarithms

The mathematical tables on this and the following pages are intended for laboratory and slide-rule working and are therefore given to three significant figures only (except for the table of logarithms). If greater accuracy is required (for example, in connection with a spectrometer) consult a book of mathematical tables.

x	$\exp x$	$\exp(-x)$	$1-\exp(-x)$	$\ln x$	x
0	1.0	1.0	0	$-\infty$	0
0.1	1.1	0.905	0.095	−2.302	0.1
0.2	1.2	0.819	0.181	−1.608	0.2
0.3	1.3	0.741	0.259	−1.203	0.3
0.4	1.5	0.670	0.330	−0.915	0.4
0.5	1.6	0.607	0.393	−0.692	0.5
0.6	1.8	0.549	0.451	−0.510	0.6
0.7	2.0	0.497	0.503	−0.356	0.7
0.8	2.2	0.449	0.551	−0.222	0.8
0.9	2.5	0.407	0.593	−0.104	0.9
1.0	2.7	0.368	0.632	0.000	1.0
1.1	3.0	0.333	0.667	0.095	1.1
1.2	3.3	0.301	0.699	0.182	1.2
1.3	3.7	0.273	0.727	0.262	1.3
1.4	4.1	0.247	0.753	0.336	1.4
1.5	4.5	0.223	0.777	0.405	1.5
1.6	5.0	0.202	0.798	0.470	1.6
1.7	5.5	0.183	0.817	0.531	1.7
1.8	6.0	0.165	0.835	0.588	1.8
1.9	6.7	0.150	0.850	0.642	1.9
2.0	7.4	0.135	0.865	0.693	2.0
2.1	8.2	0.122	0.878	0.742	2.1
2.2	9.0	0.111	0.889	0.788	2.2
2.3	10.0	0.100	0.900	0.833	2.3
2.4	11.0	0.091	0.909	0.875	2.4
2.5	12.2	0.082	0.918	0.916	2.5
2.6	13.5	0.074	0.926	0.956	2.6
2.7	14.9	0.067	0.933	0.993	2.7
2.8	16.4	0.061	0.939	1.030	2.8
2.9	18.2	0.055	0.945	1.065	2.9
3.0	20.1	0.050	0.950	1.099	3.0
∞	∞	0	1.000	∞	∞

Exp x for integer values of x

x	$\exp x$	x	$\exp x$
3	20.1	10	2.20×10^{4}
4	54.6	20	4.85×10^{8}
5	148.4	30	1.07×10^{13}
6	403.4	40	2.35×10^{17}
7	1097	50	5.18×10^{21}
8	2981	60	1.14×10^{26}
9	8103	70	2.52×10^{30}
10	22 027	80	5.54×10^{34}

The relationship $\exp(a+b) = \exp a \exp b$ may be used to calculate intermediate values of $\exp x$.

$\exp(-x) = 1/\exp x$
$\exp x \approx 1+x$ when x is small
$\ln x = 2.3026 \log_{10} x$

Logarithms

											Mean differences								
	0	**1**	**2**	**3**	**4**	**5**	**6**	**7**	**8**	**9**	**1**	**2**	**3**	**4**	**5**	**6**	**7**	**8**	**9**
10	0000	0043	0086	0128	0170	0212	0253	0294	0334	0374	4	8	13	17	21	25	29	33	37
11	0414	0453	0492	0531	0569	0607	0645	0682	0719	0755	4	8	11	15	19	23	27	30	34
12	0792	0828	0864	0899	0934	0969	1004	1038	1072	1106	4	7	10	14	17	21	24	28	31
13	1139	1173	1206	1239	1271	1303	1335	1367	1399	1430	3	6	10	13	16	19	23	26	29
14	1461	1492	1523	1553	1584	1614	1644	1673	1703	1732	3	6	9	12	15	18	21	24	27
15	1761	1790	1818	1847	1875	1903	1931	1959	1987	2014	3	6	8	11	14	17	20	23	25
16	2041	2068	2095	2122	2148	2175	2201	2227	2253	2279	3	5	8	11	13	16	18	21	24
17	2304	2330	2355	2380	2405	2430	2455	2480	2504	2529	2	5	7	10	12	15	17	20	22
18	2553	2577	2601	2625	2648	2672	2695	2718	2742	2765	2	5	7	9	12	14	16	19	21
19	2788	2810	2833	2856	2878	2900	2923	2945	2967	2989	2	4	7	9	11	13	16	18	20
20	3010	3032	3054	3075	3096	3118	3139	3160	3181	3201	2	4	6	9	11	13	15	17	19
21	3222	3243	3263	3284	3304	3324	3345	3365	3385	3404	2	4	6	8	10	12	14	16	18
22	3424	3444	3464	3483	3502	3522	3541	3560	3579	3598	2	4	6	8	10	12	14	15	17
23	3617	3636	3655	3674	3692	3711	3729	3747	3766	3784	2	4	6	7	9	11	13	15	17
24	3802	3820	3838	3856	3874	3892	3909	3927	3945	3962	2	4	5	7	9	11	12	14	16
25	3979	3997	4014	4031	4048	4065	4082	4099	4116	4133	2	3	5	7	9	10	12	14	15
26	4150	4166	4183	4200	4216	4232	4249	4265	4281	4298	2	3	5	7	8	10	12	13	15
27	4314	4330	4346	4362	4378	4393	4409	4425	4440	4456	2	3	5	6	8	9	11	13	14
28	4472	4487	4502	4518	4533	4548	4564	4579	4594	4609	2	3	5	6	8	9	11	12	14
29	4624	4639	4654	4669	4683	4698	4713	4728	4742	4757	1	3	4	6	7	9	10	12	13
30	4771	4786	4800	4814	4829	4843	4857	4871	4886	4900	1	3	4	6	7	9	10	11	13
31	4914	4928	4942	4955	4969	4983	4997	5011	5024	5038	1	3	4	6	7	8	10	11	12
32	5052	5065	5079	5092	5105	5119	5132	5145	5159	5172	1	3	4	5	7	8	9	11	12
33	5185	5198	5211	5224	5237	5250	5263	5276	5289	5302	1	3	4	5	6	8	9	10	12
34	5315	5328	5340	5353	5366	5378	5391	5403	5416	5428	1	3	4	5	6	8	9	10	11
35	5441	5453	5465	5478	5490	5502	5514	5527	5539	5551	1	2	4	5	6	7	9	10	11
36	5563	5575	5587	5599	5611	5623	5635	5647	5658	5670	1	2	4	5	6	7	8	10	11
37	5682	5694	5705	5717	5729	5740	5752	5763	5775	5786	1	2	3	5	6	7	8	9	10
38	5798	5809	5821	5832	5843	5855	5866	5877	5888	5899	1	2	3	5	6	7	8	9	10
39	5911	5922	5933	5944	5955	5966	5977	5988	5999	6010	1	2	3	4	6	7	8	9	10
40	6021	6031	6042	6053	6064	6075	6085	6096	6107	6117	1	2	3	4	5	6	8	9	10
41	6128	6138	6149	6159	6170	6180	6191	6201	6212	6222	1	2	3	4	5	6	7	8	9
42	6232	6243	6253	6263	6274	6284	6294	6304	6314	6325	1	2	3	4	5	6	7	8	9
43	6335	6345	6355	6365	6375	6385	6395	6405	6415	6425	1	2	3	4	5	6	7	8	9
44	6435	6444	6454	6464	6474	6484	6493	6503	6513	6522	1	2	3	4	5	6	7	8	9
45	6532	6542	6551	6561	6571	6580	6590	6599	6609	6618	1	2	3	4	5	6	7	8	9
46	6628	6637	6646	6656	6665	6675	6684	6693	6702	6712	1	2	3	4	5	6	7	7	8
47	6721	6730	6739	6749	6758	6767	6776	6785	6794	6803	1	2	3	4	5	5	6	7	8
48	6812	6821	6830	6839	6848	6857	6866	6875	6884	6893	1	2	3	4	4	5	6	7	8
49	6902	6911	6920	6928	6937	6946	6955	6964	6972	6981	1	2	3	4	4	5	6	7	8
50	6990	6998	7007	7016	7024	7033	7042	7050	7059	7067	1	2	3	3	4	5	6	7	8
51	7076	7084	7093	7101	7110	7118	7126	7135	7143	7152	1	2	3	3	4	5	6	7	8
52	7160	7168	7177	7185	7193	7202	7210	7218	7226	7235	1	2	2	3	4	5	6	7	7
53	7243	7251	7259	7267	7275	7284	7292	7300	7308	7316	1	2	2	3	4	5	6	7	7
54	7324	7332	7340	7348	7356	7364	7372	7380	7388	7396	1	2	2	3	4	5	6	6	7

											Mean differences								
	0	**1**	**2**	**3**	**4**	**5**	**6**	**7**	**8**	**9**	**1**	**2**	**3**	**4**	**5**	**6**	**7**	**8**	**9**
55	7404	7412	7419	7427	7435	7443	7451	7459	7466	7474	1	2	2	3	4	5	5	6	7
56	7482	7490	7497	7505	7513	7520	7528	7536	7543	7551	1	2	2	3	4	5	5	6	7
57	7559	7566	7574	7582	7589	7597	7604	7612	7619	7627	1	2	2	3	4	5	5	6	7
58	7634	7642	7649	7657	7664	7672	7679	7686	7694	7701	1	1	2	3	4	4	5	6	7
59	7709	7716	7723	7731	7738	7745	7752	7760	7767	7774	1	1	2	3	4	4	5	6	7
60	7782	7789	7796	7803	7810	7818	7825	7832	7839	7846	1	1	2	3	4	4	5	6	6
61	7853	7860	7868	7875	7882	7889	7896	7903	7910	7917	1	1	2	3	4	4	5	6	6
62	7924	7931	7938	7945	7952	7959	7966	7973	7980	7987	1	1	2	3	3	4	5	6	6
63	7993	8000	8007	8014	8021	8028	8035	8041	8048	8055	1	1	2	3	3	4	5	5	6
64	8062	8069	8075	8082	8089	8096	8102	8109	8116	8122	1	1	2	3	3	4	5	5	6
65	8129	8136	8142	8149	8156	8162	8169	8176	8182	8189	1	1	2	3	3	4	5	5	6
66	8195	8202	8209	8215	8222	8228	8235	8241	8248	8254	1	1	2	3	3	4	5	5	6
67	8261	8267	8274	8280	8287	8293	8299	8306	8312	8319	1	1	2	3	3	4	5	5	6
68	8325	8331	8338	8344	8351	8357	8363	8370	8376	8382	1	1	2	3	3	4	4	5	6
69	8388	8395	8401	8407	8414	8420	8426	8432	8439	8445	1	1	2	3	3	4	4	5	6
70	8451	8457	8463	8470	8476	8482	8488	8494	8500	8506	1	1	2	2	3	4	4	5	6
71	8513	8519	8525	8531	8537	8543	8549	8555	8561	8567	1	1	2	2	3	4	4	5	5
72	8573	8579	8585	8591	8597	8603	8609	8615	8621	8627	1	1	2	2	3	4	4	5	5
73	8633	8639	8645	8651	8657	8663	8669	8675	8681	8686	1	1	2	2	3	4	4	5	5
74	8692	8698	8704	8710	8716	8722	8727	8733	8739	8745	1	1	2	2	3	4	4	5	5
75	8751	8756	8762	8768	8774	8779	8785	8791	8797	8802	1	1	2	2	3	3	4	5	5
76	8808	8814	8820	8825	8831	8837	8842	8848	8854	8859	1	1	2	2	3	3	4	5	5
77	8865	8871	8876	8882	8887	8893	8899	8904	8910	8915	1	1	2	2	3	3	4	4	5
78	8921	8927	8932	8938	8943	8949	8954	8960	8965	8971	1	1	2	2	3	3	4	4	5
79	8976	8982	8987	8993	8998	9004	9009	9015	9020	9025	1	1	2	2	3	3	4	4	5
80	9031	9036	9042	9047	9053	9058	9063	9069	9074	9079	1	1	2	2	3	3	4	4	5
81	9085	9090	9096	9101	9106	9112	9117	9122	9128	9133	1	1	2	2	3	3	4	4	5
82	9138	9143	9149	9154	9159	9165	9170	9175	9180	9186	1	1	2	2	3	3	4	4	5
83	9191	9196	9201	9206	9212	9217	9222	9227	9232	9238	1	1	2	2	3	3	4	4	5
84	9243	9248	9253	9258	9263	9269	9274	9279	9284	9289	1	1	2	2	3	3	4	4	5
85	9294	9299	9304	9309	9315	9320	9325	9330	9335	9340	1	1	2	2	3	3	4	4	5
86	9345	9350	9355	9360	9365	9370	9375	9380	9385	9390	1	1	2	2	3	3	4	4	5
87	9395	9400	9405	9410	9415	9420	9425	9430	9435	9440	0	1	1	2	2	3	3	4	4
88	9445	9450	9455	9460	9465	9469	9474	9479	9484	9489	0	1	1	2	2	3	3	4	4
89	9494	9499	9504	9509	9513	9518	9523	9528	9533	9538	0	1	1	2	2	3	3	4	4
90	9542	9547	9552	9557	9562	9566	9571	9576	9581	9586	0	1	1	2	2	3	3	4	4
91	9590	9595	9600	9605	9609	9614	9619	9624	9628	9633	0	1	1	2	2	3	3	4	4
92	9638	9643	9647	9652	9657	9661	9666	9671	9675	9680	0	1	1	2	2	3	3	4	4
93	9685	9689	9694	9699	9703	9708	9713	9717	9722	9727	0	1	1	2	2	3	3	4	4
94	9731	9736	9741	9745	9750	9754	9759	9763	9768	9773	0	1	1	2	2	3	3	4	4
95	9777	9782	9786	9791	9795	9800	9805	9809	9814	9818	0	1	1	2	2	3	3	4	4
96	9823	9827	9832	9836	9841	9845	9850	9854	9859	9863	0	1	1	2	2	3	3	4	4
97	9868	9872	9877	9881	9886	9890	9894	9899	9903	9908	0	1	1	2	2	3	3	4	4
98	9912	9917	9921	9926	9930	9934	9939	9943	9948	9952	0	1	1	2	2	3	3	4	4
99	9956	9961	9965	9969	9974	9978	9983	9987	9991	9996	0	1	1	2	2	3	3	3	4

Powers of x

x	$2\pi x$	x^2	x^3	$1/x$	$\sqrt{x}$	$\sqrt{10x}$	$\sqrt[3]{x}$	$\sqrt[3]{10x}$	$\sqrt[3]{100x}$	$1/\sqrt{x}$	$1/\sqrt{10x}$	x
1	6.28	1	1	1.0000	1.00	3.16	1.00	2.15	4.64	1.000	0.316	1
2	12.57	4	8	0.5000	1.41	4.47	1.26	2.71	5.85	0.707	0.224	2
3	18.85	9	27	0.3333	1.73	5.48	1.44	3.11	6.69	0.577	0.183	3
4	25.13	16	64	0.2500	2.00	6.32	1.59	3.42	7.37	0.500	0.158	4
5	31.42	25	125	0.2000	2.24	7.07	1.71	3.68	7.94	0.447	0.141	5
6	37.70	36	216	0.1667	2.45	7.75	1.82	3.91	8.43	0.408	0.129	6
7	43.98	49	343	0.1429	2.65	8.37	1.91	4.12	8.88	0.378	0.120	7
8	50.27	64	512	0.1250	2.83	8.94	2.00	4.31	9.28	0.354	0.112	8
9	56.55	81	729	0.1111	3.00	9.49	2.08	4.48	9.65	0.333	0.105	9
10	62.83	100	1000	0.1000	3.16	10.00	2.15	4.64	10.00	0.316	0.100	10
11	69.12	121	1331	0.0909	3.32	10.49	2.22	4.79	10.32	0.302	0.095	11
12	75.40	144	1728	0.0833	3.46	10.95	2.29	4.93	10.63	0.289	0.091	12
13	81.68	169	2197	0.0769	3.61	11.40	2.35	5.07	10.91	0.277	0.088	13
14	87.96	196	2744	0.0714	3.74	11.83	2.41	5.19	11.19	0.267	0.085	14
15	94.25	225	3375	0.0667	3.87	12.25	2.47	5.31	11.45	0.258	0.082	15
16	100.53	256	4096	0.0625	4.00	12.65	2.52	5.43	11.70	0.250	0.079	16
17	106.81	289	4913	0.0588	4.12	13.04	2.57	5.54	11.93	0.243	0.077	17
18	113.10	324	5832	0.0556	4.24	13.42	2.62	5.65	12.16	0.236	0.075	18
19	119.38	361	6859	0.0526	4.36	13.78	2.67	5.75	12.39	0.229	0.073	19
20	125.66	400	8000	0.0500	4.47	14.14	2.71	5.85	12.60	0.224	0.071	20
21	131.95	441	9261	0.0476	4.58	14.49	2.76	5.94	12.81	0.218	0.069	21
22	138.23	484	10648	0.0455	4.69	14.83	2.80	6.04	13.01	0.213	0.067	22
23	144.51	529	12167	0.0435	4.80	15.17	2.84	6.13	13.20	0.209	0.066	23
24	150.80	576	13824	0.0417	4.90	15.49	2.88	6.21	13.39	0.204	0.065	24
25	157.08	625	15625	0.0400	5.00	15.81	2.92	6.30	13.57	0.200	0.063	25
26	163.36	676	17576	0.0385	5.10	16.12	2.96	6.38	13.75	0.196	0.062	26
27	169.65	729	19683	0.0370	5.20	16.43	3.00	6.46	13.92	0.192	0.061	27
28	175.93	784	21952	0.0357	5.29	16.73	3.04	6.54	14.09	0.189	0.060	28
29	182.21	841	24389	0.0345	5.39	17.03	3.07	6.62	14.26	0.186	0.059	29
30	188.50	900	27000	0.0333	5.48	17.32	3.11	6.69	14.42	0.183	0.058	30
31	194.78	961	29791	0.0323	5.57	17.61	3.14	6.77	14.58	0.180	0.057	31
32	201.06	1024	32768	0.0313	5.66	17.89	3.17	6.84	14.74	0.177	0.056	32
33	207.35	1089	35937	0.0303	5.74	18.17	3.21	6.91	14.89	0.174	0.055	33
34	213.63	1156	39304	0.0294	5.83	18.44	3.24	6.98	15.04	0.171	0.054	34
35	219.91	1225	42875	0.0286	5.92	18.71	3.27	7.05	15.18	0.169	0.053	35
36	226.19	1296	46656	0.0278	6.00	18.97	3.30	7.11	15.33	0.167	0.053	36
37	232.48	1369	50653	0.0270	6.08	19.24	3.33	7.18	15.47	0.164	0.052	37
38	238.76	1444	54872	0.0263	6.16	19.49	3.36	7.24	15.60	0.162	0.051	38
39	245.04	1521	59319	0.0256	6.24	19.75	3.39	7.31	15.74	0.160	0.051	39
40	251.33	1600	64000	0.0250	6.32	20.00	3.42	7.37	15.87	0.158	0.050	40
41	257.61	1681	68921	0.0244	6.40	20.25	3.45	7.43	16.01	0.156	0.049	41
42	263.89	1764	74088	0.0238	6.48	20.49	3.48	7.49	16.13	0.154	0.049	42
43	270.18	1849	79507	0.0233	6.56	20.74	3.50	7.55	16.26	0.152	0.048	43
44	276.46	1936	85184	0.0227	6.63	20.98	3.53	7.61	16.39	0.151	0.048	44
45	282.74	2025	91125	0.0222	6.71	21.21	3.56	7.66	16.51	0.149	0.047	45
46	289.03	2116	97336	0.0217	6.78	21.45	3.58	7.72	16.63	0.147	0.047	46
47	295.31	2209	103823	0.0213	6.86	21.68	3.61	7.77	16.75	0.146	0.046	47
48	301.59	2304	110592	0.0208	6.93	21.91	3.63	7.83	16.87	0.144	0.046	48
49	307.88	2401	117649	0.0204	7.00	22.14	3.66	7.88	16.98	0.143	0.045	49
50	314.16	2500	125000	0.0200	7.07	22.36	3.68	7.94	17.10	0.141	0.045	50

x	$2\pi x$	x^2	x^3	$1/x$	$\sqrt{x}$	$\sqrt{10x}$	$\sqrt[3]{x}$	$\sqrt[3]{10x}$	$\sqrt[3]{100x}$	$1/\sqrt{x}$	$1/\sqrt{10x}$	x
51	320.44	2601	132651	0 0196	7.14	22.58	3.71	7.99	17.21	0.140	0.044	51
52	326.73	2704	140608	0.0192	7.21	22.80	3.73	8.04	17.32	0.139	0.044	52
53	333.01	2809	148877	0.0189	7.28	23.02	3.76	8.09	17.44	0.137	0.043	53
54	339.29	2916	157464	0.0185	7.35	23.24	3.78	8.14	17.54	0.136	0.043	54
55	345.58	3025	166375	0.0182	7.42	23.45	3.80	8.19	17.65	0.135	0.043	55
56	351.86	3136	175616	0.0179	7.48	23.66	3.83	8.24	17.76	0.134	0.042	56
57	358.14	3249	185193	0.0175	7.55	23.87	3.85	8.29	17.86	0.132	0.042	57
58	364.42	3364	195112	0.0172	7.62	24.08	3.87	8.34	17.97	0.131	0.042	58
59	370.71	3481	205379	0.0169	7.68	24.29	3.89	8.39	18.07	0.130	0.041	59
60	376.99	3600	216000	0.0167	7.75	24.49	3.91	8.43	18.17	0.129	0.041	60
61	383.27	3721	226981	0.0164	7.81	24.70	3.94	8.48	18.27	0.128	0.040	61
62	389.56	3844	238328	0.0161	7.87	24.90	3.96	8.53	18.37	0.127	0.040	62
63	395.84	3969	250047	0.0159	7.94	25.10	3.98	8.57	18.47	0.126	0.040	63
64	402.12	4096	262144	0.0156	8.00	25.30	4.00	8.62	18.57	0.125	0.040	64
65	408.41	4225	274625	0.0154	8.06	25.50	4.02	8.66	18.66	0.124	0.039	65
66	414.69	4356	287496	0.0152	8.12	25.69	4.04	8.71	18.76	0.123	0.039	66
67	420.97	4489	300763	0.0149	8.19	25.88	4.06	8.75	18.85	0.122	0.039	67
68	427.26	4624	314432	0.0147	8.25	26.08	4.08	8.79	18.95	0.121	0.038	68
69	433.54	4761	328509	0.0145	8.31	26.27	4.10	8.84	19.04	0.120	0.038	69
70	439.82	4900	343000	0.0143	8.37	26.46	4.12	8.88	19.13	0.120	0.038	70
71	446.11	5041	357911	0.0141	8.43	26.65	4.14	8.92	19.22	0.119	0.038	71
72	452.39	5184	373248	0.0139	8.49	26.83	4.16	8.96	19.31	0.118	0.037	72
73	458.67	5329	389017	0.0137	8.54	27.02	4.18	9.00	19.40	0.117	0.037	73
74	464.96	5476	405224	0.0135	8.60	27.20	4.20	9.05	19.49	0.116	0.037	74
75	471.24	5625	421875	0.0133	8.66	27.39	4.22	9.09	19.57	0.115	0.037	75
76	477.52	5776	438976	0.0132	8.72	27.57	4.24	9·13	19.66	0.115	0.036	76
77	483.81	5929	456533	0.0130	8.77	27.75	4.25	9.17	19.75	0.114	0.036	77
78	490.09	6084	474552	0.0128	8.83	27.93	4.27	9.21	19.83	0.113	0.036	78
79	496.37	6241	493039	0.0127	8.89	28.11	4.29	9.24	19.92	0.113	0.036	79
80	502.65	6400	512000	0.0125	8.94	28.28	4.31	9.28	20.00	0.112	0.035	80
81	508.94	6561	531441	0.0123	9.00	28.46	4.33	9.32	20.08	0.111	0.035	81
82	515.22	6724	551368	0.0122	9.06	28.64	4.34	9.36	20.17	0.110	0.035	82
83	521.50	6889	571787	0.0120	9.11	28.81	4.36	9.40	20.25	0.110	0.035	83
84	527.79	7056	592704	0.0119	9.17	28.98	4.38	9.44	20.33	0.109	0.035	84
85	534.07	7225	614125	0.0118	9.22	29.15	4.40	9.47	20.41	0.108	0.034	85
86	540.35	7396	636056	0.0116	9.27	29.33	4.41	9.51	20.49	0.108	0.034	86
87	546.64	7569	658503	0.0115	9.33	29.50	4.43	9.55	20.57	0.107	0.034	87
88	552.92	7744	681472	0.0114	9.38	29.66	4.45	9.58	20.65	0.107	0.034	88
89	559.20	7921	704969	0.0112	9.43	29.83	4.46	9.62	20.72	0.106	0.034	89
90	565.49	8100	729000	0.0111	9.49	30.00	4.48	9.65	20.80	0.105	0.033	90
91	571.77	8281	753571	0.0110	9.54	30.17	4.50	9.69	20.88	0.105	0.033	91
92	578.05	8464	778688	0.0109	9.59	30.33	4.51	9.73	20.95	0.104	0.033	92
93	584.34	8649	804357	0.0108	9.64	30.50	4.53	9.76	21.03	0.104	0.033	93
94	590.62	8836	830584	0.0106	9.70	30.66	4.55	9.80	21.10	0.103	0.033	94
95	596.90	9025	857375	0.0105	9.75	30.82	4.56	9.83	21.18	0.103	0.032	95
96	603.19	9216	884736	0.0104	9.80	30.98	4.58	9.86	21.25	0.102	0.032	96
97	609.47	9409	912673	0.0103	9.85	31.14	4.59	9.90	21.33	0.102	0.032	97
98	615.75	9604	941192	0.0102	9.90	31.30	4.61	9.93	21.40	0.101	0.032	98
99	622.04	9801	970299	0.0101	9.95	31.46	4.63	9.97	21.47	0.101	0.032	99
100	628.32	10000	1000000	0.0100	10.00	31.62	4.64	10.00	21.54	0.100	0.032	100

Trigonometric functions: radians

x/rad	*x*/°	sin *x*	cos *x*	tan *x*	cot *x*	sec *x*	cosec *x*	$\log_{10}\sin x$	$\log_{10}\cos x$	*x*/rad
0.02	1.146	0.020	1.000	0.020	49.993	1.000	50.003	$\bar{2}.301$	0.000	0.02
0.04	2.292	0.040	0.999	0.040	24.987	1.001	25.007	$\bar{2}.602$	0.000	0.04
0.06	3.438	0.060	0.998	0.060	16.647	1.002	16.677	$\bar{2}.778$	$\bar{1}.999$	0.06
0.08	4.584	0.080	0.997	0.080	12.473	1.003	12.513	$\bar{2}.903$	$\bar{1}.999$	0.08
0.10	5.730	0.100	0.995	0.100	9.967	1.005	10.017	$\bar{2}.999$	$\bar{1}.998$	0.10
0.12	6.875	0.120	0.993	0.121	8.293	1.007	8.353	$\bar{1}.078$	$\bar{1}.997$	0.12
0.14	8.021	0.140	0.990	0.141	7.096	1.010	7.166	$\bar{1}.145$	$\bar{1}.996$	0.14
0.16	9.167	0.159	0.987	0.161	6.197	1.013	6.277	$\bar{1}.202$	$\bar{1}.994$	0.16
0.18	10.313	0.179	0.984	0.182	5.495	1.016	5.586	$\bar{1}.253$	$\bar{1}.993$	0.18
0.20	11.459	0.199	0.980	0.203	4.933	1.020	5.033	$\bar{1}.298$	$\bar{1}.991$	0.20
0.22	12.605	0.218	0.976	0.224	4.472	1.025	4.582	$\bar{1}.339$	$\bar{1}.989$	0.22
0.24	13.751	0.238	0.971	0.245	4.086	1.030	4.207	$\bar{1}.376$	$\bar{1}.987$	0.24
0.26	14.897	0.257	0.966	0.266	3.759	1.035	3.890	$\bar{1}.410$	$\bar{1}.985$	0.26
0.28	16.043	0.276	0.961	0.288	3.478	1.041	3.619	$\bar{1}.441$	$\bar{1}.983$	0.28
0.30	17.189	0.296	0.955	0.309	3.233	1.047	3.384	$\bar{1}.471$	$\bar{1}.980$	0.30
0.32	18.335	0.315	0.949	0.331	3.018	1.053	3.179	$\bar{1}.498$	$\bar{1}.977$	0.32
0.34	19.481	0.333	0.943	0.354	2.827	1.061	2.999	$\bar{1}.523$	$\bar{1}.974$	0.34
0.36	20.626	0.352	0.936	0.376	2.657	1.068	2.839	$\bar{1}.547$	$\bar{1}.971$	0.36
0.38	21.772	0.371	0.929	0.399	2.504	1.077	2.696	$\bar{1}.569$	$\bar{1}.968$	0.38
0.40	22.918	0.389	0.921	0.423	2.365	1.086	2.568	$\bar{1}.590$	$\bar{1}.964$	0.40
0.42	24.064	0.408	0.913	0.447	2.239	1.095	2.452	$\bar{1}.610$	$\bar{1}.961$	0.42
0.44	25.210	0.426	0.905	0.471	2.124	1.105	2.348	$\bar{1}.629$	$\bar{1}.957$	0.44
0.46	26.356	0.444	0.896	0.495	2.018	1.116	2.253	$\bar{1}.647$	$\bar{1}.952$	0.46
0.48	27.502	0.462	0.887	0.521	1.921	1.127	2.166	$\bar{1}.664$	$\bar{1}.948$	0.48
0.50	28.648	0.479	0.878	0.546	1.830	1.139	2.086	$\bar{1}.681$	$\bar{1}.943$	0.50
0.52	29.794	0.497	0.868	0.573	1.747	1.152	2.013	$\bar{1}.696$	$\bar{1}.938$	0.52
0.54	30.940	0.514	0.858	0.599	1.668	1.166	1.945	$\bar{1}.711$	$\bar{1}.933$	0.54
0.56	32.086	0.531	0.847	0.627	1.595	1.180	1.883	$\bar{1}.725$	$\bar{1}.928$	0.56
0.58	33.232	0.548	0.836	0.655	1.526	1.196	1.825	$\bar{1}.739$	$\bar{1}.922$	0.58
0.60	34.377	0.565	0.825	0.684	1.462	1.212	1.771	$\bar{1}.752$	$\bar{1}.917$	0.60
0.62	35.523	0.581	0.814	0.714	1.401	1.229	1.721	$\bar{1}.764$	$\bar{1}.911$	0.62
0.64	36.669	0.597	0.802	0.745	1.343	1.247	1.674	$\bar{1}.776$	$\bar{1}.904$	0.64
0.66	37.815	0.613	0.790	0.776	1.288	1.266	1.631	$\bar{1}.788$	$\bar{1}.898$	0.66
0.68	38.961	0.629	0.778	0.809	1.237	1.286	1.590	$\bar{1}.799$	$\bar{1}.891$	0.68
0.70	40.107	0.644	0.765	0.842	1.187	1.307	1.552	$\bar{1}.809$	$\bar{1}.884$	0.70
0.72	41.253	0.659	0.752	0.877	1.140	1.330	1.517	$\bar{1}.819$	$\bar{1}.876$	0.72
0.74	42.399	0.674	0.738	0.913	1.095	1.354	1.483	$\bar{1}.829$	$\bar{1}.868$	0.74
0.76	43.545	0.689	0.725	0.950	1.052	1.380	1.452	$\bar{1}.838$	$\bar{1}.860$	0.76
0.78	44.691	0.703	0.711	0.989	1.011	1.407	1.422	$\bar{1}.847$	$\bar{1}.852$	0.78
0.80	45.837	0.717	0.697	1.030	0.971	1.435	1.394	$\bar{1}.856$	$\bar{1}.843$	0.80

x/rad	x/°	$\sin x$	$\cos x$	$\tan x$	$\cot x$	$\sec x$	$\operatorname{cosec} x$	$\log_{10} \sin x$	$\log_{10} \cos x$	x/rad
0.82	46.983	0.731	0.682	1.072	0.933	1.466	1.368	$\bar{1}.864$	$\bar{1}.834$	0.82
0.84	48.128	0.745	0.667	1.116	0.896	1.498	1.343	$\bar{1}.872$	$\bar{1}.824$	0.84
0.86	49.274	0.758	0.652	1.162	0.861	1.533	1.320	$\bar{1}.880$	$\bar{1}.815$	0.86
0.88	50.420	0.771	0.637	1.210	0.827	1.569	1.297	$\bar{1}.887$	$\bar{1}.804$	0.88
0.90	51.566	0.783	0.622	1.260	1.794	1.609	1.277	$\bar{1}.894$	$\bar{1}.794$	0.90
0.92	52.712	0.796	0.606	1.313	0.761	1.651	1.257	$\bar{1}.901$	$\bar{1}.782$	0.92
0.94	53.858	0.808	0.590	1.369	0.730	1.696	1.238	$\bar{1}.907$	$\bar{1}.771$	0.94
0.96	55.004	0.819	0.574	1.428	0.700	1.744	1.221	$\bar{1}.913$	$\bar{1}.759$	0.96
0.98	56.150	0.830	0.557	1.491	0.671	1.795	1.204	$\bar{1}.919$	$\bar{1}.746$	0.98
1.00	57.296	0.841	0.540	1.557	0.642	1.851	1.188	$\bar{1}.925$	$\bar{1}$ 733	1.00
1.02	58.442	0.852	0.523	1.628	0.614	1.911	1.174	$\bar{1}.930$	$\bar{1}.719$	1.02
1.04	59.588	0.862	0.506	1.704	0.587	1.975	1.160	$\bar{1}.936$	$\bar{1}.704$	1.04
1.06	60.734	0.872	0.489	1.784	0.560	2.046	1.146	$\bar{1}.941$	$\bar{1}.689$	1.06
1.08	61.879	0.882	0.471	1.871	0.534	2.122	1.134	$\bar{1}.945$	$\bar{1}.673$	1.08
1.10	63.025	0.891	0.454	1.965	0.509	2.205	1.122	$\bar{1}.950$	$\bar{1}.657$	1.10
1.12	64.171	0.900	0.436	2.066	0.484	2.295	1.111	$\bar{1}.954$	$\bar{1}.639$	1.12
1.14	65.317	0.909	0.418	2.176	0.460	2.395	1.101	$\bar{1}.958$	$\bar{1}.621$	1.14
1.16	66.463	0.917	0.399	2.296	0.436	2.504	1.091	$\bar{1}.962$	$\bar{1}.601$	1.16
1.18	67.609	0.925	0.381	2.427	0.412	2.625	1.082	$\bar{1}.966$	$\bar{1}.581$	1.18
1.20	68.755	0.932	0.362	2.572	0.389	2.760	1.073	$\bar{1}.969$	$\bar{1}.559$	1.20
1.22	69.901	0.939	0.344	2.733	0.366	2.910	1.065	$\bar{1}.973$	$\bar{1}.536$	1.22
1.24	71.047	0.946	0.325	2.912	0.343	3.079	1.057	$\bar{1}.976$	$\bar{1}.512$	1.24
1.26	72.193	0.952	0.306	3.113	0.321	3.270	1.050	$\bar{1}.979$	$\bar{1}.485$	1.26
1.28	73.339	0.958	0.287	3.341	0.299	3.488	1.044	$\bar{1}.981$	$\bar{1}.457$	1.28
1.30	74.485	0.964	0.267	3.602	0.278	3.738	1.038	$\bar{1}.984$	$\bar{1}.427$	1.30
1.32	75.630	0.969	0.248	3.903	0.256	4.029	1.032	$\bar{1}.986$	$\bar{1}.395$	1.32
1.34	76.776	0.973	0.229	4.256	0.235	4.372	1.027	$\bar{1}.988$	$\bar{1}.359$	1.34
1.36	77.922	0.978	0.209	4.673	0.214	4.779	1.023	$\bar{1}.990$	$\bar{1}.321$	1.36
1.38	79.068	0.982	0.190	5.177	0.193	5.273	1.018	$\bar{1}.992$	$\bar{1}.278$	1.38
1.40	80.214	0.985	0.170	5.798	0.172	5.883	1.015	$\bar{1}.994$	$\bar{1}.230$	1.40
1.42	81.360	0.989	0.150	6.581	0.152	6.657	1.011	$\bar{1}.995$	$\bar{1}.177$	1.42
1.44	82.506	0.991	0.130	7.602	0.132	7.667	1.009	$\bar{1}.996$	$\bar{1}.115$	1.44
1.46	83.652	0.994	0.111	8.989	0.111	9.044	1.006	$\bar{1}.997$	$\bar{1}.044$	1.46
1.48	84.798	0.996	0.091	10.983	0.091	11.029	1.004	$\bar{1}.998$	$\bar{2}.957$	1.48
1.50	85.944	0.997	0.071	14.101	0.071	14.137	1.003	$\bar{1}.199$	$\bar{2}.850$	1.50
1.52	87.090	0.999	0.051	19.670	0.051	19.695	1.001	$\bar{1}.999$	$\bar{2}.706$	1.52
1.54	88.236	1.000	0.031	32.461	0.031	32.477	1.000	0.000	$\bar{2}.488$	1.54
1.56	89.381	1.000	0.011	92.621	0.011	92.626	1.000	0.000	$\bar{2}.033$	1.56

Trigonometric functions: degrees

$x/°$	x/rad	$\sin x$	$\cos x$	$1-\cos x$	$\tan x$	$\cot x$	$\sec x$	$\operatorname{cosec} x$	$\log_{10} \sin x$	$\log_{10} \cos x$	$x/°$
1	0.017	0.017	1.000	0.000	0.017	57.290	1.000	57.299	$\bar{2}.242$	0.000	1
2	0.035	0.035	0.999	0.001	0.035	28.636	1.001	28.654	$\bar{2}.543$	0.000	2
3	0.052	0.052	0.999	0.001	0.052	19.081	1.001	19.107	$\bar{2}.719$	$\bar{1}.999$	3
4	0.070	0.070	0.998	0.002	0.070	14.301	1.002	14.336	$\bar{2}.844$	$\bar{1}.999$	4
5	0.087	0.087	0.996	0.004	0.087	11.430	1.004	11.474	$\bar{2}.940$	$\bar{1}.998$	5
6	0.105	0.105	0.995	0.005	0.105	9.514	1.006	9.567	$\bar{1}.019$	$\bar{1}.998$	6
7	0.122	0.122	0.993	0.007	0.123	8.144	1.008	8.206	$\bar{1}.086$	$\bar{1}.997$	7
8	0.140	0.139	0.990	0.010	0.141	7.115	1.010	7.185	$\bar{1}.144$	$\bar{1}.996$	8
9	0.157	0.156	0.988	0.012	0.158	6.314	1.012	6.392	$\bar{1}.194$	$\bar{1}.995$	9
10	0.175	0.174	0.985	0.015	0.176	5.671	1.015	5.759	$\bar{1}.240$	$\bar{1}.993$	10
11	0.192	0.191	0.982	0.018	0.194	5.145	1.019	5.241	$\bar{1}.281$	$\bar{1}.992$	11
12	0.209	0.208	0.978	0.022	0.213	4.705	1.022	4.810	$\bar{1}.318$	$\bar{1}.990$	12
13	0.227	0.225	0.974	0.026	0.231	4.331	1.026	4.445	$\bar{1}.352$	$\bar{1}.989$	13
14	0.244	0.242	0.970	0.030	0.249	4.011	1.031	4.134	$\bar{1}.384$	$\bar{1}.987$	14
15	0.262	0.259	0.966	0.034	0.268	3.732	1.035	3.864	$\bar{1}.413$	$\bar{1}.985$	15
16	0.279	0.276	0.961	0.039	0.287	3.487	1.040	3.628	$\bar{1}.440$	$\bar{1}.983$	16
17	0.297	0.292	0.956	0.044	0.306	3.271	1.046	3.420	$\bar{1}.466$	$\bar{1}.981$	17
18	0.314	0.309	0.951	0.049	0.325	3.078	1.051	3.236	$\bar{1}.490$	$\bar{1}.978$	18
19	0.332	0.326	0.946	0.054	0.344	2.904	1.058	3.072	$\bar{1}.513$	$\bar{1}.976$	19
20	0.349	0.342	0.940	0.060	0.364	2.747	1.064	2.924	$\bar{1}.534$	$\bar{1}.973$	20
21	0.367	0.358	0.934	0.066	0.384	2.605	1.071	2.790	$\bar{1}.554$	$\bar{1}.970$	21
22	0.384	0.375	0.927	0.073	0.404	2.475	1.079	2.669	$\bar{1}.574$	$\bar{1}.967$	22
23	0.401	0.391	0.921	0.079	0.424	2.356	1.086	2.559	$\bar{1}.592$	$\bar{1}.964$	23
24	0.419	0.407	0.914	0.086	0.445	2.246	1.095	2.459	$\bar{1}.609$	$\bar{1}.961$	24
25	0.436	0.423	0.906	0.094	0.466	2.145	1.103	2.366	$\bar{1}.626$	$\bar{1}.957$	25
26	0.454	0.438	0.899	0.101	0.488	2.050	1.113	2.281	$\bar{1}.642$	$\bar{1}.954$	26
27	0.471	0.454	0.891	0.109	0.510	1.963	1.122	2.203	$\bar{1}.657$	$\bar{1}.950$	27
28	0.489	0.469	0.883	0.117	0.532	1.881	1.133	2.130	$\bar{1}.672$	$\bar{1}.946$	28
29	0.506	0.485	0.875	0.125	0.554	1.804	1.143	2.063	$\bar{1}.686$	$\bar{1}.942$	29
30	0.524	0.500	0.866	0.134	0.577	1.732	1.155	2.000	$\bar{1}.699$	$\bar{1}.938$	30
31	0.541	0.515	0.857	0.143	0.601	1.664	1.167	1.942	$\bar{1}.712$	$\bar{1}.933$	31
32	0.559	0.530	0.848	0.152	0.625	1.600	1.179	1.887	$\bar{1}.724$	$\bar{1}.928$	32
33	0.576	0.545	0.839	0.161	0.649	1.540	1.192	1.836	$\bar{1}.736$	$\bar{1}.924$	33
34	0.593	0.559	0.829	0.171	0.675	1.483	1.206	1.788	$\bar{1}.748$	$\bar{1}.919$	34
35	0.611	0.574	0.819	0.181	0.700	1.428	1.221	1.743	$\bar{1}.759$	$\bar{1}.913$	35
36	0.628	0.588	0.809	0.191	0.727	1.376	1.236	1.701	$\bar{1}.769$	$\bar{1}.908$	36
37	0.646	0.602	0.799	0.201	0.754	1.327	1.252	1.662	$\bar{1}.779$	$\bar{1}.902$	37
38	0.663	0.616	0.788	0.212	0.781	1.280	1.269	1.624	$\bar{1}.789$	$\bar{1}.897$	38
39	0.681	0.629	0.777	0.223	0.810	1.235	1.287	1.589	$\bar{1}.799$	$\bar{1}.891$	39
40	0.698	0.643	0.766	0.234	0.839	1.192	1.305	1.556	$\bar{1}.808$	$\bar{1}.884$	40
41	0.716	0.656	0.755	0.245	0.869	1.150	1.325	1.524	$\bar{1}.817$	$\bar{1}.878$	41
42	0.733	0.669	0.743	0.257	0.900	1.111	1.346	1.494	$\bar{1}.826$	$\bar{1}.871$	42
43	0.750	0.682	0.731	0.269	0.933	1.072	1.367	1.466	$\bar{1}.834$	$\bar{1}.864$	43
44	0.768	0.695	0.719	0.281	0.966	1.036	1.390	1.440	$\bar{1}.842$	$\bar{1}.857$	44
45	0.785	0.707	0.707	0.293	1.000	1.000	1.414	1.414	$\bar{1}.849$	$\bar{1}.849$	45

$x/°$	x/rad	sin x	cos x	$1-\cos x$	tan x	cot x	sec x	cosec x	$\log_{10}$ sin x	$\log_{10}$ cos x	$x/°$
46	0.803	0.719	0.695	0.305	1.036	0.966	1.440	1.390	$\bar{1}.857$	$\bar{1}.842$	46
47	0.820	0.731	0.682	0.318	1.072	0.933	1.466	1.367	$\bar{1}.864$	$\bar{1}.834$	47
48	0.838	0.743	0.669	0.331	1.111	0.900	1.494	1.346	$\bar{1}.871$	$\bar{1}.826$	48
49	0.855	0.755	0.656	0.344	1.150	0.869	1.524	1.325	$\bar{1}.878$	$\bar{1}.817$	49
50	0.873	0.766	0.643	0.357	1.192	0.839	1.556	1.305	$\bar{1}.884$	$\bar{1}.808$	50
51	0.890	0.777	0.629	0.371	1.235	0.810	1.589	1.287	$\bar{1}.891$	$\bar{1}.799$	51
52	0.908	0.788	0.616	0.384	1.280	0.781	1.624	1.269	$\bar{1}.897$	$\bar{1}.789$	52
53	0.925	0.799	0.602	0.398	1.327	0.754	1.662	1.252	$\bar{1}.902$	$\bar{1}.779$	53
54	0.942	0.809	0.588	0.412	1.376	0.727	1.701	1.236	$\bar{1}.908$	$\bar{1}.769$	54
55	0.960	0.819	0.574	0.426	1.428	0.700	1.743	1.221	$\bar{1}.913$	$\bar{1}.759$	55
56	0.977	0.829	0.559	0.441	1.483	0.675	1.788	1.206	$\bar{1}.919$	$\bar{1}.748$	56
57	0.995	0.839	0.545	0.455	1.540	0.649	1.836	1.192	$\bar{1}.924$	$\bar{1}.736$	57
58	1.012	0.848	0.530	0.470	1.600	0.625	1.887	1.179	$\bar{1}.928$	$\bar{1}.724$	58
59	1.030	0.857	0.515	0.485	1.664	0.601	1.942	1.167	$\bar{1}.933$	1.712	59
60	1.047	0.866	0.500	0.500	1.732	0.577	2.000	1.155	$\bar{1}.938$	$\bar{1}.699$	60
61	1.065	0.875	0.485	0.515	1.804	0.554	2.063	1.143	$\bar{1}.942$	$\bar{1}.686$	61
62	1.082	0.883	0.469	0.531	1.881	0.532	2.130	1.133	$\bar{1}.946$	$\bar{1}.672$	62
63	1.100	0.891	0.454	0.546	1.963	0.510	2.203	1.122	$\bar{1}.950$	$\bar{1}.657$	63
64	1.117	0.899	0.438	0.562	2.050	0.488	2.281	1.113	$\bar{1}.954$	$\bar{1}.642$	64
65	1.134	0.906	0.423	0.577	2.145	0.466	2.366	1.103	$\bar{1}.957$	$\bar{1}.626$	65
66	1.152	0.914	0.407	0.593	2.246	0.445	2.459	1.095	$\bar{1}.961$	$\bar{1}.609$	66
67	1.169	0.921	0.391	0.609	2.356	0.424	2.559	1.086	$\bar{1}.964$	$\bar{1}.592$	67
68	1.187	0.927	0.375	0.625	2.475	0.404	2.669	1.079	$\bar{1}.967$	$\bar{1}.574$	68
69	1.204	0.934	0.358	0.642	2.605	0.384	2.790	1.071	$\bar{1}.970$	$\bar{1}.554$	69
70	1.222	0.940	0.342	0.658	2.747	0.364	2.924	1.064	$\bar{1}.973$	$\bar{1}.534$	70
71	1.239	0.946	0.326	0.674	2.904	0.344	3.072	1.058	$\bar{1}.976$	$\bar{1}.513$	71
72	1.257	0.951	0.309	0.691	3.078	0.325	3.236	1.051	$\bar{1}.978$	$\bar{1}.490$	72
73	1.274	0.956	0.292	0.708	3.271	0.306	3.420	1.046	$\bar{1}.981$	$\bar{1}.466$	73
74	1.292	0.961	0.276	0.724	3.487	0.287	3.628	1.040	$\bar{1}.983$	$\bar{1}.440$	74
75	1.309	0.966	0.259	0.741	3.732	0.268	3.864	1.035	$\bar{1}.985$	$\bar{1}.413$	75
76	1.326	0.970	0.242	0.758	4.011	0.249	4.134	1.031	$\bar{1}.987$	$\bar{1}.384$	76
77	1.344	0.974	0.225	0.775	4.331	0.231	4.445	1.026	$\bar{1}.989$	$\bar{1}.352$	77
78	1.361	0.978	0.208	0.792	4.705	0.213	4.810	1.022	$\bar{1}.990$	$\bar{1}.318$	78
79	1.379	0.982	0.191	0.809	5.145	0.194	5.241	1.019	$\bar{1}.992$	$\bar{1}.281$	79
80	1.396	0.985	0.174	0.826	5.671	0.176	5.759	1.015	$\bar{1}.993$	$\bar{1}.240$	80
81	1.414	0.988	0.156	0.844	6.314	0.158	6.392	1.012	$\bar{1}.995$	$\bar{1}.194$	81
82	1.431	0.990	0.139	0.861	7.115	0.141	7.185	1.010	$\bar{1}.996$	$\bar{1}.144$	82
83	1.449	0.993	0.122	0.878	8.144	0.123	8.206	1.008	$\bar{1}.997$	$\bar{1}.086$	73
84	1.466	0.995	0.105	0.895	9.514	0.105	9.567	1.006	$\bar{1}.998$	$\bar{1}.019$	84
85	1.484	0.996	0.087	0.913	11.430	0.087	11.474	1.004	$\bar{1}.998$	$\bar{2}.940$	85
86	1.501	0.998	0.070	0.930	14.301	0.070	14.336	1.002	$\bar{1}.999$	$\bar{2}.844$	86
87	1.518	0.999	0.052	0.948	19.081	0.052	19.107	1.001	$\bar{1}.999$	$\bar{2}.719$	87
88	1.536	0.999	0.035	0.965	28.636	0.035	28.654	1.001	0.000	$\bar{2}.543$	88
89	1.553	1.000	0.017	0.983	57.290	0.017	57.298	1.000	0.000	$\bar{2}.242$	89
90	1.571	1.000	0	1.000	∞	0	∞	1.000	0.000	$-\infty$	90

References

It would require too much space to list all the works consulted in the preparation of this *Book of Data*. Sources most likely to be of use if you require similar information to that contained in this book but for a wider range of substances are listed below. Those marked with an asterisk * would be useful in a school laboratory. Reference numbers such as R5 relate to the source references given in footnotes to the tables. The principal tables derived from each source are noted on this page using the standard reference letters. GEN denotes a general reference used for many tables.

Most of these references were compiled in pre-SI days and the data appear in a variety of units. These were converted to the appropriate SI units before inclusion in this book: this may make direct comparison difficult. When we were preparing the *Book of Data*, we found a large number of disagreements between sources which were difficult to resolve. Generally we adopted the most recent determination, if this could be ascertained, or alternatively that in the most recently published source. No attempt was made to ensure that data drawn from different sources were compatible.

R1*	Kaye, G. W. C. and Laby, T. H. (1966) *Tables of physical and chemical constants*, 13th edition, Longman.	**GEN**
R2*	Weast, R. C. and Selby, S. M. (1969) *Handbook of chemistry and physics*, 48th edition, The Chemical Rubber Company, Blackwell. (In recent years, this useful work has been revised and extended almost annually. The latest editions contain a very valuable list of sources of data.)	**GEN**
R4*	Gray, D. E., ed. (1963) *American Institute of Physics Handbook*, 2nd edition, McGraw Hill.	**GEN**
R7	Rossini, F. D., Wayman, D. D., Evans, W. K., Levine, S., and Jaffe, I. (1952, 1965, and 1968) *Selected values of chemical thermodynamic properties*, U.S. National Bureau of Standards, Circular 500 and two supplements.	**GEN** **PTI** **PTO** **TEI**
R14	Harrison, G. R., ed. (1939) *Wavelength tables*, 1st edition, M.I.T.	**EMS**
R15*	McGlashan, M. L. (1968) *Physico-chemical quantities and units*, Monographs for Teachers No. 15, Royal Institute of Chemistry.	**UCS**
R17	Smithells, C. J. (1962) *Metals reference book*, 3rd edition, Butterworths.	**SLD**
R19	Stull, D. R. and Sinke, G. C. (1956) *Thermodynamic properties of the elements*, Advances in Chemistry Series, Volume 18, American Chemical Society.	**TCE** **PTI**
R22	Kittel, C. (1966) *Introduction to solid state physics*, 3rd edition, John Wiley.	**SIZ**
R24	Lederer, C. M., Hollander, J. M., and Perlman, I. (1967) *Table of isotopes*, 6th edition, John Wiley.	**PPE** **NUC**
R34	Cotton, F. A. and Wilkinson, G. (1967) *Advanced inorganic chemistry, a comprehensive text*, 2nd edition, Interscience.	**GEN**
R44	Timmermans, J. (1965) *Physico-chemical constants of pure organic compounds*, 2 volumes, Elsevier.	**PTO**
R45	Dreisbach, R. R. (1955, 1959, and 1961) *Physical properties of chemical compounds*, Advances in Chemistry Series, Volumes 15, 22, and 29, American Chemical Society.	**PTO**
R46 and R47	The Thermodynamics Research Centre (1961 onwards) has been compiling thermochemical and other data. (Thermodynamics Research Centre, Texas A and M University, U.S.A.) Some of this data was previously published as A.P.I. Project 44, *Selected values of properties of hydrocarbons and related compounds* (R46); and M.C.A. Project, *Selected values of properties of chemical compounds (organic)* (R47). Additions and revisions are published regularly in loose-leaf form.	**PTO** **LIQ** **GAS**
R48	American Society for Testing Materials *Special Technical Publication 48-J* is one of a number of yearly supplements to *STP 48 – X-ray diffraction data cards for chemical analysis* (1941).	**TCE** **PTI**
R49	Stephen, H. and Stephen, T. (1963–64) *Solubilities of inorganic and organic compounds*, 2 volumes, Pergamon.	**PTI**
R50	Linke, W. F. (1959) *Solubilities*, 4th edition, Van Nostrand.	**PTI**

R51 Gray, C. H., ed. (1966) *Laboratory handbook of toxic agents*, 2nd edition, Royal Institute of Chemistry. **TCE PTI PTO**

R52 Pieters, H. A. J. and Creyghton, J. W. (1957) *Safety in the chemical laboratory*, 2nd edition, Butterworths. **TCE PTI PTO**

R53 American Society for Metals (1961–67) *Metals Handbook*, Volume I, 8th edition. **SLD**

R54 Hampel, C. A., ed. (1961) *Rare metals handbook*, 2nd edition, Reinhold. **SLD**

R55 Woolman, J. and Mottram, R. A. (1964–66) *The mechanical and physical properties of British Standard En steels*, British Iron and Steel Research Association, Pergamon. **SLD**

R56 The Copper Development Association (1964) *Copper Data*, No. 12. **SLD**

R57 Siegbahn, K., ed. (1965) *α, β, and γ-ray spectroscopy*, North Holland.

R60 Symbols Committee of the Royal Society (1969) *Symbols, signs and abbreviations recommended for British scientific publications*, The Royal Society. **UCS**

R61 Kuhn, H. G. (1969) *Atomic spectra*, 2nd edition, Longman. **EIA**

R62 Benjamin, L. and Gold, V. (1954) 'A table of thermodynamic functions of ionic hydration.' *Transactions of the Faraday Society*, **50,** 797.

R63 Institution of Electrical Engineers (1967) *Regulations for the electrical equipment of buildings*, 14th edition. **SLD**

R65 Chemical Society, London (1958) *Interatomic distances*, Special publication No. 11; and (1965) *Interatomic distances supplement*, Special publication No. 18. **SIZ**

R66 Cottrell, T. L. (1958) *The strengths of chemical bonds*, 2nd edition, Butterworths. **SIZ**

R67 Pauling, L. (1967) *The nature of the chemical bond*, Oxford University Press. **SIZ**

R68 Latimer, W. M. (1952) *The oxidation states of the elements and their potentials in aqueous solutions*, 2nd edition, Constable. **TEI**

R69 Sillen, L. G. and Martell, A. E. (1964) *Stability constants of metal-ion complexes*, Special publication No. 17, Chemical Society, London. **CHM**

R70 British Standards Institute (1967) *Marking codes for values and tolerances of resistors and capacitors*, BS 1852; and (1969) *Enamelled copper conductors polyvinyl base with high mechanical properties. Part I: Round wire*, BS 4516. **SLD**

R71 Moelwyn-Hughes, E. A. (1961) *Physical chemistry*, 2nd edition, Cambridge University Press. **GEN**

R72 *International Encyclopaedia of chemical science*, (1964), Van Nostrand. **SIZ CHM**

R73 U.S. National Bureau of Standards (1951) *Tables of chemical kinetics, homogenous reactions*: Circular 510; Supplement No. 1 (1956); Supplement No. 2 (1960); Monograph 34, volumes 1 and 2 (1961 and 1964). **TEI**

R74 U.S. National Bureau of Standards (1953) *Electrochemical constants*, Circular 524. **TEI**

R75 Parsons, R. (1959) *Handbook of electrochemical constants*, Butterworth. **EIA**

Index

Most references in this index are to *properties*, such as density or molar mass, rather than to substances.

* FEP is now pages 150-151; BEP is now page 152.

Physical and mathematical constants

Values are quoted to the maximum precision attained by 1965 and are internationally recommended figures. The estimated error (three times the statistical standard error to allow for the possibility of systematic error) is given in brackets in units of the last digit quoted. D denotes an exact value by definition. Quantities named in bold type were determined directly. Other quantities were obtained from these and other experiments by calculation.

Atomic constants

Quantity	Symbol	Value		Error	Unit	$\log_{10}$
Speed of light in vacuum	c	**2.997** 925	$\times 10^{8}$	(3)	$m\,s^{-1}$	8.4768
permeability of vacuum	μ_0	**1.256** 637	$\times 10^{-6}$	(D)	$H\,m^{-1}$	$\overline{6}.0992$
permittivity of vacuum	ε_0	**8.854** 186	$\times 10^{-12}$	(9)	$F\,m^{-1}$	$\overline{12}.9471$
electrostatic force constant	$1/4\pi\varepsilon_0$	**8.98** 7 555	$\times 10^{9}$	(9)	$N\,m^2\,C^{-2}$	9.9537
Faraday constant	F	**9.64** 8 70	$\times 10^{4}$	(16)	$C\,mol^{-1}$	4.9845
Avogadro constant	L, N_A	**6.02** 2 52	$\times 10^{23}$	(28)	mol^{-1}	23.7798
unified atomic mass unit	m_u	**1.660** 43	$\times 10^{-27}$	(6)	kg	$\overline{27}.2202$
Boltzmann constant	k	**1.380** 54	$\times 10^{-23}$	(18)	$J\,K^{-1}$	$\overline{23}.1400$
elementary charge	e	**1.602** 10	$\times 10^{-19}$	(7)	C	$\overline{19}.2047$
rest mass of electron	m_e	**9.109** 08	$\times 10^{-31}$	(40)	kg	$\overline{31}.9595$
charge:mass ratio of electron	e/m_e	**1.758** 796	$\times 10^{11}$	(19)	$C\,kg^{-1}$	11.2452
mass : charge ratio of electron	m_e/e	**5.685** 708	$\times 10^{-12}$	(62)	$kg\,C^{-1}$	$\overline{12}.7548$
mass of proton	m_p	**1.672** 52	$\times 10^{-27}$	(8)	kg	$\overline{27}.2234$
charge:mass ratio of proton	e/m_p	**9.578** 00	$\times 10^{7}$	(2)	$C\,kg^{-1}$	7.9813
mass : charge ratio of proton	m_p/e	**1.043** 960	$\times 10^{-8}$	(2)	$kg\,C^{-1}$	$\overline{8}.0187$
mass ratio proton : electron	m_p/m_e	**1.836** 10	$\times 10^{3}$	(3)	—	3.2639
rest mass of neutron	m_n	**1.674** 82	$\times 10^{-27}$	(8)	kg	$\overline{27}.2240$
rest mass of hydrogen atom	m_H	**1.673** 43	$\times 10^{-27}$	(8)	kg	$\overline{27}.2235$
Rydberg constant	R_∞	**1.097** 373 1	$\times 10^{7}$	(3)	m^{-1}	7.0404
	$R_\infty c$	**3.289** 842	$\times 10^{15}$	(4)	Hz	15.5832
	$R_\infty ch$	**2.179** 72	$\times 10^{-18}$	(17)	J	$\overline{18}.3385$
Rydberg constant (hydrogen)	R_H	**1.096** 775 8	$\times 10^{7}$	(3)	m^{-1}	7.0401
Planck constant	h	**6.625** 59	$\times 10^{-34}$	(50)	J s	$\overline{34}.8212$
	$h/2\pi = \hbar$	**1.054** 494	$\times 10^{-34}$	(70)	J s	$\overline{34}.0230$
ratio Planck constant : elementary charge	h/e	**4.135** 56	$\times 10^{-15}$	(12)	$J\,s\,C^{-1}$	$\overline{15}.6165$
Bohr radius	a_0	**5.291** 67	$\times 10^{-11}$	(7)	m	$\overline{11}.7236$

Other physical constants

Quantity	Symbol	Value		Error	Unit	$\log_{10}$
gravitational constant	G	**6.673**	$\times 10^{-11}$	(9)	$N\,m^{-2}\,kg^{-2}$	$\overline{11}.8241$
Hubble constant		**2.5**	$\times 10^{-18}$		$m\,s^{-1}/m$	$\overline{18}.3979$
standard gravity[A]	g_n	**9.806** 65		(D)	$m\,s^{-2}$ or $N\,kg^{-1}$	0.9915
density of mercury	$\rho(Hg)$	**1.359** 51	$\times 10^{4}$		$kg\,m^{-3}$	4.1334
maximum density of water	$\rho(H_2O, 277.13\,K)$	**0.999** 973	$\times 10^{3}$		$kg\,m^{-3}$	3.0000
temperature of 'ice point'	T_{ice}	**273.15** 0 0		(1)	K	2.4364
molar volume of ideal gas[B]	$V_m^{\ominus}$	**2.24** 1 36	$\times 10^{-2}$	(30)	$m^3\,mol^{-1}$	$\overline{2}.3506$
gas constant	R	**8.314** 34		(120)	$J\,K^{-1}\,mol^{-1}$	0.9198
speed of sound in air	$c(273\,K)$	**3.313** 6	$\times 10^{2}$		$m\,s^{-1}$	2.5202

Quantity	Symbol	Value		Unit	$\log_{10}$
radius of Earth[C]	$r_\oplus$ or r_E	**6.371** 02	$\times 10^{6}$	m	6.8042
mass of Earth	$m_\oplus$ or m_E	**5.976**	$\times 10^{24}$	kg	24.7764
mean distance Earth to Sun[C]	au or A	**1.496** 00	$\times 10^{11}$	m	11.1749
solar constant[D]		**1.40** (± 0.03)	$\times 10^{3}$	$W\ m^{-2}$	3.1461
Earth's horizontal magnetic field[E]	H	**1.87**	$\times 10^{-5}$	T	$\bar{5}.2718$
Earth's vertical magnetic field[E]	Z	**4.36**	$\times 10^{-5}$	T	$\bar{5}.6395$
Earth's equivalent dipole	m	**8.1**	$\times 10^{22}$	$A\ m^2$	22.9085

Conversion factors

inch	0.0**25 4**	m
foot	0.**304** 8	m
mile	**1.609** 344	km
mile per hour	0.**447** 04	$m\ s^{-1}$
UK gallon[F]	**4.546** 09	dm^3
pound	0.**453** 592 37	kg
pound force	**4.448** 22	N
foot pound force	**1.355** 82	J
British thermal unit	**1.055** 06	kJ
calorie (thermochemical)[F]	**4.184**	J
horsepower[F]	0.**745** 7	kW
pound force per square inch	**6.894** 76	kPa
millimetre of mercury	**133**.322 4	Pa
standard atmosphere	**101**.325	kPa
electrostatic unit of charge	$\triangleq$ **3.336** $\times 10^{-10}$	C
electrostatic unit of potential	$\triangleq$ **3.00** $\times 10^{2}$	V
debye unit	$\triangleq$ **3.336** $\times 10^{-30}$	C m
electronvolt	$\triangleq$ **96.48**7	$kJ\ mol^{-1}$
reciprocal metre (wave number) m^{-1}	$\triangleq$ **1.987** $\times 10^{-25}$	J (per atom)
atomic mass unit	**1.660** 4 $\times 10^{-27}$	kg
	$\triangleq$ **931**.5	MeV
$RT^{\ominus} \ln 10/F$[G]	0.**059 17**	V

Mathematical constants

$\sqrt{2}$ = **1.414** 2	π = **3.141** 59	e = **2.718** 28 = 1/0.**367** 88
$\sqrt{3}$ = **1.732** 1	π^2 = **9.869** 6	$\log_{10}e$ = 0.**434** 3
$\sqrt{10}$ = **3.162** 3	$\sqrt{\pi}$ = **1.772** 5	ln2 = 0.**693** 15
$\sqrt[3]{10}$ = **2.154** 4	$\log_{10}\pi$ = 0.**497** 1	ln10[H] = **2.302** 59
1° = 0.0**17 4**53 rad	1 rad = **57.296**°	

Notes

[A] This quantity is used only in certain definitions.
The local value of g should be used for precise experimental work.
[B] At 273.15 K and 101.3 kPa.
[C] The exact value depends on the definition. The mean distance Earth-Sun given here is the astronomical unit.
[D] Maximum solar total radiant power above atmosphere at a distance of 1 au from the Sun. Natural variability quoted.
[E] For London, 1960. Z positive downwards.
Students are advised to ascertain the current local value.
[F] Units with similar names have different values. Beware.
[G] Used in the measurement of pH; $T^{\ominus}$ = 298.15 K.
[H] Conversion factor for $\log_{10}$ to ln.

References: R1, R4, R60.

Periodic Table

1s	1 H																			2 He
2s	3 Li	4 Be												2p	5 B	6 C	7 N	8 O	9 F	10 Ne
3s	11 Na	12 Mg												3p	13 Al	14 Si	15 P	16 S	17 Cl	18 Ar
4s	19 K	20 Ca	3d	21 Sc	22 Ti	23 V	24 Cr	25 Mn	26 Fe	27 Co	28 Ni	29 Cu	30 Zn	4p	31 Ga	32 Ge	33 As	34 Se	35 Br	36 Kr
5s	37 Rb	38 Sr	4d	39 Y	40 Zr	41 Nb	42 Mo	43 Tc	44 Ru	45 Rh	46 Pd	47 Ag	48 Cd	5p	49 In	50 Sn	51 Sb	52 Te	53 I	54 Xe
6s	55 Cs	56 Ba	5d	57 La	72 Hf	73 Ta	74 W	75 Re	76 Os	77 Ir	78 Pt	79 Au	80 Hg	6p	81 Tl	82 Pb	83 Bi	84 Po	85 At	86 Rn
7s	87 Fr	88 Ra	6d	89 Ac	104 Ku															

4f	58 Ce	59 Pr	60 Nd	61 Pm	62 Sm	63 Eu	64 Gd	65 Tb	66 Dy	67 Ho	68 Er	69 Tm	70 Yb	71 Lu
5f	90 Th	91 Pa	92 U	93 Np	94 Pu	95 Am	96 Cm	97 Bk	98 Cf	99 Es	100 Fm	101 Md	102 No	103 Lr